Laughter, War and Feminism

Writing About Women
Feminist Literary Studies

General Editor

Esther Labovitz
Pace University

Advisory Board

Marie Collins
Rutgers-Newark University

Doris Guilloton
New York University

Lila Hanft
Case Western Reserve University

Mark Hussey
Pace University

Helane Levine-Keating
Pace University

Vol. 11

PETER LANG
New York • Washington, D.C./Baltimore • San Francisco
Bern • Frankfurt am Main • Berlin • Vienna • Paris

Gabriela Castellanos

Laughter, War and Feminism

Elements of Carnival in Three of Jane Austen's Novels

PETER LANG
New York • Washington, D.C./Baltimore • San Francisco
Bern • Frankfurt am Main • Berlin • Vienna • Paris

Library of Congress Cataloging-in-Publication Data

Castellanos, Gabriela.
   Laughter, war and feminism: elements of carnival in three of Jane
Austen's novels / Gabriela Castellanos.
     p.   cm. — (Writing about women; vol. 11)
    1. Austen, Jane, 1775–1817—Criticism and interpretation.
2. Feminism and literature—England—History—19th century. 3. Women
and literature—England—History—19th century. 4. Bakhtin, M. M.
(Mikhail Mikhaïlovich), 1895–1975. 5. Laughter in literature.
6. Carnival in literature. 7. War in literature. I. Title. II. Series.
PR4038.F44C37   1994   823'.7—dc20   93-42550
ISBN 0-8204-2351-3   CIP
ISSN 1053-7937

Die Deutsche Bibliothek-CIP-Einheitsaufnahme

Castellanos, Gabriela:
Laughter, war and feminism: elements of carnival in three of Jane Austen's
novels / Gabriela Castellanos. - New York; Washington, D.C.; Baltimore;
San Francisco; Bern; Frankfurt am Main; Berlin; Vienna; Paris: Lang, 1994
   (Writing about women; Vol. 11)
   ISBN 0-8204-2351-3
NE: GT

Cover design by Jean Morley.

The paper in this book meets the guidelines for permanence and durability of
the Committee on Production Guidelines for Book Longevity of the
Council on Library Resources.

© Peter Lang Publishing, Inc., New York 1994

Printed in the United States of America.

To my husband, Luis Eduardo Valencia,
and to our children, Victoria, Santiago and Virginia Valencia Castellanos,
who help to make all my efforts worthwhile.

ACKNOWLEDGEMENTS

I am grateful to Elizabeth Langland, Alistair Duckworth and Daniel Cottom for their support and advice. My gratitude extends to Brandon Kershner, who read and commented on one of the drafts, and to my parents, Jorge and Carmela Castellanos, who read various drafts and made invaluable comments. They also helped with many of the details of the editing and publishing process, which was made difficult by my residing in Cali, Colombia while it was going on. My sister, Isabel Castellanos, also helped.

Finally, I am indebted to Dr. Jaime Galarza S., Rector of the Universidad del Valle, in Cali, for his support.

TABLE OF CONTENTS

LIST OF ABBREVIATIONS

Works by Jane Austen:

S	*Sense and Sensibility*
NA	*Northanger Abbey*
PP	*Pride and Prejudice*
E	*Emma*
MW	*Minor Works*
MP	*Mansfield Park*
P	*Persuasion*

Works by Mikhail Bakhtin:

DN	"Discourse in the Novel"
FTCN	"Forms of Time and of the Chronotope in the Novel"
PDP	*Problems of Dostoevski's Poetics*
RHW	*Rabelais and his World*

Chapter 1
Introduction

Jane Austen's main resource, her most basic attitude, was laughter. Because her voice was never strident, her manner never discordant, the peculiar shape of her laughter allowed many to smile at her wit, without feeling the force of her irony. As D. W. Harding said, for a long time "her books [were] . . . read and enjoyed by precisely the sort of people whom she disliked."[1] The attitudes of critics as well as those of the general public had to evolve before they could realize how original she was, how daring, in saying what she had been saying, while seemingly engrossed only in the surface of her world. Because her solutions to the problems a woman writer of her times inevitably faced were highly creative, it was not easy to see how she responded to a social reality that allowed little room for the intelligent independence of a woman, to a culture where the ideal human being was male. Multiple readings are necessary to discover the complexity of her response in the seeming ease of her narrative language.

Indeed, careful consideration reveals the plurality of social voices in dialogue in her work. This description, of course, is based on Bakhtin's definition of the novel not in terms of a single structural model, but as a combination of languages, "a diversity of speech types . . . and a diversity of individual voices, artistically organized," used "to form a structured artistic system."[2] Typically, novels combine the languages of different literary and extra-literary genres, as well as a diversity of approaches to the major ideological problems of the author's age. Austen's novels also combine the languages of different genres and social groups, focusing on the differences of gender and generation, and delving deeply and dialogically into class conflicts among the "middling classes,"[3] rather than presenting the whole spectrum of social classes.

A woman novelist, in addition to transforming a combination of styles into literary speech, must deal with a very specific problem: most of the literary and extra-literary stylistic sources at a novelist's disposal are tinted by at least nuances, if not strong colors, of misogynist bias.[4] Furthermore, the fact that the pen has been almost always in the hands of men, the lack of a parallel tradition of women writers, poses a serious problem. For not only are the traditional sources full of negative images of woman;[5] even if positive qualities are attributed to her, the richness and complexity of male characters is denied to feminine ones. In traditional literature, as in other types of discourse, "humanity," implicitly male, is recognized as a complex and deep object of study, while femininity is often accorded simplistic, stereotyped treatment. When Austen began to write, feminist novelists had been using different approaches to solve the problem of feminine authorship in the midst of male domination; her solution, however, was highly original.

One source of Austen's originality can be found in her peculiar use of the cultural opposition between popular carnival and official ideology. In this opposition lay a potential for meaning that, according to Bakhtin, found artistic fruition in Rabelais. The latter, as Bakhtin demonstrated,[6] translated into literary form the festive stance of carnival pageantry and artistic manifestations, as well as the language of the people in the marketplace. The carnival rites and linguistic innovations collectively created by certain dominated groups in medieval and Renaissance Europe did not oppose a "truth of the people" to official verities; such a move would have meant founding a new dogmatism. Rather, these popular manifestations constituted an alternative to officialdom, imbued as they were with a joyful ambivalence. Their exuberant, irreverent attitude slyly undermined official "truths," giving the common people symbolic room to play and laugh at domination. Making literary use of many of the images, themes and stylistic traits of carnival, Rabelais produced what Bakhtin called a "carnivalization" of his fictional world. His peculiar laughing stance acquired the major characteristics of popular, festive laughter: first, a sense of utopian community or "oneness," in which all hierarchies and distancing among people dissolve; second, a joyful ambivalence in which death and negation become symbolic rebirth and affirmation; and third, a universal derision that is often self-directed, as the reveler himself is ironically included in his own mockery. Through a series of mediations, the same elements that appear in Rabelais' "carnivalized" novel (as in picaresque novels, much of the work of Cervantes, Jean-Paul, even Shakespeare) influenced such authors as Dostoevski. His fictional world evokes in the reader a feeling of standing at the threshold of quotidian reality, immersed in the topsy-turvy realm of carnivalesque inversion. The work of this novelist, though far from Rabelaisian exuberance, bore the imprint of carnival in such traits as mésalliances (the combination or juxtaposition of opposites), eccentricity, free and familiar contact among characters whose different social standing called for hierarchical distancing, and profanation, or the debasing of "sacred elements."[7]

What Austen did was to transpose some elements of the cultural opposition between carnival and officialdom, with carnival's characteristic mingling of many social classes, to the tension between male and female within a limited range of classes. Austen's, then, is a *feminist* laughter rather than the bawdy guffaw of popular carnival. Her irony, however, subverts dominant views of women's characters, relationships and social roles in a uniquely ambivalent way, through a laughing stance she could only have derived, albeit indirectly, from carnival.

Of course, in her work the male-dominant emphasis on bawdiness and the grotesque body that was typical of carnival cannot be found. Austen, however, made cunning use of many of the resources by which carnivalesque language, by opposing an ambivalent attitude to the dogmatism of official ideology, allows dominated groups to superimpose their ideological perspective on authorized "truths," and thus to produce their own meaning. Much of her work shows carnivalesque elements, such as, for example, mésalliance in the ludicrous juxtaposition of foolish and wise characters, a delight in a variety of eccentric behavior, and a tendency to portray situations in which the worldly reverence for wealth, rank, and male dominance is ridiculed. Austen's novels build upon traditional Christian morals but turn official ideologies of male superiority upside down by laughing at heroism. Austenian satire pokes fun at the perfection of heroes and heroines in sentimental novels, creating fallible protagonists who, in spite of their often excellent qualities, can and do make laughable and painful mistakes. Thus Austen subverts idealized novelistic heroism, while symbolically regenerating human fallibility by showing that even "superior" characters are often deluded yet eminently redeemable. This ironic attitude toward heroism becomes a form of profanation as the ideal of the moral and intellectual superiority of men over women is undermined. Her joyfully ambivalent narrative stance allows her to show women's strengths and to grant her central characters an utopian "perfect felicity," as the oppressive dominance of men over women is fictionally suspended.

Austen's narration thus puts into play artistic possibilities by which women, as members of a subordinate group, are empowered to produce their own meaning. From this perspective, I will analyze three of Austen's novels, *Northanger Abbey, Pride and Prejudice,* and *Emma.* I have chosen to analyze these works because they provide the best grounds for explicating what I will call Austenian irony. Each of the three novels, like all her works, considers how a different type of woman from "the middling classes" might achieve some measure of happiness in a society inimical to women. In the three novels chosen, the search for happiness is simultaneously a process of serio-comic humiliation of the protagonist culminating in her personal growth. Austen, I will argue, achieved her unique mixture of ludicrous and serious narrative purposes by adding certain elements of carnivalesque laughter, which she shrewdly adapted to her narrative needs, to the basic, canonical ingredients of the sentimental novel, the genre in whose tradition she worked.

In these three novels, her most explicitly satiric *Bildungsromane*, as in her juvenilia, we find a greater relative weight of the carnivalesque elements that are always present in Austen's work. In *Northanger Abbey* Austenian laughter undermines the pathos of victimized virtue of the protagonists of sentimental and Gothic novels and thus their established form of heroism. In this sense, the novel exhibits the greatest tendency to carnivalesque parody of all of Austen's work. For not only is the protagonist, Catherine Morland, if not an anti-heroine, at least a resolutely un-heroic protagonist. In addition, the work consistently mocks many of the typical images, themes, episodes and sequences which usually serve to establish the exquisite superiority of traditional heroines in sentimental novels and their cruel persecution by unworthy characters. Thus, unlike typical satire, *Northanger Abbey* does not hold up the vulgar, ordinary characters to ridicule by contrasting them to a heroic, epic greatness. Rather, in the mode of carnivalesque irreverence, what is satirized is the normative, "respectable" fictional figure: in this case, the angelic ideal of ethereal femininity of the novels of Austen's predecessors. I will analyze this novel, then, as a parodical, carnivalesque response to both official patriarchal ideology regarding young women and the novelistic ideal of feminine perfection of the sentimental tradition.

In *Pride and Prejudice* parody underlies the whole work without relying on reiterated allusions to the idealized heroines of preceding novels. Rather, a parodical intention is evident as the most basic tenet of women's sentimental fiction, the sweet, sacrosanct innocence of the heroine, is violated. For Elizabeth Bennet is not one of those exceptional women whose soft, delicate tenderness is only comparable to their unerring judgment, whose qualities allow them to escape the fallibility of ordinary mortals. On the contrary, in this novel the heroine is a lively, outspoken character who is capable of making serious mistakes; furthermore, a number of situations lead to the humiliation of both the protagonist and her lover as each is made to realize her/his own folly. Elizabeth's uncommon intellectual and moral qualities do not exempt her from occasionally erring as much as her unenlightened neighbors. In consequence, some strands in the thematic fabric of the novel are colored by an ironic sense of carnivalesque community, of the universality of folly, as moral and intellectual hierarchies are symbolically toppled. Indeed, the very possibility of unequivocal moral certainty is denied, as perception is shown to be influenced by self-interest even in the most intelligent and honest characters. From beginning to end "universally acknowledged truths" are seen to be suspect, although they may be not only inescapable but necessary. The complexity of this narrative attitude calls for ambivalent laughter at people's partial blindness.

In *Emma* we encounter a basically kind, yet charmingly perverse heroine whose exceptional cleverness does not make her any wiser; rather, it appears to feed her enormous capacity for self-delusion. Emma finally realizes her mistakes, but not because her mentor, Mr. Knightley, points them out to her; to achieve wisdom she must undergo her own personal and painful process. In my reading, the narrator's attitude toward the main character's errors and flaws is a profoundly dialogic one; no single perspective on the narrative events is privileged or presented as normative. All characters in the novel make different types of mistakes at different times, but the narrator does not pass judgment on them, allowing us as readers to discover their mistakes in the same way we discover those we and our associates make: by observing and analyzing what transpires among people. Readers accustomed to find intelligent characters perceiving situations clearly and lovable ones being frequently right will find their expectations reversed. Emma is often wrong, but her flaws do not make her any less attractive. As we follow her inner evolution, the more outrageously mistaken she is, the more interesting and closer to the reader's affections she becomes. This inversion is only one of the many ways in which the novel creates a "world-upside-down" typical of carnival. The passages of the heroine's humiliation can be interpreted in terms of a carnivalesque "crowning and uncrowning," which Bakhtin defines as a literary adaptation of a symbolic rite of popular feasts in which a mock-king is at once honored and debased (cf. RHW, 8-10, 197).

All the analyses summarized above are meant as approximations to Austen's resilient, unique laughter, her most characteristic answer to the problems women encountered in her world. On the other hand, Austen's laughter does not blind her to negative conditions for women. All her novels depict social situations and institutions most adverse to women's exercise of their abilities. Frequently, a careful reading of Austen's fiction may unveil the subtle ways in which the seemingly powerless participate in the circulation of the same power that dominates them. Thus, according to Foucault, those who appear to be oppressed share in upholding the power that places them in a subordinate position. Women, like other subordinate social groups, share in the control of certain discursive practices that represent the dissemination of knowledges, which in turn are related to social power. Through everyday, "commonsense" ways of understanding social life, people uphold and reproduce certain clichés that act as homogenizing, controlling forces, subtly but relentlessly promoting conformity to social norms. This perspective will add an important ingredient to the analysis of Austen's shrewd use of discourse, including characters' speech and other social practices.

This type of analysis is not at variance with Bakhtinian categories, in spite of his current image among literary critics as the apostle of optimism. Bakhtin is often seen, in the words of Graham Pechey, as overestimating "the political effectivity of the disunifying and carnivalising forces to which [a monoglot hegemony] is opposed."[8] And yet, Bakhtin is not a rhapsodist of festive freedom, nor is he oblivious to the weight of the homogenizing, monologic forces. In "Discourse in the Novel," for instance, Bakhtin posits the existence of a "centripetal force" in language, a social tendency to unify modes of expression, to institute a common speech; this tendency is in constant interaction with its opposite, a "centrifugal force," which pulls in the direction of social diversity in language (DN, 254). A reader, applying these Bakhtinian concepts, may hear in Austen's narrating voices laughter at "centripetal" ideological themes, i.e. at the clichés of everyday social intercourse. These clichés appear as invalid generalizations rooted in cultural attitudes that, indispensable as they may be, often impoverish the mind, leading characters to error. The use of the same Bakhtinian categories will allow us to see how pervasive and influential these centripetal tendencies are in the social life of Austen's novels.

As Caryl Emerson puts it, the dominant image of Bakhtin among critics is the image of the libertarian,

> the apostle of freedom who rejoices, Bakunin-like, in the undoing of rules, in centrifugal energy, in carnival clowning, in novels as loopholes, and in sly denials of authorship. . . . But Bakhtin in fact insulates himself against that sort of thought better than it at first appears. Judging him not only by the essays of his best-known middle period but by the evolution of his work as a whole, Bakhtin is, if anything, an apostle of *constraints*.[9]

Indeed, Bakhtin and his circle realize that individuals cannot differentiate themselves radically from their culture; even the personal accents of their words are merely the result of a reworking of "ideological themes."[10] Inventive freedom, which can "liberate from the prevailing point of view in the world, from conventions and established truths," can be achieved only through "the combination of a variety of different elements and their rapprochement" (RHW, p. 34). Even when people are "inventing," the available elements for the inventions are similar to ideological garments in which a person must dress herself and which are "always too tight, and thus comical."[11] If we apply this conceptualization of the interaction between creative needs and social material to Austen's fiction, we become aware of the ways in which her narrators' word is often engaged in dialogue with conventions that may lead to characters' alienation. The utopian solutions Austen reaches in her endings can be compared to new forms of motley dress, comical recombinations of old clothes.

At times, however, one feels that Bakhtin's theories, with their novel, original approach from the perspective of the seemingly powerless, are indeed insufficient to explore the ways in which official ideologies interact with popular or feminist contestation. The limitation in Bakhtin, however, is a consequence of precisely what constitutes his great original contribution: his determination to investigate diversity, what Bakhtin called the centrifugal forces in language (forces that traditional linguists and cultural and literary analysts had persistently overlooked) more often than he explored centripetal ones. In order to respond to Austen's awareness of the centripetal pull, of the force and attractiveness of established truths, we must make use of other theoretical tools, to serve as complements to Bakhtin's and fill in the gaps left by the application of his concepts.

One obvious choice for such a counter-balancing of Bakhtinian ideas is Foucault, whose analysis of power may help us to understand how "officialdom" may react to carnival. I believe one reason why Bakhtin's views on the liberating possibilities of carnival have been rejected as naive is the fact that some critics have interpreted him as saying that the "disunifying and carnivalising forces" entail a radical undermining of the *status quo* leading to its eventual overthrow. From such a perspective, freedom is only reached after a decided victory; if the dominant group remains strongly in power, it must be because carnivalesque freedom has been an alienating illusion, and carnival has failed. Foucault, on the other hand, proposes an understanding of freedom, not as an either/or pursuit, but "as an agonism, . . . a relationship which is at the same time reciprocal incitation and struggle; less of a face-to-face confrontation which paralyzes both sides than a permanent provocation."[12] Domination, also, is not merely a crushing of an underclass by those above, but "a general structure of power whose ramifications and consequences can sometimes be found descending to the most incalcitrant fibers of society." Rather than achieving a decided victory or defeat, the structure of power is "more or less taken for granted and consolidated by means of a long-term confrontation between adversaries."[13]

Within this perspective, we may see the laughter of carnival as a form of resistance cunningly taking advantage of weak points in the ideological structure, as a form of response that the dominant ideology must in turn reckon with, respond to, attempt to neutralize. As a result, this ideology does not remain monolithic and unchanged. The changes, it is true, are not equal to a triumph, to a defiant declaration of independence, to a definitive achievement of freedom, among other things because the "two sides" are probably not as clearly demarcated as the labels "official" and "carnival" would seem to suggest. But however complex and fragmented the opposition to dominant strategies, these are forced to transform themselves, and the alterations become evidence against the eternal validity of official ideology, cutting fine but perhaps enlarging cracks in the monolith. Such an understanding of the interaction between dominance and resistance can lead us to regard such cultural manifestations as popular-festive traditions and jest-books in a different light. These forms of "comic relief," which for a long time have been analyzed as serving only as a valve for discontent, and thus to work for stability, can now be seen to have "a potentially subversive force, needing careful control."[14]

Austenian laughter may be seen as a carnivalesque subversion of patriarchal tenets, in this sense of subtle, multifarious challenge to certain misogynist positions. In the novels' endings, for example, Austen's heroines will willingly enter into an egalitarian marital relationship, in which a combination of circumstances create an exceptionally favorable situation. Although each novel pointedly provides evidence of severe social and personal limitations for married women, each protagonist is gaily promised a life of utopian happiness. This utopia is one of the carnivalesque elements at play in the three novels, for the reader is led to adopt an ambivalent attitude towards it. On the one hand, in each case there are certain exceptional circumstances that seem to exempt the protagonists from some of the common pitfalls of ordinary female life. On the other hand, the plausibility of the "perfect felicity" promised is belied both by the ironic language of these endings and by the generally skeptical tone of the entire works. *Emma*, furthermore, may serve to investigate the private and public role of women as "mistresses" of their homes, since from the beginning of the novel we see the protagonist playing the role of mistress of her father's house. It is in the analysis of *Emma*, then, that the discussion of women's exercise of power through domestic roles and women's powerlessness will be concentrated.

I will not attempt to deny that very different readings of *Emma* are possible, for Austen is one of those privileged authors who invite many and varied reactions. I only claim that her texts are rare in that they allow readers so inclined to laugh at situations surrounding women without acquiescing in a single misogynist premise. Many might and have read her from an anti-feminist perspective; and yet her novels allow feminist readings as deep and as fruitful as any.

An approach to Austen's works that stresses both their feminism and the importance of carnivalesque elements in them must immediately contend with Austen's traditional image, which has been painted in colors of gentility and conventional morality. One example will portray how her works have been represented in the minds of some readers: for a long time, American schoolboys used to be "forcibly exposed to *Pride and Prejudice* in the lower grades,"[15] apparently in the hope that they would learn good manners as much as a controlled and elegant writing style. In the case of one schoolboy, at least, such reading only led to a lifelong disgust for her novels; in Mark Twain's famous phrase, to enter her fictional world made him feel as awkward as "a barkeeper entering the Kingdom of Heaven."[16]

Critics have done much to promote Austen's "heavenly" image by characterizing her style in terms of her "deliberate and detailed" rhetorical patterns,[17] and by interpreting her work as a ladylike, lighthearted revelation of, to use D. W. Harding's ironic words again, "the comic foibles and amiable weakness" of her world.[18] It is undeniable that Austen's language strove for correctness; however, many critics have tended to overemphasize the classical harmony of her wording, her syntax and her rhetoric, and to overlook the tension between the elegant precision of her narrators' reports of characters' utterances and the disorder of these utterances. This disorder includes her use of syntactical fragments, of stylistic quirks, of illogicality and folly in the voices, reported in indirect or free indirect style, of individuals or the collectivity. The hypercorrectness of Austen's narrators can be seen as a comic foil for this disorder; the characters' mannerisms often subvert the rhetorical equilibrium of her prose.

And yet the joyful energy of her writing has been explained as a result of her delight in being fastidiously accurate. Mary Lascelles, for instance, observes Austen's "scrupulous phrasing," concluding that she must have "positively enjoyed" rewriting and polishing.[19] Typically, critics remain insensitive to Austen's narrators' obvious pleasure in shattering platitudes and shaking up prejudice and common assumptions, both official and unofficial, academic and popular. While to some of us Austen's great achievement is her uniquely irreverent, many-faceted laughter, in the view of Norman Page Austen's success as a novelist is a consequence of her "finely controlled use of language."[20] K. C. Philips finds in her prose evidence of a distaste for slang and of "a craftsmanlike interest in English words" that convinces him that "she agrees with Henry Tilney in his strictures, made in the best Johnsonian manner, on illogical expressions."[21] Philips sees no self-mockery in the passage from *Northanger Abbey* to which he alludes, a passage which can be read as both ironic and profoundly dialogic.

For a long time, not only Austen's language but her whole approach to the novel were considered affirmations of her conservatism, her untroubled reliance on the status quo. It is true that D. W. Harding, the founder of the "subversive" school of Austen criticism, described Austen as a sardonic ironist, emphatically refuting the view of her work as delicate, amiable satire. Nevertheless, Harding, like Q.D. Leavis,[22] exaggerated the individualism of her social critique. Similarly, Marvin Mudrick would later stress her individualistic ideology,[23] apparently assuming that the only socially critical stance that could be taken at her time was a Romantic one.[24]

Partly in reaction to the excesses of the "subversives," Alistair Duckworth presented Austen as a Burkeian Conservative whose heroines' moral choices support their cultural heritage, the "improvement" of their "estate." Such hereditary property is seen as a symbol of the ideal society, buttressed by stable secular institutions and founded on the religious principles of Christian rationalism.[25]

There are undoubtedly some similarities between Austen's view of the inevitability of community as the framework for interpersonal relationships and Burke's social philosophy, which "In opposition to individualist democracy ... set the idea of a People," as a corporation from which "no man can abstract himself."[26] Nevertheless, in Austen community does not mean a Platonic ideal, or, in Burke's terms, a grand "inheritance from our forefathers," a "noble and venerable castle" to be defended at all costs, although its walls be in need of repair.[27] Rather, community in Austen's narratives is typically actualized only in a "small band of true friends" (E, 484). The novelist's understanding of the term seems to point to the moral imperative to keep oneself open to the possibility of love as *agape*, even though the potential is seldom realized. At the same time, in her novels social rules and commonsense views also appear as a source of false certainty leading to ludicrous error and moral torpitude, and as a comic cover for hostility. Austen often uses war as the underlying metaphor for many relationships between individuals from different social classes or families, between friends, even between members of the same family.[28] A similar carnivalesque ambivalence may be noted in Austen's attitude to the problem of women's social situation.

Following Duckworth, Marilyn Butler even placed Jane Austen squarely with the dreary anti-Jacobin novelists, with their propaganda in defense of the status quo and their reaction against individualistic subversion of traditional values.[29] Butler interprets Austen's attack on sentimentality in *Sense and Sensibility* and elsewhere as a reaction against the revolutionary individualism that appeared to conservatives to be threatening orthodox morality. In spite of its merits, Butler's well-documented study fails to do justice to the complex attitude to social institutions found in Austen's fiction. Butler characterizes two "camps," conservatives and progressive individualists, partly on the basis of attitudes toward sentiment. And yet Butler herself recognizes that these attitudes were very complex during the eighteenth and early nineteenth centuries. While some conservative moralists identified Jacobin novelists with an emphasis on sentiment, actually many revolutionary writers were opposed to sentimentalism as well, for they saw it as an emphasis on the involuntary side of human conduct which encouraged inactivity and thus precluded active opposition to the status quo. Many radicals regarded sentiment as especially dangerous for women, since "the stress on feeling rather than reason, and on fine sensation rather than on activity" encouraged passivity which led to submission.[30] Indeed, a radical such as Mary Wollstonecraft was particularly repelled by sentimentality, which she felt to be often a "romantic unatural delicacy of feeling" fostered in women by "the herd of novelists."[31] Conservative writers, on the other hand, were often sentimentalists who stressed, as did Hume, Gibbon and Burke, the impotence of individuals, their inability to change the course of history.[32] Both

sentimentalism and its rejection, therefore, were eighteenth-century ideological phenomena that cut across all political lines. Jane Austen's attack on
sentimentality, in *Sense and Sensibility* and elsewhere, need not be seen, as does
Butler, as a reaction against the revolutionary individualism that appeared to
conservatives to be threatening orthodox morality. Rather, with Margaret
Kirkham, we can regard Austen's distaste for sentiment as a rejection of anti-
rational leanings that could particularly affect women.[33]

 Indeed, Butler emphasized conservative ideology in Austen's work to
a degree that obscured her awareness of the conflicts and hypocrisy of a society
that calls itself Christian and yet respects only wealth and status, and is
animated by greed and snobbery. Such a critical position thus fails to do
justice to the plurality of ideological voices in her novels. As Duckworth
himself states in an essay published twelve years after *The Improvement of the
Estate*, if Austen has been read in so many diverse and even contradictory ways,
it is because she starts from many contextual origins, and does not "achieve
'univocal' certainties."[34]

 It can be argued that the very wealth of contradictory readings of her
works is an indication of the complexity of her writing, of her ability to lend
credibility to diverse ideological positions in her narrative. Austen achieves
diversity by contextualizing the different moral perspectives of her characters
in a fabric of social relations by virtue of which personal choices acquire
broader and deeper meanings. Many different positions vis à vis the major
historical conflicts of her times are thus represented in her work, in such a way
that readers may form divergent images of the symbolic and semantic
implications of her novels. Paraphrasing Bakhtin on Dostoevski (cf. PDP,
35), we may conjecture that her personal position before the great changes,
movements and controversies of her historical epoch was ambivalent, and that
this ambivalence, perhaps deplorable from a political viewpoint, allowed her
to construct an artistic position which gave rise to her multi-voiced novel.

 As we shall see, in spite of the precision of most of Austen's prose and
in spite of her apparent respect for established customs, there are strong
elements of disruption in her narrative language which subvert the superficial
order of her writing. This study will argue that, the conclusions of many
analysts notwithstanding, Austen's style, as well as her handling of themes,
plot and characters, show the mark of the prevalent tendency of her narrating
voices, one of skepticism towards, rather than concurrence with, established
truths. Her skepticism is not grim or pessimistic, however, but imbued with
a sense of gay relativity.

 Before tackling this line of argument, however, we must contemplate
the question of *why* Austen's esthetic position was so long seen as primly
conservative. Some answers to this query are internal to her texts, involving
the critics' misinterpretation of the unique use of carnival in her narrative as
well as certain historical characteristics of the fictional tradition in which she

worked. Other plausible reasons for Austen's traditional image are external to the novels, having to do with typical attitudes to women during her times and with her position in the history of laughter.

An interesting trait of carnival is its tendency to appear coupled with a peculiar brand of conservatism: while those kept largely outside dominant groups mock an official ideology that justifies their exclusion, they are also highly skeptical of radical idealism. This position is a direct consequence of their skepticism vis à vis iconoclastic individualism and their respect for tradition, since, they suspect, most individuals are in some sense deluded. The laughter of popular festivity flourishes by opposition to the solemn rituals celebrating official truths, but, as stated above, it does not oppose a new dogma (say, the Truth of the People) to authority and officialdom; rather, in Bakhtin's view, it counters dogmatism with gay ambivalence (cf. RHW, 8-11). This ambivalence allows popular celebrations, with their mocking pageantry and their praising/insulting language, simultaneously to undermine certitude and to affirm belief. Similarly, in Austen we find an irreverent picture of the folly of "the neighbourhood" or of that collective character, "every body," coupled with a deeply ingrained sense of the inescapability of cultural and social ties. In her narrative, observance of traditional ways ("manners") is used as a stable point of reference when reporting relationships, and to provide some basis for making moral choices.

Another reason why Austen has been read as a staunch conservative has to do with the fact her novels mostly deal, as do many eighteenth-century novels, with the activities of gentlemen and ladies during their leisure time. The nature of this content has been misinterpreted as a sign of, if not frivolity, at least a bias toward privileged idleness, an unconcern for the affairs of people from the lower classes. It is true that, though Austen would probably include many more people in her definition of "gentleman" or "lady" than would her own heroine, Emma Woodhouse, Austen's fictional world is peopled mostly by those whose social standing allows them to visit each other. As Raymond Williams put it, "To be face to face in [Austen's] world is already to belong to a class." But then, it was not until George Eliot that the novel could include a recognition of "other kinds of people, other kinds of country, other kinds of action,"[35] of a certain bond of community between squires and tenants. And it was probably not until this century that a character born to a rich family (though in another English-speaking country) could, as Laura did in Katherine Mansfield's "The Garden Party," describe workers living in a cottage nearby as "practically neighbors!" Before the late nineteenth century, popular characters ware generally used only for comic effect (which, to her credit, Austen never did); part of the comedy was achieved by making fun of the speech of "common people." Such is the case, for example, with the caricaturesque letters written by the servants in *Humphrey Clinker.* The nearly illiterate style of these letters constitutes what Bakhtin calls "objectified discourse" (cf. PDP, pp. 181-204). In such discourse the voice of certain social types is heard, as it were, from the outside, as though the narrator were asking us to observe a specimen; it is a voice with which no dialogue is possible, for we have no real access to the character as subject. It was not until Mark Twain that English-language fiction could grant a central place to the subjectivity of a semi-literate rustic.

In spite of Austen's concentration on the social dealings among members of a certain class, she used her material, as David Daiches aptly put it, to expose "the economic basis of social behavior," unveiling "the economic objectives pursued by members of her class." Her picture of a heroine's happiness included sharing "the truly civilized life" which required to be "completely free from economic cares," and "in a position to enjoy . . . the arts . . . in perfect peace of mind." Daiches calls this the "country house ideal," observing that it was so far from being incompatible with a liberal frame of mind that it was the ideal which, in another continent, Jefferson would live. It was part of Austen's great originality to see, before Karl Marx, the relations among artistic, ideological and political ideals, and their inseparability from economic organization.[36] This "civilized ideal" of enlightened, humanistic leisure was nevertheless enmeshed with what can only be called an influence of the work ethic, for idleness in Austen is invariably frowned upon. Furthermore, her focus on social intercourse during mostly leisure moments was not incompatible with a tendency to side, not as much with the gentry, as with a less wealthy, non-landed group David Spring has called the "pseudo-gentry,"[37] against the aristocracy and the idle rich.

The conservative image of Austen has also been encouraged by factors external to her work. Many critics, in spite of Austen's ironic attitude toward society, have failed to see the need for a more dynamic reading of the novelist's conception of manners as a discourse framing relationships rather than as an intrinsically normative code. One reason for this failure has been her image as a conventional woman who would not have dared to challenge established social views. This image was partly due to the fact that most readers in the past have been conditioned to see women as mostly comformists and followers, never as innovators. The "sweet spinster" image was also largely based on her depiction by her family: her brother and nephew each published short biographies of the "authoress" stressing her "regular habits . . . and quiet and happy occupations," and extolling her self-denial and resignation.[38] The fact that after her death her sister, Cassandra, burned many of her letters and censored the rest must have helped to create the myth of her innocuous elegance, for it may be safely conjectured that Cassandra preserved only what was inoffensive.[39]

Another factor contributing to Austen's image as a kindly spinster was the typical Victorian conception of humor as benevolence.[40] As Stuart Tave tells us, for such Victorians as Carlyle, "the essence of humor is sensibility:

Janeites

warm, tender fellow-feeling with all forms of existence."[41] This conception is evident, for example, in G. H. Lewes' expression of what he considers Austen's "teachings": "charity for the ordinary failings of ordinary people, and sympathy with their goodness."[42] Such descriptions helped to build the foundation for Austen's image among "Janeites," those sentimental admirers of the novelist who extolled her "exquisite" penetration into comic foibles as well as her tender regard for all humanity. According to this position, Austen is a genteel, conservative author, incapable of challenging any received views.

Although this image has been largely superseded by a more complex view of her novels, its stubborn remnants survive interwoven with more sophisticated approaches to Austenian texts. And yet these texts lend themselves to a very different construction, as animated by a brand of laughter in which carnival is an important, indeed an indispensable ingredient. Furthermore, the function played by carnivalesque elements in her work is that of an iconoclastically feminist contestation to the status quo.

The question of Austen's feminism has been explored by several contemporary critics.[43] Unfortunately, some of the feminist readings of Austen seem startlingly unlike her. This misrepresentation may be due to the clash between many feminists' stress on women's cultural "secondariness" and Austen's lack of overt protest, the complexity of her resources in handling the "woman problem." Critics such as Gilbert and Gubar, who stress women's radical exclusion from culture, tend to see all writing by women as expressions of anger, fear and loathing. As Elaine Showalter points out, "Gilbert and Gubar . . . accept the essential psychoanalytic definition of the woman artist as displaced, disinherited, and excluded."[44] This viewpoint, while allowing them to achieve brilliant insights in reading secluded or tormented authors like the Brontës or Mary Shelley, seems flawed when they turn to Jane Austen.

Gilbert and Gubar picture Austen as an angry woman who camouflaged and repressed her impulse to rebellion. In their view, this impulse nevertheless surfaced in her supposed admiration for Mrs. Norris as "the vitriolic shrew" in *Mansfield Park*, or in the "monstrosity" of such characters as Catherine Morland in *Northanger Abbey*. Catherine is described as full of the gothic "terror and self-loathing that results when a woman is made . . . to accept as real what contradicts her perception of her own situation."[45] Such a dark image is hard to square with Catherine's gaiety and animal spirits. The novel's insistence on her ordinariness repeatedly mocks the extraordinariness of heroines in both gothic and sentimental novels. Catherine's "perception of her own situation," moreover, is improved and strengthened in the narrative. She does, it is true, learn she had been extravagant in her romantic musings about the *manifestations* of General Tilney's wickedness, but she finally comes to see that the substance of her appraisal of him had been correct. Gilbert and Gubar's failure to see Catherine's strengths can be regarded as an emblem of their difficulties in handling Jane Austen's fiction.

laughter as resistance

Other feminist critics have attempted to temper the view of Austen's "dark rage" against women's exclusion with a recognition of the stoicism of her moral stance. Thus, Allison Sulloway forces us to face the extreme intellectual and even physical privation Austen must have endured, and her smiling grace under such conditions. To Sulloway, the novelist's work is all the more admirable for the magnificent restraint of her passionate protest. Two of Sulloway's striking metaphors may give an idea of her approach: Austen as outcast ("Austen was classified with a category of noncitizens that included the mad, the indentured servant, the untutored . . . and even infants under maternal care")[46] and as soldier ("Austenian joy" is "a comedic gift" that shows her resilience "under prolonged adversity. It is a capacity similar to the instinctive courage of a soldier who rejoices when a single bird sings during a lull in the bombing.")[47] These images stress the limitations Austen encountered as a woman of her times, but they ignore the strengths she drew upon. If in many social senses she was a nonperson, and was denied the training her powers demanded, she made the most of her scanty formal education and proceeded to teach herself. If she bravely stood up to many privations as a woman of her times, her courage was not limited to her capacity to find some beauty in the midst of adversity, but it further moved her to use language as a means to shape her very personal, very effective response. We need, in sum, a more positive analysis of Austen's achievement than that offered by some feminist critics who stress the victimization of women.

Not all feminist critics of Austen have taken the dark, exclusionary view; probably the most influential of the recent feminist readings of Austen is one that stresses her rationalism. The success of this view has been such that the old image of the conventional, spinsterly Jane Austen has been superseded by a new, more complex figure, perhaps equally mythical, "a curious cross between Burke and Mary Wollstonecraft: a politically sophisticated and highly committed Tory idealist . . . *and*, simultaneously, a passionate supporter of contemporary radical ideas [about] women."[48]

imp

It was Margaret Kirkham who gave lasting form to this trend when she tacitly accepted Marilyn Butler's depiction of the novelist as a Tory in all other matters, while proposing that Austen held revolutionary views with regard to the identity and social roles of women. Although the conception of Austen as a staunch conservative needs to be tempered with a realization of the influence of carnivalized literature on her work, the postulation of her radical feminism represents a breakthrough in the evolution of Austen criticism. Kirkham accepts the picture of Austen as a "true daughter of the Church of England," but argues that the thought of such men as Bishop Butler had reconciled Christian beliefs with a natural grounding of morality on Reason, thus making religion compatible with rationalism. This made it possible for conservative feminists like Austen to "hold common ground on morals with less orthodox ones like Mary Wollstonecraft."[49]

We may never know whether Austen was influenced by Mary Wollstonecraft's ideas, or whether the two authors' attitudes to women had been shaped through convergent reactions to their historical context and through shared influences. Nevertheless, there are indeed many similarities between the two. For example, reading Wollstonecraft's repeated denunciations of the idea that pleasing men is women's major role in life brings to mind Miss Bingley's efforts to flatter Darcy. *Vindication*'s many injunctions to women to maintain robust health through exercise may remind a reader, not only of Elizabeth Bennet's brisk walk across muddy fields to see the ailing Jane,[50] but also of Catherine Morland's love of "rolling down the green slope at the back of the house" when she was a child (NA, 14). Some conservative writers of conduct books for women may have shared Austen's positive view of feminine exercise, but they, like Henry Tilney, tended to paint young ladies' physical exertions in delicate colors. Catherine herself naively disabused Henry of the notion that she needed such dainty feelings as an admiration for flowers in order to be induced to exercise: "I do not want any such pursuit to get me out of doors. The pleasure of walking and breathing fresh air is enough for me, and in fine weather I am out more than half my time.- Mamma says, I am never within" (NA, 174).

In some cases, some important episodes in Austen's novels are judged by reliable characters, and in ways that seem persuasive, on the basis of attitudes that are strikingly similar to those shown by Wollstonecraft. For example, at Box Hill Emma insults Miss Bates, who, as Mr Knightley says, has become dependent on her neighbors' generosity, and who has known Emma in better days, when Miss Bates was rich and "her notice was an honour" (E, 375). Emma's attitude is repudiated by Knightley; Emma herself comes to admit that she has behaved very badly. Their combined view of the situation is nearly identical to Wollstonecraft's appraisal, in the following passage in *Vindication*, of the effect of idleness on spoiled young women:

> I have seen [a young lady] insult a worthy old gentlewoman, whom unexpected misfortunes had made dependent on her ostentatious bounty, and who, in better days, had claims on her gratitude.[51]

We can also hear in Austen echoes of Wollstonecraft's criticism of sycophantic attitudes toward the landed class:

> One class presses on another; for all are aiming to procure respect on account of their property: and property, once gained, will procure the respect due only to talents and virtue. (V, 246)

Compare this statement to Elizabeth Bennet's determination not to be swayed by the almost overpowering alarm felt by Maria and Sir William Lucas as they prepare to meet the very rich and powerful Lady Catherine: Elizabeth had heard nothing of Lady Catherine that spoke her awful from any extraordinary talents or miraculous virtue, and the mere stateliness of money and rank she thought she could witness without trepidation. (PP, 161) Austen's condemnation of those who subordinate the value of individuals to considerations of rank and fortune places her close to Wollstonecraft. Furthermore, in Austen's fictional world social relationships are not seen as wholly settled and traditional. Austen's plots record, not unfavorably, many "changes of fortune--the facts of general change and of a certain mobility-which were affecting the landed families at this time."[52]

There are, obviously, differences between Austen and Wollstonecraft. For one thing, it seems irrefutable that Austen was more inclined to stress the value of the network of social relationships, of the community as the proper framework for the individual, than was Wollstonecraft. Also, in Wollstonecraft's writings the reader often gets a glimpse of her unconventional attitude toward female sexual freedom;[53] although sexuality represents a central energy in Austen's fiction, she rarely alludes to it directly. Wollstonecraft's greater openness may seem to us to be more in tune with the individualism of urban, industrial culture, than Austen's general attitude; Austen, however, was probably obeying a later trend toward reticence in sexual matters, a trend that would reach its zenith during Victorian times.

And yet, upon reflection, some of these differences between the two authors do not seem so marked. Austen's conception of women's sexuality does not differ radically from Wollstone-craft's. Several of Austen's characters act motivated by sexual desire, disregarding conventions. Although their actions are not condoned, two of them, Colonel Brandon's ward (SS) and Miss Darcy (PP), are presented as victims of their own inexperience and of male unscrupulousness. Austen does not condemn women's sexual feelings as unnatural or degrading, as conservative moralists tend to do. Even a shameless young woman like Lydia Bennet is never described with the loathing anti-Jacobins used when refering to female "vice": rather, she appears to be modeled after Wollstonecraft's condemnation of a style of young women's education in which, "Every thing that they see or hear serves to fix impressions, call forth emotions, and associate ideas, that give a sexual character to the mind" (V, 59). In similar terms, in *Pride and Prejudice* Elizabeth explains Lydia's "consent to live with Wickham" before marriage as a result of her idleness and frivolity:

> "Since the — shire were first quartered in Meryton. . . [she] has been doing every
> thing in her power, by thinking and talking [only about flirtation and officers],
> to give greater — what shall I call it? susceptibility to her feelings; which are
> naturally lively enough." (PP, 283-4)

Perhaps because Lydia is a victim of a mistaken education, Austen allows her to be received in Longbourn after her marriage, to Lady Catherine and Mr. Collins' scandal, and permits her to go on merrily with her vacuous life.

Another topic on which there is more similarity between Austen and Wollstonecraft that it would at first appear is women's maternal and conjugal function. Women's domestic role is not a degrading factor, either in Austen's novels or, in spite of Wollstonecraft's popular image, in the latter's work. One reason for this acceptance of domestic roles may be found in the fact that in the eighteenth century, especially in rural areas, women still enjoyed a certain economic independence from men, though the rapid industrialization would in the following century put an end to most domestic industries. This independence was a legacy of the seventeenth century, in which, according to Alice Clark, "the idea is seldom encountered that a man supports his wife; husband and wife were then mutually dependent and together supported their children."[54] Thus in *Pride and Prejudice* we see Charlotte Lucas enjoying the charms of "her home and her housekeeping, her parish and her poultry"; her employment in administrating these "concerns" and, presumably, the returns she obtained from the sale of dairy products, apparently compensated for her marriage to the absurd Collins (PP, 216).

Apparently we are still very far, in the late eighteenth century, from a sense of claustrophobia in the "feminine mystique." Although in *Vindication* Wollstonecraft warns that mothers should not make children the sole reason for their existence, she admits that child-rearing "has justly been insisted on as the peculiar destination of woman" (V, 331). The constant urgings to women in *Vindication* to acquire "sufficient serious employment" generally refer us to contented domestic scenes:

> I have then viewed with pleasure a woman nursing her children, and discharging the duties of her station. . . , the happiest as well as the most respectable situation in the world, . . . [adding] a taste for literature to throw a little variety and interest into social converse. (V, 249)

Ironically, in spite of Austen's image as more conventional, this idyllic picture of conjugal felicity will not be found in her work. When, in a rare passage, she does give us a brief glimpse of a happy marital relationship, it is not a vision similar to Wollstonecraft's idyll of the sexual division of labor; rather, she paints a comically egalitarian picture of Admiral and Mrs Croft sharing the reins of their carriage during a ride in the country:

> "Very good humoured, unaffected girls, indeed," said Mrs Croft. . . ."--My dear admiral, that post!--we shall certainly take that post."
> But by coolly giving the reins a better direction herself, they happily passed the danger; and by once afterwards judiciously putting out her hand, they neither

fell into a rut, nor ran foul of a dung-cart; and Anne, with some amusement at
their style of driving, which she imagined no bad representation of the general
guidance of their affairs, found herself safely deposited by them at the cottage.
(P, 92)

Outside of the exceptionally happy case of the Crofts in *Persuasion,* in
Austen's fiction very few individuals play either the conjugal or the parental
role sucessfully. In consequence, although the ending of each novel predicts
that the protagonists will achieve perfect marital happiness, their chances
appear slim, judging by the examples we have been shown.

However, on the need for additional social roles for women, a topic on
which Wollstonecraft takes a crusader's attitude, the novelist is silent. While
the author of *Vindication* laments that women of superior talents "have not a
road open by which they can pursue more extensive plans of usefulness and
independence" (p. 145), it is clear that Austen's heroines do not show "any
ambition to be admitted into the professions, to manage an estate or to join
the army."[55] Not one of the female characters in Austen's novels ever expresses
yearnings that could be considered the precursors to Jane Eyre's passionate
apology for her own discontent.[56] This silence is the more surprising because,
although they do not dwell on the fact, several of Austen's women seem to
have a clear perception of their restrictions. In *Pride and Prejudice,* for example,
the narratorial voice acknowledges that marriage "was the only honorable
provision for well-educated young women of small fortune," and that
"however uncertain of giving happiness, it must be their pleasantest preservative
from want" (PP, 122-3).[57] In *Emma,* Jane Fairfax feels doomed to a career as
governess, the same pursuit which Jane Eyre found so constricting; Miss
Fairfax compares it to slavery (E, 300). In *Persuasion,* Anne Elliot rejects the
old stereotype of woman's inconstancy and attributes the feminine tendency
to love longer than men, beyond hope, to a lack of mobility and of interesting
occupations (P, 232). Why then, do these women fail to protest against their
situation?

Part of the reason why Austen is nearly silent about the injustice of
women's social situation may be found in her determination to write
comedies about women whose fates are ordinary, rather than tragedies about
unconventional crusaders. If there are no feminist philippics in Austen it
might be because she recognized the inefficacy of such tactics in the
reactionary climate that followed the French Revolution; she must have seen
little use in indignantly denouncing women's plight to an audience that
would have almost unanimously deplored her views. What is most important,
however, is that Austen's general attitude as a narrator is far removed from
indignant discoursing or extended social commentary. Rather, Austen's
favorite political strategy was contestatory laughter, which she achieved by
her unique uses of satire and irony.

Thus, her works can be read as engaging her readers in a relationship in which the predominant attitude is an ironic one, although her irony is not of the acerbic, individualistic brand. Austenian ironic laughter is animated by a peculiar type of opposition to traditional views of women's situation and abilities, an opposition whose feminism is best understood by recourse to the ambivalent stance typical of carnival. Indeed, in her novels, especially in *Pride and Prejudice* and *Emma*, the whole of social reality is both minutely regulated by the omnipresent surveillance of "every body" and engulfed in comic, generalized hostility, in merry war. In fact, the carnivalesque ingredients in her prose make many of the traditional critical and theoretical approaches seem inappropriate to explain her irony. This study will show the significance of certain carnivalesque elements in her narrative, focusing both on her feminism and on the peculiar shapes of social satire and ironic language in Austenian laughter.

NOTES

1. D.W. Harding, "Regulated Hatred: An Aspect of the Work of Jane Austen," *Scrutiny* 8 (March, 1940), p. 147. Harding was referring fundamentally to the snobbish and sentimental cult of Austen by devotees who came to be known as "Janeites." (For a discussion of the controversy between "Janeites and Anti-Janeites" see Brian Southam, "Criticism, 1870-1940," in *The Jane Austen Companion*, ed. J. David Grey (New York: Macmillan, 1986), pp. 102-9.)

2. Mikhail Bakhtin, "Discourse in The Novel," *The Dialogic Imagination: Four Essays by M.M. Bakhtin*, ed. Michael Holquist, tr. Caryl Emerson and Michael Holquist (Austin: University of Texas Press, 1981), p. 262. All further references to this work will be marked DN and included in the text.

3. Sir Walter Scott, quoted in Claudia Johnsons's *Jane Austen: Women, Politics and the Novel* (Chicago: University of Chicago Press, 1988). Johnson adds that Madame de Staël "nailed Austen's work with devastating concision, *'vulgaire'* " (p. xviii).

4. See, for example, Katherine Rogers, *The Troublesome Helpmate: A History of Misogyny in Literature* (Seattle: University of Washington Press, 1966).

5. As Sandra Gilbert and Susan Gubar have put it, before a woman writer can find "literary autonomy, she must come to terms with the images on the surface of the glass, with, that is, those mythic masks male artists have fastened over her human face" (*The Madwoman in the Attic: The Woman Writer and the Nineteenth-Century Literary Imagination* (New Haven: Yale University Press, 1979), p. 17).

6. See Mikhail M. Bakhtin's *Rabelais and His World*, tr. Helene Iswolsky (Bloomington, Indiana: Indiana University Press, 1984). Further references to this work will be marked RWH and included in the text.

7. See Mikhail M. Bakhtin, *Problems of Dostoevski's Poetics,* ed. and tr. Caryl Emerson (Minneapolis, Minn.: University of Minnesota Press, 1984), especially pp. 156-7 and 160-78. Further references to this work will be marked PDP and included in the text. (Bakhtin's conceptions of carnival and of carnavalesque influence on literature will be discussed in greater depth in the following chapter).

8. Graham Pechey, "On the Borders of Bakhtin," *Bakhtin and Cultural Theory*, eds. Ken Hirschkop and David Shepherd (Manchester and New York: Manchester University Press, 1989), p. 52.

9. Caryl Emerson, "Problems with Baxtin's Poetics," *Slavic and East European Journal* 32 (Winter 1988), p. 507.

10. Vladimir Volosinov, *Marxism and the Philosophy of Language*, (Cambridge, Mass.: Harvard University Press, 1986), p. 22. (This and other texts have been attributed to Bakhtin, but there is no conclusive evidence. The "disputed texts" by Medvedev and Volosinov do seem to mesh easily with Bakhtin's thought.)

11. Mikhail Bakhtin, "Epic and the Novel," in *Dialogic Imagination*, p. 37.

12. Michel Foucault, "The Subject and Power," in *Michel Foucault: Beyond Structuralism and Hermeneutics*, eds. Hubert L. Dreyfus and Paul Rabinow (Chicago: University of Chicago Press, 1983), p. 212.

13. Foucault, "Subject and Power," p. 226.

14. Keith Thomas, "The Place of Laughter in Tudor and Stuart England," *Times Literary Supplement*, (Jan. 21, 1977), p. 79.

15. Ian Watt, "Introduction," *Jane Austen: A Collection of Critical Essays*, ed. Ian Watt (Englewood Cliffs, N.J.: Prentice-Hall, 1963), p. 7.

16. From a Mark Twain manuscript entitled "Jane Austen," quoted in Ian Watt, *Jane Austen*, p. 7.

17. Howard S. Babb, *Jane Austen's Novels: The Pattern of Dialogue* (Columbus, Ohio: Ohio State University Press , 1962), p. 25.

18. D.W. Harding, p. 346.

19. *Jane Austen and Her Art* (London: Oxford University Press, 1939), p. 101.

20. Norman Page, *The Language of Jane Austen* (Oxford: Brasil Blackwell, 1972), p. 9.

21. K.C. Philips, *Jane Austen's English* (London: Andre Deutsch, 1970), p. 17.

22. See Q.D. Leavis, "A Critical Theory of Jane Austen's Writings," *Scrutiny* 10 (1942). Leavis' positions, nevertheless, represent a significant contribution to the critical tradition, for they assail the image of Austen

as a facile, spontaneous, intuitive novelist, arguing that she was a mature, methodical writer who was deeply engaged in responding to the work of other novelists. Leavis also countered the view of Austen as prim and possessed of a "sunny temper," and argued against those critics who felt a need to "apologize for her inability to dwell on guilt and misery, the French Revolution and the Napoleonic Wars" (p. 64).

23. See Marvin Mudrick, *Jane Austen: Irony as Defence and Discovery* (Berkeley: University of California Press, 1952).

24. For a short review of other significant works of the "subversive" school of Austen criticism, see Alistair Duckworth, *The Improvement of the Estate* (Baltimore: The Johns Hopkins Press, 1971), pp. 5-10.

25. For an alternative view of "two meanings of improvement" in Austen, as a physical work involved in turning nature into economic growth and as the social improvement by which economic advantage is turned into "what is seen as a cultivated society," see Raymond Williams, *The English Novel: From Dickens to Lawrence* (London: Chatto & Windus, 1970), pp. 18-24. Williams sees in Austen "the development of an everyday uncompromising morality which is in effect separable from its social basis."

26. Raymond Williams, *Culture and Society: 1780-1950* (New York: Columbia University Press, 1958), p. 9.

27. See Edmund Burke, *Reflections on the Revolution in France*, ed. G.A. Pockock (Indianapolis: Hacket, 1987), pp. 27, 38.

28. For a discussion of generational conflict in Austen see Patricia Meyer Spacks, "Muted Discord: Generational Conflict in Jane Austen," *Jane Austen in Social Context*, ed. David Monaghan (Totowa, N.J.: Barnes & Noble, 1981), pp. 159-78.

29. Marilyn Butler, *Jane Austen and the War of Ideas* (Oxford: Clarendon Press, 1975), pp. 164-5.

30. Katherine M. Rogers, *Feminism in Eighteenth Century England* (Urbana: University of Illinois , 1982), p. 43.

31. Mary Wollstonecraft, *A Vindication of the Rights of Woman* (New York: Garland, 1974), p. 62.

32. Marilyn Butler, Chapter II.

33. Margaret Kirkham, *Jane Austen: Feminism and Fiction* (Sussex: The Harvester Press, 1983).

34. A. Duckworth, "Jane Austen and the Conflict of Interpretations," in *Jane Austen: New Perspectives* (New York: Holmes & Meier, 1983), pp. 29-38.

35. Raymond Williams, *The English Novel: From Dickens to Lawrence* (London: Chatto & Windus, 1979), pp. 18-24.

36. David Daiches, "Jane Austen, Karl Marx and the Aristocratic Dance," in *The American Scholar*, p. 189-90.

37. Spring shows that most of Austen's characters belonged, not to the gentry, but to a slightly lower class, that nevertheless tended to associate with the gentry. ("Interpreters of Jane Austen's Social World: Literary Critics and Historians," in *Jane Austen: New Perspectives* (New York: Holmes and Meier, 1983)). For this reason, throughout the present study the term "member of the middling classes" or even "middle class" is preferred to "gentry."

38. From her brother Henry Austen's "Biographical Notice of the author," first published as a preface to the posthumous volume containing *Persuasion* and *Northanger Abbey* in 1817; it was reprinted in Chapman's Oxford edition of *The Novels of Jane Austen* in 1933. J.E. Austen Leigh, her nephew, included his "Memoir" in his publication of the *Lady Susan* manuscript in 1869. Even as late as 1913, this nephew's son, William, and the latter's nephew, Richard Arthur Austen-Leigh, wrote *Jane Austen: Her life and Letters: A Family Record*, wich, according to Park Honan, "neglects nearly every reference to family tensions," and "offers a benign Austen-Leigh family version of Jane Austen's character" (Honan, *Jane Austen: Her life* (New York: St. Martin's Press, 1987), pp. 413-4.

39. For a discussion of how the "received" biography of Jane Austen helped to hide her rationalist feminism, see Margaret Kirkham's "The Austen Portraits and the Received Biography," in Jane Todd, ed. *Jane Austen: New Perspectives* (New York: Holmes & Harvester Press, 1983), pp. 53-60. Margaret Kirkham also outlines the severity of social condemnation of "free women" when she dicusses public reaction to Godwin's revelation about Mary Wollstonecraft's life; this reaction helps explain the need felt by Jane Austen's family to stress the "domesticated" image of the author.

40. For a discussion of the evolution of ideas of humor, see Chapter 2 below.

41. Stuart Tave, *The Amiable Humorist: A Study in the Comic Theory and Criticism of the Eighteenth and Early Nineteenth Centuries* (Chicago: The University of Chicago Press, 1960), p. 239.

42. G.H. Lewes, "The Novels of Jane Austen," reprinted from *Blackwood Magazine* 86 (1859), in *Pride and Prejudice*, ed. Donald J. Gray, Norton Critical Edition (New York: W.W. Norton, 1966), p. 323.

43. David Monaghan reviews feminist criticism of Austen in "Jane Austen and the Feminist Critics," *A Room of One's Own*, 4 (Spring 1979), pp. 34-9.

44. Elaine Showalter, "Feminism Criticism in the Wilderness," in *Writing and Sexual Difference*, ed. E. Abel (Chicago: The University of Chicago Press, 1982), p. 24.

45. Sandra Gilbert and Susan Gubar, *The Madwoman in the Attic* (New Haven: Yale University Press, 1979), p. 143.

46. Allison Sulloway, *Jane Austen and the Province of Womanhood* (Philadelphia: University of Pennsylvania Press, 1989), p. 27.

47. Sulloway, p. 84.

48. Kate Fulbrook, "Jane Austen and the Comic Negative," in *Women Reading Women's Writing*, ed. Sue Roe (New York: St. Martin's Press, 1987), p. 39.

49. Kirkham, *Jane Austen*, p. 23.

50. *Pride and Prejudice*, in *The Novels of Jane Austen*, ed. R.W. Chapman (Oxford: Oxford University Press, 1988), p. 41. All further references to Jane Austen's novels will be to this edition and will be included in the text.

51. Wollstonecraft, *Vindication*, p. 80. Further references to this work will be found in the text.

52. R. Williams, *The English Novel*, p. 19.

53. For example, Wollstonecraft ridicules the idea that "the common appetites of human nature" are indelicate in women (*Vindication*, p. 61).

54. Alice Clark, *Working Life of Women in the Seventeenth Century,* Reprints of Economics Classics (New York: Frank Cass, 1968), p. 12.

55. David Monaghan, "Jane Austen and the Position of Women," in *Jane Austen in a Social Context*, p. 110.

56. See Charlote Brontë, *Jane Eyre* (London: Clarendon Press, 1969), pp. 131-3.

57. Austen must have felt deeply the injustice of women's situation, which was apparent even to Richardson. In his novel *Sir Charles Grandison* (well known to the Austens, and satirized by Jane in a play by the same name written in her youth), Mrs Reeves comments that "in England many a poor girl [marries a man] she would little care for, if the state of the single woman were not here so peculiary unprovided and helpless." Sir Charles' proposed solution to this problem is to create "Protestant Nunneries ... in which single women of small or no fortunes might live with all manner of freedom, under such regulations as it would be a disgrace for a modest or good woman not to comply with." (*Sir Charles Grandison* (London: Oxford University Press, 1972), Part 2, Vol IV, Letter XVII, p. 355). Such a solution, of course, meant a forced renunciation of sexuality which would have been abhorrent to Austen.

Chapter 2
Carnival and Austen's Feminism

At first glance, nothing seems farther from Austen's novels than carnival. Undeniably, her style is diametrically opposed to the typical bawdiness of popular-festive traditions which, according to Bakhtin, influenced Rabelais, and which many critics regard as *sine qua non* condition for a literary work to qualify as carnivalesque. And yet in many senses her writings exhibit that "transposition of carnival into the language of literature" that Bakhtin described in Dostoevski. Indeed, as I read her work, there are some aspects of Austen's stance as a narrator that can only be analyzed with the aid of Bakhtin's conception of the "carnivalization of literature." Austen's attitude toward culture was colored by her complex response to conditions which denied women full accession to power, a right also denied to the common people, though in different ways. Bakhtin discusses popular festivities as a form of contestation to official, ritual celebrations of the "truths" amenable to the power structure; a similar approach can illuminate the ingenious ways in which Austen resisted "truths" that were inimical to women. Of course, she does not portray the body in terms of grotesque or hyperbolic references to eating, drinking, defecation, or to the genitals, as did most carnivalesque literature; nevertheless, certain aspects of her personal situation and education favored her use of some carnivalesque elements.

Indeed, the concept of carnival can help us to analyze the contestatory, joyful ambivalence of Austen's work. By "carnival" Bakhtin alludes not only to medieval festivities imbued with an "obvious sensuous character" and a "strong element of play" (RHW, 7), but also to the philosophic outlook embodied in these traditions. Carnival grew by opposition to "official feasts,"[1] in which participants solemnly celebrated "the triumph of a truth already established, . . . eternal and indisputable," and to which "laughter was alien" (RHW, 8-9). By contrast, "popular-festive traditions" were fluid, characterized by a temporary suspension of feudal structures as everyone in town "for a time entered the utopian realm of community, freedom, equality, and abundance" (RHW, 9).[2] These traditions built upon everyday manifestations of folk culture such as verbal parodies and gay representations of death, degradation and uncrowning. In carnival, figures of authority were mocked, while a fool (or a clown playing the role of a fool) was crowned and allowed to reign. In the apparent confusion, everything was debased so it could be reborn, and the most important regeneration was that of truth. Paradoxically, by suspending the validity of official truth, which proclaimed that God had ordained the people's exclusion from power, carnival made it possible for the people to believe. As "the true feast of time, the feast of becoming, of change, of renewal" (RHW, 10), carnival celebrated the people's faith in their difference from the powerful, in their own capacity to grow and the world's ability to be transformed.

As Keith Thomas explains, referring to Tudor England, although popular laughter was often a conservative force, "there was also a current of radical, critical laughter which . . . sought to give the world a nudge in a new direction."[3] This conception of popular laughter is substantiated by Emmanuel Le Roy Ladurie, who states that carnival acts as an instrument of "satiric, lyric, epic knowledge for groups in their complexity; therefore, [as] an instrument of action, with eventual modifying force in the direction of social change and possible *progress*, with respect to society as a whole."[4] Although, as Ladurie recognizes, carnival may be used for repressive or reactionary ends, the culture of marketplace and popular feasts was potentially subversive, for it turned the official ideology upside down so the people could believe in it without doing violence to themselves.

Finally, while popular interaction produced its own language and art forms, these in turn influenced the work of academically trained philosophers and artists who, like Rabelais, reveled in the democratic vision of popular festivity as "a banquet for all the world" (RHW, 185).[5] According to Bakhtin, carnival traditions gave rise to an artistic conception that flowered in the Renaissance and that was radically opposed to classical order. In modern times, some writers, who felt the deadening weight of official ideologies, received the influence of carnival indirectly, through literary sources (through the works of such writers as Rabelais and Cervantes, for example). Such writers incorporated in their work categories that together make up what Bakhtin called the "carnivalization of literature." These categories include, first, "free and familiar contact among people," with a suspension of hierarchical barriers; second, eccentricity, shown when a suspension of authority frees "behavior, gesture and discourse"; third, mésalliances, a combining of opposites, "the sacred with the profane, the lofty with the low, the great with the insignificant, the wise with the stupid"; and fourth, profanation, "a whole system of carnivalistic debasings and bringing down to earth," often coupled with the use of blasphemies and obscenity (PDP, 123). Typical of "carnivalization" is a tendency to parody sacred, lofty texts, and a peculiar type of laughter:

> Carnivalistic laughter . . . is directed toward something higher—toward a shift of authorities and truths, a shift of world orders. Laughter embraces both poles of change, it deals with the very process of change, with crisis itself. Combined in the act of carnival laughter are death and rebirth, negation (a smirk) and affirmation (rejoicing laughter). (PDP, 127)

This laughter is ambivalent, both destroying certainties and affirming belief, ridiculing the gods and "the highest earthly authority . . . to force them to *renew themselves*" (stress in the original—PDP, 126-7). Thus it is mocking, deriding, and yet triumphantly regenerative: "It asserts and denies, it buries and revives" (RHW, 10). It is a laughter which is "universal in scope, directed at all and everyone," and therefore often self-directed. In carnival no one is excluded from mockery, no one is spared, not even the one who laughs. Thus carnival sets its all-inclusive laughter in opposition to the celebrations of the people's exclusion from power typical of official feasts.

During the Middle Ages, the lower classes were made to participate in rites celebrating an official truth that sanctioned their social subordination as divinely ordained. Similarly, women of Austen's times were asked to acquiesce in a culture that had excluded them at many levels for ages.[6] Therefore, in spite of the misogyny of some conceptions of women in the popular subculture, a cunning contestatory attitude like that of folk carnival could be fruitfully applied to the feminine predicament. Through carnival the common people could subvert official ideology without immediately and obviously threatening the established order, without surrendering to their oppressors but also without suffering reprisals. These are all needs that women shared.

Before a woman can feel an affinity toward the irreverent attitude of carnivalesque literature, however, it might be necessary for her class position to reinforce her sense of being an outsider due to gender. It also seems imperative for her to be not only well-educated, but also endowed with enough intellectual self-confidence to be very daring. Her intelligence, furthermore, must exhibit a strong comical bent. In Austen all these conditions were met. From the viewpoint of class, she was something of an outsider because of the conjunction of several circumstances: her status was that of a gentlewoman, but her father, the Rev. George Austen, the descendant of an old Kentish family of woollen cloth manufacturers, had been orphaned at six and was propertyless. Her mother, Cassandra Leigh, "had ancestral ties with Oxford" and aristocratic relations, but was apparently portionless. (At Steventon Rectory, where George took her, Cassandra took to rural life without a murmur, tending her cows and pigs with admirable good humor.) While Jane was growing up, the family lived under "the shadow of hard poverty."[7] And "she spent her most productive years as what Barbara Pym would call 'a distressed gentlewoman.'"[8] Having been made to feel that she was of estimable origin yet poor, and having suffered the snubs and condescension of her fashionable relatives and their friends,[9] Austen could have either taken the atittude of insisting on rank as her due, or accepted the position of partial outsider. The former is the position of Sir Walter Elliot, ridiculed in *Persuasion*; the latter is the stance many of her heroines are forced to assume.

Austen, furthermore, was unusually well educated. Her family provided a propitious intellectual environment, since everyone loved to read, and it was not thought necessary to limit severely the range of female knowledge. Her father, himself academically successful at Oxford, cared "for the education of his daughters." Her mother, herself the daughter of a scholarly Rector, was enterprising enough to write spirited comic verses about everyday family affairs.[10] When Austen amused her family by penning *Love and Freindship*,[11] she already possessed astonishing intellectual self-assurance. In the face of a culture that from every corner proclaimed feminine inferiority, Jane Austen, a child, chose to laugh. Her juvenilia shows, as Virginia Woolf puts it, that "at fifteen she had few illusions about other people and none about herself"; and yet her writing was "spirited, easy, full of fun verging with freedom upon sheer nonsense."[12] Such a mind was highly compatible with the irreverence of carnivalesque literature; even as a child she was capable of laughing, not just at some ludicrous objects, but at everyone, including herself. Somehow she must have found in her readings a carnivalesque stance that she could use, and somehow she knew that she was doing something radically new. For Austen wrote not merely "for home consumption," but

> for everybody, for nobody, for our age, for her own; in other words, even at that early age Jane Austen was *writing*. . . —but what is this note which merges in with the rest, which sounds distinctly and penetratingly all through the volume? It is the sound of laughter. The girl of fifteen is laughing in her corner at the world.[13]

In the earliest fragments of her juvenilia, written when Austen was twelve, we find the strongest, most direct and unmixed influence of carnival of all her works, with the possible exception of *Sanditon*, her posthumous fragment. Those early dramatic sketches and brief narratives can be analyzed as clear illustrations of the four "carnivalistic categories" that make up carnivalization. If we except the use of obscenity, which is not found in the juvenilia (or, of course, anywhere in Austen), carnivalesque manifestations are so common in these childhood compositions that the latter appear almost as a catalogue of carnival influences on literature. Let us examine, as an example, an account of a first visit by one family to newcomers in the neighborhood, from the very first piece, "Frederic and Elfrida":

> [Elfrida and her companions] were struck with the engaging Exterior and beautifull outside of Jezalinda, the eldest of the young ladies; but e'er they had been many minutes seated, the Wit & Charms which shone resplendent in the conversation of the amiable Rebecca, enchanted them so much that they all with one accord jumped up and exclaimed,

> "Lovely & too charming Fair one, notwithstanding your forbidding Squint, your greasy tresses & your swelling back, which are more frightfull than imagination can paint or pen describe, I cannot refrain from expressing my raptures at the engaging Qualities of your Mind, which so amply atone for the Horror, with which your first appearance must ever inspire the unwary visitor.

> "Your sentiments so nobly expressed on the different excellencies of Indian and English Muslins, & the judicious preference you give to the former, have excited in me an admiration of which I can alone give an adequate idea, by assuring you it is nearly equal to what I feel for myself."

> Then making a profound Curtesy to the amiable and abashed Rebecca, they left the room and hurried home. (*Volume the First*, MW, p. 6)

One of the absurdities that first strike the reader is the visitors' open avowal of their impressions of the young ladies; the remarks both praising and abusing Rebecca are spoken with the freedom and familiarity the characters in the juvenilia so often exhibit. Two paragraphs below those here quoted, another instance of "free and familiar contact" can be found; in it we are told that the intimacy between the families "grew to such a pitch that they did not scruple to kick one another out of the window on the slightest provocation." The barrier thus hurdled, however, is not that of a social hierarchy, as in popular carnival, but that of manners, social conventions which demand that individuals show respect for others. In typical carnivalesque reversal, violence becomes a mark of loving intimacy.

Secondly, the whole passage, as indeed the whole composition, is fraught with obvious eccentricity; the socially unacceptable remarks addressed to Rebecca, for example, are underlined by the visitors' bizarre behavior in "jumping up" and speaking in unison. Thirdly, in the contrast between the "beautifull" Jezalinda and the "frightfull" Rebecca, we see one of the many mésalliances in which the childish writer delights. In the visitors' reactions to Rebecca herself, moreover, there is a further combination of opposites, as horror at her physical appearance gives way to "raptures" provoked by her "Mind." The incongruence between the "noble sentiments" and their object, the qualities of domestic and foreign muslins, is another instance of mésalliance. Fourthly, the emphasis on "noble sentiments" and reference to what "pen cannot describe" and "admiration of which I can alone give an adequate idea" constitute evidence of the parodic intention of the piece, which profanes the ridiculous solemnity of much sentimental fiction. This burlesque tone is, in the words of one critic, "the prevailing mode of the *Juvenilia*," where we see "Jane Austen taking off on practically every feature of the sentimental novel so popular at the time, from its cult of sensibility to its narrative techniques."[14] In the passage from the *Juvenilia* quoted above, the concluding sentence of the speech addressed to Rebecca derides not only the speakers' affectation of sensibility but also the typical self-centeredness of romantic heroes and heroines. However, laughter here is not merely based on ridicule. Since there is no sensible standpoint from which all absurdity can be judged, the whole is engulfed in a childish, joyful reveling in nonsense.

Of course, in Austen's adult works such traits appear only after having been substantially modified. In one of the later pieces in the juvenilia, "Catherine, or the Bower," we already find the author combining elements of carnival and features of narratives typical of the sentimental tradition. In this piece she was obviously making an effort to incorporate "the rules of composition," as she puts it herself when, in *Northanger Abbey*, she ironically refers to rhetorical demands for classical unity in stories (NA, 251). Such efforts would never lead her to classicism, but she did strive to work both in oposition to and within the mainstream of contemporary narrative. In the process of adapting the overall structure of the contemporary novel to her personal needs as a writer, her use of the carnival categories would be modified.

In Austen's mature fiction the first of these categories, "free and familiar contact," appears mostly in the tearing down of the barrier dominant culture has erected between the sexes, through the creation of, in the words of one critic, "a bright atmosphere in which men and women speak to each other as equals."[15] There are, however, other instances of jocose freedom and familiarity that are frequent in Austen, in the speech and behavior of some of her fools. The second category, eccentricity, became a feature of Austen's comic villains, like General Tilney and Lady Catherine, and of her many fools, clowns and rogues. The fool, with his/her stupid incomprehension of lying conventions, the rogue, whose lies are justified because she or he lies to liars or hypocrites, and the clown, a rogue who disguises as a fool in order to unveil social lies while seeming not to understand them, are three ancient literary devices serving to undermine conventional pathos or sentimentality (DN, 400-10). Austen modernizes these masks, combining their functions with a realistic depiction of characters.

One sense in which Austen's use of fools is carnivalesque is related to their opposition to the novel's own "official ideology." Thus, for instance, ludicrous characters previously held up to our ridicule express, from a feminist position, views that no one else accepts. Sometimes these views are directly stated by the character in question, as is the case of Mrs Bennet on the subject of the injustice of entailing property away from the female line. Both Lady Catherine (who insensitively boasts, before Elizabeth, that an entail "was not thought necessary in Sir Lewis De Bourgh's family"—PP, 164) and Mrs Bennet refer the problem to the will of individual men. On the other hand, Jane and Elizabeth Bennet, the two intelligent daughters, take the officially sanctioned position in trying to make their mother understand that neither Mr Collins nor Mr Bennet is personally to blame for the entail. Only Mrs Bennet expresses, mixed with a most unreasonable resentment toward the men involved, the very sensible view that there is no reason for such entails. Indeed, this argument stands, apparently overlooked, for no one in the novel counters it. A similar case is that of Catherine Morland naively feeling sorry for the writers of "real, solemn History" (NA, 108), and aiming very convincing criticism at contemporary historical methods, while the eminently sensible Eleanor Tilney defends the more conventional academic position. Again, no arguments are offered against the most cogent and original aspects of Catherine's critique.

On other occasions, a character whose lack of decorum the novel explicitly decries will treat misogynist fools in ways that a well-mannered young lady could never allow herself. Such is the case, for example, in Lydia's interruption while the insufferable Collins reads Fordyce's *Sermons to Young Ladies*. Collins has just committed a sin of the kind most likely to rankle his creator, the author herself: he has contemptuously declined the offer of a novel as material to be read aloud to the ladies. When he chooses, instead, Fordyce's *Sermon*s, he is compounding his offense by submitting his "fair hearers" to the soppiness and veiled misogyny of what Wollstonecraft called "most sentimental rant."[16] Only Mrs Bennet, intent on marrying Collins to one of her daughters, could submit to an evening of such reading without rancor. And, if neither Elizabeth nor Jane, our two dutiful young ladies, would condone Lydia's rudeness, they must rejoice in its effects when Mr Collins refuses to go on reading and challenges Mr Bennet to a game of backgammon (PP, 68-69). Thus Lydia, acting as an unruly woman, and thus as a female version of the carnivalesque type of the irresponsible "rake," becomes the means by which misogynous morality and decorum are subverted with impunity.

Austen's mature fiction abounds in all kinds of mésalliances, the third category of carnivalization. Her novels, for instance, often place characters with comically contrasting traits in interaction with each other or combine opposite traits in the same character. A recurring type of Austenian mésalliance shows one character attempting to solve a romantic problem, or a deficiency in a relationship, by some reference to food. The effect is an undermining of the seriousness of important moments or a bringing romantic love down to earth. Three brief examples: Mrs Morland surmises that Catherine's lovesickness is a pining for the culinary delicacies of Northanger Abbey (NA, 241); Mrs Bennet resolves to seek a reconciliation with her future son-in-law, Darcy, by asking Elizabeth what he likes to eat (PP, 378); Mr Woodhouse suggests to Emma that the best way to do Mr Elton a service is not to find him a wife but to invite him to dinner (E, 14). All three examples seem to confuse love and digestion, so that mésalliance mingles with profanation of sentimental love. Similarly, a show of altruism can be juxtaposed with references to cooking, as it happens when both Mr Knightley and Emma are tenderly contemplating the latter's generosity in sending a whole hind of pork to the Bateses; Mr Woodhouse's description of how pork must be boiled so it will not be unwholesome, and his reference to the effects of pork on the stomach comically debase the scene (E, 172). (The debasing effect does not mean that the tenderness becomes totally ineffective. In typical carnivalesque ambivalence, both the emotion and the act of ridiculing it can exist side by side.)

As examples of profanation, the last category of carnivalization, we can mention such debasings as Catherine's love of dirt in childhood, her naive assertion, when hoping for a walk with the Tilneys on a rainy day, that she "never minds dirt," together with Mrs Allen's placid concurrence, "No, . . .I know you never mind dirt" (NA, 14, 82), and Elizabeth Bennet's dirty petticoats after her walk to Netherfield (PP, 36). Furthermore, demolitions of the heroine's romantic stature occur everywhere in Austen, for everyone must occasionally submit to the folly of the John Thorpes, Collinses, Mrs Bennets, Miss Bates, Mr Woodhouses of her fictional world. Austen's narratives, however, are as far from depicting "dunces" the narrator can look down upon as they are from creating "villains" to be opposed to the purity and sense of the heroine. Rather, human fallibility appears to be generalized, for even the most sensible or the cleverest of characters will occasionally be shown to make fools of themselves. Thus, in the three novels we will consider all Austen's major characters, including the "super-excellent" Mr Knightley, are ultimately forced to face their own folly. Such encounters with their delusions and flaws constitute instances of moral "uncrowning," comparable to those the Lords of Misrule or Kings of Fools suffered during carnival.

This humiliation is not of a solemn cast, however, for her protagonists and her narrators laugh at themselves as much as at the world around them. As we laugh with them, that world is renewed, transformed into a place where women can live and grow. Laughter in Austen's works is very similar to "the people's festive laughter" of Bakhtin's account because it is, like the people's,

> also directed at those who laugh. The people do not exclude themselves from the
> wholeness of the world. . . . This is one of the essential differences of the people's
> festive laughter from the pure satire of modern times. The satirist whose
> laughter is negative places himself above the object of his mockery, he is opposed
> to it. The wholeness of the world's comic aspect is destroyed, and that which
> appears comic becomes a private reaction. The people's ambivalent laughter, on
> the other hand, expresses the point of view of the whole world; he who is
> laughing also belongs to it. (RHW, 12)

The generalized, often self-directed laughter of Austen's narrators undermines the established, official ideology regarding women and love (see the following chapter for a brief account of this ideology), and it does so by means of feminist carnivalesque irony.

There is, however, one aspect of Austen's work which is almost as far from popular carnival as her more traditional critics would have it: her approach to the image of human corporality. In Austen's fictions there are none but the sketchiest physical descriptions, and certainly no earthy blending of the body with the world around it through bodily functions. Two types of limitations precluded Austen's use of carnival images of the grotesque body: its male bias and the increasing prudery affecting literature, a movement which would culminate in a shunning of all allusions to sexuality in Victorian times. Indeed, many aspects of the folk culture of carnival were inimical to women, proposing a celebration of corporality that mutilated the female body. As Ronald Paulson tells us, the conventional image of a headless woman on a tavern signboard under the name "Good Woman" presented one "subliminal image of woman . . . at this popular level of consciousness: the 'good woman' is all body, without head, tongue, mind or spirit."[17] The word "body" here is synonymous of "headless trunk." Such images of women must have influenced Rabelais, in whose work, as Wayne C. Booth has said, we observe a sexist exclusion of women, both literal and symbolic, for "even the passages most favorable to women are spoken by and addressed to men who are the sole arbiters of the question [of the *querelle des femmes*]."[18] Although Bakhtin's reading of Rabelais does not acknowledge it, there is obvious misogyny in such episodes as that in which the Lady of Paris is followed and pissed on by 600,014 dogs, in punishment for rejecting Panurge's advances. As Mary Russo puts it, "Bakhtin . . . fails to acknowledge or incorporate the social relations of gender in his semiotic model of the body politic."[19]

Furthermore, Rabelais' use of popular images of eating, drinking, urinating, defecating, spitting, etc., like those images themselves, not only suggests a merging of the body with the world but also represents an attitude of mastery, of appropriation (cf. RHW, 282-3) that is triumphantly male.

This triumph, though Bakhtin only refers it to banquet imagery, appears in relation to a public display of bodily functions in which typically only some males participate. While medieval and Renaissance priests raged from the pulpit about women's bodies as the gates of hell, it does not seem possible that the attitudes of people of both sexes to their own bodies could have been the same. On the other hand, it is difficult to imagine how a defiant public show of the male body could be made without *both* challenging its repression by officialdom *and* triumphing over women.[20] And of course, *women* can hardly hear or read males' use of such imagery without feeling, at best, excluded from the audience. The grotesque images of "eating, drinking, defecation and other elimination" cannot be fully dissociated from their misogynous meaning.[21]

In addition to the incompatibility between male-dominant images of the body and her artistic objectives as a woman writer, Austen also faced another historical constraint: the reticence in the handling of sexual matters that came to be expected of all authors, male or female. By the first decade of the nineteenth century literary allusions to the body and sexuality were becoming increasingly less frequent. This cultural change in attitudes to corporality in turn affected readers' attitudes towards the carnivalized "grotesque body." As European culture was affected by a gradual rise in individualism, academically educated writers lost the ability to understand the meaning of sexual and scatological obscenity in the tradition of folk culture or in Rabelais' work: "Obscenity [had] become narrowly sexual, isolated, individual, and [had] no place in the new official system of philosophy and imagery" (RHW, 109).

Not only bawdiness, but also any reference to sexuality in literary works, were increasingly frowned upon. I do not mean to enter here into the controversy over what Foucault has called "the repressive hypothesis."[22] I merely state the obvious: towards the beginning of the nineteenth century we find fewer references to pregnancies or to the genitals, in any style or form, than there appeared in previous works. Finally, during the Victorian era, the point was reached when a character like Catherine Earnshaw Linton in *Wuthering Heights* could suddenly deliver a baby in the midst of a passionate episode of ecstatic reunion and stormy jealousy, without the readers having been given a single previous clue about her pregnancy. The body had become unspeakable.

Furthermore, women writers of Austen's times needed to exhibit even more restraint than men in references to the body, especially to what Bakhtin quaintly calls "the material bodily lower stratum." There is probably more frankness in Austen's fictions regarding pregnancies[23] and even the possibility of a Lydia Bennet "coming upon the town" than most fictional works will allow during the remainder of the nineteenth century. Nevertheless, her frankness was never such as to risk offending her contemporaries. We must remember that she lived during times when antifeminist repression was most explicitly linked to fears of what was supposed to be the sexual debauchery and general lack of restraint of Jacobins and revolutionaries. Any woman author's free reference to sexuality would invoke images of libertinism, especially in the wake of the publication of Godwin's *Memoirs of the Author of "Vindication of the Rights of Woman,"* a work which revealed Wollstonecraft's liaison with Imlay, her conceptions out of wedlock and her suicide attempts.[24]

In spite of the limitations imposed by these historical situations, in Austen's novels a form of overcoming "the confines between bodies and between the body and the world" (RHW, 317) was indeed achieved, though by means very different from those of traditional carnival. Her evident interest in the material world is usually linked to cultural reality, to the economic, political and ideological framework of the society of her time. In her works physicality is strong,[25] but the walks in the countryside, the dances, the offering and taking of hands among characters, are all part of interactions in which they often both seek pleasure and aspire to create ties of love and a spirit of community. Thus the body is placed at the center of a semiotic of social intercourse and inter-subjectivity, relating to the world, not as the popular-festive "grotesque body," but as the point of intersection for all social relationships.

At the same time, in both popular and literary traditions in Europe we find another source of carnivalesque images, that of the sexual reversals Natalie Zemon Davis has called "women on top," whose subversive potential could be put to feminist use. In broadsheets or carnival farces, sexually active, disorderly women appeared "going beyond what can ordinarily be expected of a mere female," ruling themselves "and thus deserving to be like men."[26] These images, originating in old myths and festive customs, could be used for both reinforcement and subversion of the status quo. The "disorderly woman" was "a multivalent image and could operate to widen behavioral options for women within and even outside marriage, and to sanction riot and political disobedience for both men and women in a society that allowed the lower orders few normal means of protest." It was not easy, however, to use carnivalesque images for feminist ends while these images remained strongly tied to misogynist ideas. For this reason, Davis tells us, "one strain in early feminist thought argued that women were *not* by nature more unruly, disobedient and fickle than men." Christine de Pisan, for example, would argue that "If anything, it was the other way around"; that is, most women were more modest and sober than most men.[27] Although Austen saw virtue and vice, as well as abilities, about equally distributed between the two sexes, in her work she would adapt the carnivalesque figure of the disobedient female for feminist ends.

During the seventeenth and eighteenth centuries, this imagery was widely disseminated through books, in the theater, and in "stories, poems, proverbs and broadsheets,"[28] and therefore accessible to Austen as she constructed certain aspects of her feminine characters. Austen dressed the image of the "unruly" or "disorderly" woman in respectable clothes in creating Catherine Morland, whose sexual drive is strong and assertive yet naively expressed; she selectively robed a giddy young woman with only some of the garments of disorder to produce Lydia Bennet, who lusted after "officers," but who, after living with Wickham out of wedlock, would marry him and remain monogamous.

Lydia's reiterated disregard for social and moral norms is clearly related to what Davis describes as "the unruly woman unmasking the truth," exhibiting sexual licence and ridiculing the men who should be restraining her. Such an attitude provided "a chance for temporary release from traditional and stable hierarchy." It also acted as "part and parcel of conflict over efforts to change the basic distribution of power within the society." The unruly "woman on top" constituted a reversal of orthodox femininity; play with this ambivalent image in popular art "not only reconfirmed certain traditional ways of thinking about society, it also facilitated innovation in historical theory and political behavior"[29]

Austen's lusty young women are viewed sympathetically, like Catherine, or at least allowed to get away with their actions, like Lydia, when they are spontaneous; however, her narrators will frown upon self-assertive young women who take the sexual initiative when they are also greedy and calculating, like Isabella Thorpe or Mary Crawford. Nevertheless, whether Austen's narrators approve of or derogate these unruly "women on top," the texts use the image of giddy or headstrong women as initiators of sexual relations or as outspoken and disobedient moral agents, unintimidated by men, to deride the ideology underlying women's social function and at the same time to force it to be utopically renewed. As will be discussed below, Austen's heroines refuse to bow to fathers or suitors; their process of psychological and moral growth submits them to a humiliating "uncrowning" which, in typically carnivalesque fashion, debases their status as novelistic heroines, but which does not lead them to subordination to any man. Indeed, Austen was breaking ground when she incorporated carnivalesque elements into her fiction.

In some respects, carnival was particularly amenable to Austen's presentation of her moral and philosophical position. In gay, carnivalesque ambivalence, her novels reaffirm the social value of matrimony and filial respect, but only after certain unprecedented conditions have been established: only after the protagonists have matured and asserted their freedom of choice and perception, and after the people around them have been brought to recognize this freedom. Such happy endings are possible because Austen's novels rest on an ideological structure in which a sense of community prevails and where concern for others is a dominant value. Austen's characters are placed in situations in which, as Elizabeth Langland observes, "tension between social demands and individual needs [is] mutually enriching."[30] For Austen, individuals can only exist in dialogue with a community and its conventions; and yet neither are individuals "naturally" good, nor is community intrinsically benevolent. Only a vigilant skepticism, often forcing individuals to mistrust their own motives as much as their neighbors', will allow for individual growth.

Austen's feminine characters undergo a process of growth that can be compared to the classic conception of *Bildung*, for they realize at least some of their emotional, intellectual and moral potentialities and are invariably brought to the point where they can "accept a responsible role in a friendly social community,"[31] although the friendliness is limited to a "small band" of well-wishers within the larger village. The role heroines accept is always a conjugal and domestic one; if Austen's novels went no further than this, they would indeed be liable to the familiar critical accusation of their being "limited." For characters to develop in order to fill predetermined slots, to undergo pain and conflicts only in order to accept ready-made roles, would be senseless. If such were the case, Austen would almost qualify as the writer of "Greek adventure novels," in which, according to Bakhtin, time leaves no traces on the hero, for "at the end of the novel that initial equilibrium that had been destroyed by chance is restored once again."[32]

Austen's solution to this quandary was complex. For one thing, the protagonists of the three novels analyzed here do not grow simply by learning and accepting societal norms. Rather, their *Bildung* occurs in comic moments of revelation equivalent to carnivalesque "uncrownings"; as such, they reveal a philosophic truth about human fallibility. What's more, Austen effected a radical transformation of the ideological world as she found it by making women the subjective centers of her novels, the unapologetic subjects of perception, emotion and moral choice. In her three satiric *Bildungsromane*, then, we find that the "emergence of a new man" Bakhtin considers the mark of this genre[33] acquires an unexpected twist: The feminine characters do not *become* "new" human beings, the equals of men in their abilities for thought and discourse. Rather, they are revealed to be such, in spite of common beliefs and expectations, as both the men and the women characters evolve. The reader, then, is asked to adopt a novel attitude: to regard women as fully "human," as the term was generally defined in the eighteenth and nineteenth centuries, that is, as "rational creatures." In this sense, we might say that the "emergence of a new man" (or woman) occurs subjectively in the reader.

Austen's feminism is discernible in her favorite political strategies: in contestatory laughter, which she achieved by her unique uses of satire and irony, and in the ways in which she built the consciousness of her heroines. Indeed, the subjectivity of her heroines was, in a sense, unprecedented in novels. Although Austen's protagonists owed much to the depiction of the heroines of sentimental novels by her "sister authors," she seems to have built many of her characters more by contrast to those of her literary predecessors than by following their lead. We must place Austen's resolute affirmation of women's equality through the delineation of her heroines' subjectivity in the context of attitudes toward women characters shown by the novelists who preceded her. Indeed, the whole question of the subjective treatment of characters, in Austen and others, is related both to women's writing and to important historical changes.

During the seventeenth and eighteenth centuries, more women wrote literary works in England than ever before. One reason for this increase can be found in certain ideological changes of the time. According to Foucault, these centuries saw the appearance of a new subjectivity through the exercise of disciplinary, infinitesimal, constant control.[34] Foucault finds a relation between these changes and the rise of the modern European states, in which both a new strategy for economic production and a new form of warfare appeared, producing new forms of social control and new conceptions and modes of operation of the individual conscience, a new subject. A new military type of discipline emerged and became the model for pedagogy (and for the hospital and the prison), leading to the constitution of the modern subject.[35] The model man was no longer the violent, individualistic warrior who overwhelmed his opponents by force, but a modest, disciplined man. This change may have tended to close the gap between males and females, perhaps allowing authors to see women more readily as fictional protagonists, and allowing women to see themselves as potential authors.

If Foucault's analysis is correct, however, the resulting disciplinary style for the production of subjectivity must have created a paradoxical situation with regard to women. Children, both male and female, gradually entered a school system where a generalized form of discipline, aimed at achieving social control, acted by means of techniques and procedures that produced "docile bodies." Power now became attainable and could be exercised through controlled, disciplined action. This new model was not antithetical to women's cultural modes of action and sensibility, was indeed rather amenable to them; the education of the two genders no longer produced beings as different from each other as the warrior and the matron of classical antiquity. After all, to induce docility was probably the primary goal of the education of women. This fact has led Nancy Armstrong to posit the emergence of an epoch-making ideological reality in eighteenth-century novels. Armstrong argues that Richardson's *Pamela*, that milestone in the sentimental novelistic tradition, introduces a form of feminine subjectivity that will become normative, a model for the bourgeois individual of either sex.[36] However that may be, women were still excluded from warfare and from dominance for economic, social and ideological reasons. It was still expected that they should accept their subordination to males, as a consequence of a supposed female nature that had its basis on tradition. In time, however, it would become more and more difficult to uphold women's submission to men, or to appeal to a male superiority that could be considered radical and innate. Asked to revere a masculinity that could only boast of constitutive superiority in its physical strength and its ability to wage war, some women became increasingly rebellious. These contradictions in the social relations between the genders became one of the ingredients that would lead to the feminist revolt of modern times.[37]

It was inevitable for the fictional works of the time to reflect this ideological unrest. Of course, the ages-old abeyance of feminine to masculine subjects slowly changed modes, but it was not abolished. In the typical sentimental novel by Austen's predecessors, although the "woman problem" had its influence in a number of ways, the normative position continued to be to accept the subordination of feminine characters to masculine ones. The contrast between this generalized subjective subordination and the moral and intellectual self-reliance of Austen's protagonists shows the originality of Austen's feminist response.

The subjectivity of Richardson's heroines, for example, was strongly colored by what J. M. S. Tompkins calls the "gesture of submission" to males.[38] In Richardson's epistolary novels the action is seen and reported by the heroine; thus it may seem that her subjectivity establishes the moral and intellectual norm. Nevertheless, although Pamela, for instance, tells her own story, her voice does not originate in her own desire, for Pamela does not desire[39] and does not act, except in reaction to Mr. B's desire. Her consciousness is almost all response within a socially sanctioned moral and religious framework. Pamela, in fact, follows the dictum of another of Richardson's characters, Harriet Byron in *Sir Charles Grandison*, who recommends that women after marriage turn from "over-lively mistresses" to "obliging wives."[40]

It is a fruitful exercise to compare Austen's presentation of her protagonists' subjectivity to Richardson's approach to feminine characters in this novel, which was a great favorite in the Austen household (and which Austen already satirized in a comic play written when she was a child). Richardson, furthermore, was a decisive influence on women novelists who continued to work in the sentimental tradition. A discussion of how women and their relations to men are presented in this novel can provide a proper background against which to appraise Austen's achievement.

Harriet Byron, for one thing, is far from being over-lively; she will be even more obliging after her marriage to Sir Charles Grandison. This great man is Richardson's manly paragon, created in order to satisfy those among the reading public who wanted the novelist to produce a "good" hero in contrast to the profligates Mr. B and Lovelace. Sir Charles, that model of discipline and control, is everywhere the leader, the man who decides and shapes everyone's destiny. For all his chivalrous, mild gentility, this "most noble of males" holds strongly to the need for total subservience of females to males. He frowns upon women authors; women are often "disgraced" by the "title of Wit and Poetess" (Part 1, Vol. II, Letter XXXI, p. 431); he holds that women were created in order to delight men, "not to torment us" (Part 2, Vol. IV, Letter IV, p. 274).

Sir Charles Grandison (which, like all of Richardson's novels, had a great ideological influence on the general reading public, in Britain and in all of Europe) was also in tune with its times in that it included a feminist, Grandison's sister, Charlotte. This young lady is destined to tame her lively sense of humor in deference to her ridiculous, adoring husband. Though Charlotte resists her brother's influence, his greatness dwarfs the women. As Harriet says to Charlotte: "O how great is he! And how little are we!" (Part 2, Vol. III, Letter XVIII, pp. 108-9). Charlotte's witty feminist discourse, based on her presumption to wilfully dominate men or to consider herself men's equal, is not difficult for her brother to counter. Through Sir Charles' gentle remonstrance and direction and Harriet's example of submission, Charlotte escapes the terrible fate of becoming a termagant like Lady Beauchamp. But the novel disarms both Charlotte's insubordinate wit and Lady Beauchamp's "shrewish" anger. In Sir Charles' verbal battle with the latter, he explains why women's rebelliousness against men is so absurd. Women, being unable to fight or use violence but "in words," are ultimately innocuous; furthermore, their words cannot wound. Only fools take women's anger seriously, when it is so easy to turn "the lady's displeasure into a jest." Any man "of common penetration may see to the bottom of a woman's heart"; if many are baffled, he explains, it is because women may often "not know your own minds." Finally, women fall into such states because

> Women, madam, were designed to be *dependent*, as well as *gentle*, creatures; and
> of consequence, when left to their own wills, they know not what to resolve
> upon. (Part 2, Vol. IV, Letter IV, pp. 274-80—stress in the original)

Sir Charles' picture of women as weak of will and poor in self-understanding is of a piece with the attitudes of those of Richardson's women characters that are most admired in the novel. Furthermore, Sir Charles Grandison is convinced that even weak and stupid men, such as Charlotte's husband, are somehow to be revered and submitted to by their wives for the sheer fact of their being male.

It is thus not surprising that Harriet Byron, that model of feminine perfection, should see her reason for being in revering the superiority of Sir Charles, the gentle but resolute warrior. This position of the heroine's subjectivity was continued in novelistic fiction by Fanny Burney, whose *Evelina*, for example, stands in awe and reverence of "the best of men," her adoptive father, Mr Villars, and later of the man who will be her husband, Lord Orville. Thus her subjectivity, though central in the novel, is also subsumed under a superior (male) one.

Women novelists, however, did not simply adopt Richardson's models. Faced with the humiliating image of femininity they encountered at every turn, women authors adhering to different political camps literally made a virtue of necessity, idealizing their own attitude of obedience as evidence of a sublime, uniquely feminine spirituality. Thus, paradoxically, the innate superiority of males was both upheld and countered precisely through submission, which became a new criterion of excellence. According to J. M. S. Tompkins, mere submission, a trademark of sentimentalism, was not enough:

> By an act of will [oppressed females] abrogate reason, quell discrimination, and not only accept but approve the fiat they bow to ... Fanny Burney's Mrs Tyrold "considered the vow taken at the altar to her husband as a voluntary Vestal would have held one taken to her Maker; and no dissent in opinion exculpated, in her mind, the least deviation from his will."[41]

In spite of such unabashed servility on the part of some of their characters, women novelists tended to counterbalance recommendations of submission with unconventional attitudes toward sexist stereotypes. Burney's Mrs Tyrold herself was the strong spouse in her marriage, for instance, while her husband was the weak one: "Mr Tyrold revered while he softened the rigid virtues of his wife, who adored while she fortified the melting humanity of her husband."[42] Mrs Tyrold, then, becomes a living paradox, an iron-willed warrior who worships and follows a soft-hearted commander.

In addition, as Claudia Johnson has shown, many women novelists used ridicule of freakish feminist characters (such as Harriot Freke in Edgeworth's *Belinda*) as a rhetorical device producing an ambivalent effect; feminist speeches at times convincingly "expose what genuinely *is* irrational about the code of female delicacy." Similarly, in Burney's *The Wanderer, or Female Difficulties* "the anti-heroine's feminist ravings, though duly dismissed by 'sensible' characters, provide accurate running commentary on the humiliation and injustice suffered throughout the novel by the heroine, Ellis."[43] In all Burney's novels heroines appear to be in constant jeopardy due to men's lasciviousness; the novels seem to protest against the injustice of sexual harassment while emphasizing female weakness and helplessness. On the other hand, the heroines' constant need of male protection against sexual harrassment can be seen as a denunciation of "women's social vulnerability": as Judy Simons puts it, "Women's identity [seems] reliant on male status, but this in itself is shown as a hazardous source of security."[44] Nevertheless, even novels by radical feminists tended to present women as feeble, although in works by Mary Wollstonecraft and Mary Hays it is "the evils [women] are subject to endure,"[45] rather than feminine nature itself, that degrade and weaken them.

Austen's treatment of the heroine's subjectivity presents a strong contrast. In her fiction we find, uncompromisingly and unapologetically, women as subjects, as the focus of perception, who relate to men on the grounds of equality. Thus, for example, both Elizabeth Bennet and Darcy will have to mature before they reach an understanding, although Darcy, by his own admission, needs a more profound and painful reformation. Even in *Northanger Abbey* and *Emma*, where the heroes act as the heroines' mentors, the irony ultimately turns against them; as we shall see, both hero and heroine are forced to grow in moral terms. All Austen's heroes and heroines, in these three novels at least, will become the butts of the narrator's irony.

In many of Austen's novels the intellectual and/or moral excellence of the feminine protagonists also allowed the author to present a series of ironies, notably the incongruence of a social situation in which women could not assume roles for which they seemed eminently capable. Who could deny that Elizabeth Bennet, for example, would preside over the Longbourn estate, with its farm and tenants, better than Collins could ever hope to do? Or that Elinor Dashwood, if given the required education, could come to preach better sermons than Edward Ferrars? The fact that so many of Austen's excellent feminine characters will not only be barred from authority or from the professions, but will also have to submit to immoral or inept males, contradicts the perfect happiness promised at the conclusion of each novel. What is more important, Austen creates characters whose gender does not determine their powers of perception or their will; all other things being equal, men and women may be equally adept at bellicose exchanges, equally capable of being minutely and rigorously disciplined. Thus, for example, for an Emma who is less disciplined than her Mr Knightley we have a Jane Fairfax who is much more controlled, prudent and constant than her Frank. Moreover, the contradiction between women's abilities and their conventional destinies is built into each of the narratives in a different way.

Furthermore, in Austen's novels we find elements of an alternative type of subjectivity, one that is not wholly based on the power to lead docile bodies through a collective, atomized, militaristic discipline (cf. Foucault's *Discipline and Punish*), and one most resolutely *not* based on worshipping the warrior/ male. Such is Anne Elliot's subjectivity of service, based, not on submission, but on the *power* to lead in a crisis when it is necessary, not to dominate, but to help others (cf. P, 110-1). Anne Elliot's strength is not generally recognized, but Captain Wentworth, just back from making a fortune on war and initially scornful of any virtues not based on a certain unbending "fortitude and strength of mind" (P, 88), will learn to admire it. Similarly, Fanny Price, the heroine of *Mansfield Park*, derives her strength from her resolute reliance on the Christian morality everyone preaches but which almost all sacrifice to worldly convenience. Even Edmund, a Christian minister, is initially blind to Mary Crawford's faults not simply because he is attracted to her, but also because his living in a corrupt society has made him more sensitive to her disrespect against patriarchs than to the ugliness of her greed and snobbery (cf. MP, 60-64). But if he does not recognize her mercenary attitudes, her contempt for the lower orders, as sins, it is because in this society Christian equality and community are myths, for they do not directly contribute to what articulates social forces. Christian ideology, indeed, needs a lot of retooling before it can help to promote that type of discipline which is an art "of composing forces in order to obtain an efficient machine."[46] The greed and snobbery of the higher classes, on the other hand, can be aids in the composition of forces leading to bourgeois efficiency, and thus they are tolerated or overlooked. In the end, however, both Sir Thomas and Edmund will recognize the moral superiority of Fanny's alternative, unwordly, non-domineering subjectivity, while Fanny herself will discover the lie of the moral leadership of the patriarch.

A very similar type of subjectivity, of course, is commonly taught as an ideal of submission to subjugate women—but in Austen's fictional worlds it does not achieve this end. For her narratives always end by instituting a partial, carnivalesque utopia, in which equality between the genders is possible and domination is defused, but which, like all utopias, also represents an indictment of social reality. (For utopias, from Thomas More onwards, posit a non-place, an impossible state which presupposes and derives from a deep dissatisfaction with actual places and possible states.)

At the same time, Austen's fiction recognizes that many forces in her culture assert male superiority. Austen treats this assertion as myth through her satiric assault on heroism. In accordance with Austen's ironic attitude toward heroism, the terms "heroine" and "hero" need to be understood in her novels in a sense devoid of presumptions of superiority. (Some of her male and female protagonists, for instance, excell in virtue or talents, which, far from making them exceptionally infallible, generally make their errors more significant.) In this study these terms refer to characters who act as centers of the action and foci of perception, but not as champions of moral or intellectual battles. Her novels both make fun of the martial mentality that produces novelistic heroism *and* show that war pervades society, since it is waged by men and women through many forms of social intercourse, and not only by men on battlefields.

Moreover, Austen's portrayal of social conflict is unique, in that it is meshed with a strong awareness of the ties of social cohesion. In her novels the sense of community is strong, and social relations are a very important part of characters' lives. In those episodes in which characters are shown to evolve, for instance, their relations to their social milieu are strongly implicated. The texts clearly deplore the haughtiness of a Darcy or the snobbery and manipulativeness of an Emma as obstacles to possible communication with others or to potential feelings of community. However, the actual communities (Meryton, Highbury) themselves are profoundly flawed. These communities (or the "neighbourhood" Austen wrote about, a group of neighbors from the "middling" classes, the gentry and the pseudo-gentry) are not idyllic villages, but rest on a network of invidious relationships among often grasping and greedy neighbors perpetually in covert competition and conflict, indeed in a type of serio-comic social war. In addition, social intercourse occurs in a field of mutual, generalized surveillance. Henry Tilney alludes to such surveillance in his famous phrase about "a neighbourhood of voluntary spies" (NA, 198). Elizabeth Bennet briefly acknowledges it in her comment on neighbors "triumphing over us at a distance" when Lydia elopes, and the narrator refers to it in ironic remarks about the disappointment of Meryton's "spiteful old ladies" when Lydia neither becomes a prostitute nor returns to be secluded forever in a distant farm house (PP, 293, 309). It is, finally, implied in all the obstacles Jane Fairfax and Frank Churchill encounter, mostly in the form of kindness from their well-meaning friends. These friends, from Mrs Weston to Mr John Knightley, without meddling as directly as Mrs Elton in Jane's affairs, do argue, for instance, against Jane's walking in rainy weather to the post-office for her letters. Although their motivation is protecting her health, they are unwittingly endangering her secret communication with Frank. Even the excellent Mr Knightley will interfere in the two lovers' enjoyment of their rare moments together, asking Miss Bates to stop a duet by Jane and Frank when Jane's voice thickens after only two songs (E, 229). Frank and Jane, who have very few opportunities for being together, throughout their short duet must also be reminiscing about the time when they sang these same songs at Weymouth, where they fell in love and became engaged (E, 227-9). Therefore, Jane's voice thickening (to Mr Knightley a symptom of fatigue) is probably a result of her emotion as the two lovers communicate covertly through their singing. Thus, Mr Knightley's paternalistic instincts lead him to cut short a precious moment of intimacy between the two lovers. In such a community as Highbury, both males and females cooperate to control relations between the sexes.

The flaws in the social structure, furthermore, are especially evident in the circumstances surrounding women's domestic and conjugal roles. In spite of the evolution by which the "heroes" learn to accept woman's equality, individual males who respect the woman they marry cannot abolish all the social conditions that conspire against equality in marriage, nor can they create a society where women's powers may be usefully employed outside of child-rearing. That Austen was aware of such severe limitations on a woman's possibilities for happiness is evident in her portraits of older women who often provide intimations of what may befall the heroine. Thus we have, for Catherine, the portrait of Mrs Morland exhausted "at the end of a morning" spent teaching her many children (NA, 110); for Elizabeth Bennet, the image of Mrs Gardiner at Pemberley, feeling the heat and tired from their walk, still having to wait while her husband looks at the trout (PP, 254); for Emma, the near-mirror of Mrs Weston, married to a happy-tempered man, but needing to exert herself like a "sweet-tempered woman and a good wife" to fulfil her duties (cf. E, 38, 255; see also Miss Bates' comments about "how much trouble" Mrs Weston has had in preparing the party at the Crown, E, 322). Perhaps the most poignant portrait is that of Mrs Croft, "as intelligent and keen as any of the officers around her" (P, 168), and yet lacking her own field of employment on which to exercise her powers.

In spite of all of these problems, Austen's heroines do not rebel against social demands. When these fictional women, who lead ordinary lives, encounter the myriad social conventions that proclaim women's inferiority, they do not tilt at these windmills. Often, they do something more revolutionary: they laugh. The resolution of the conflicts acting in the narrative justify their levity, for a happy ending is inevitably reached. In the Austenian plot, Christian utopias of personal growth in a propitious milieu are reached in the end; women mature, marry men to whom they relate as equals, and are promised "perfect happiness." Thus in Austen's conventionalized endings readers enter the realm of "free and familiar contact" that, according to Bakhtin, constitutes the proper medium for unofficial, festive laughter, in the sense that the requirements that women show deferential respect and abeyance to men are lifted.

The novels themselves recognize the situations of "perfect happiness" reached at the end of the novels as worlds which cannot exist. (And rightly so, for a milieu which purports to be part of early nineteenth century English society and at the same time guarantees "perfect happiness" to all, and particularly to married women, would be by definition impossible.) This recognition is achieved by separating the endings from the "real" fictional world of the preceding narratives through ironic narrative devices. The narrative techniques in question achieve by other means what Bakhtin describes in a medieval play as the erasing of boundaries between dramatic action and life. Instead of symbolically eliminating "footlights" that "separate the play from real life" (RHW, 257), what Austen's final chapters do is call attention to the presence of the footlights, to the strings that move the puppets, to all the *trompe l'oeil* devices. The happiness promised is not only at variance with the overall skeptical tone of the preceding action, but is also shown to be a fictional convention, revealed as part of the dramatic illusion-creating devices (scenery, props, lighting, etc.).

Austen's skepticism, moreover, is not limited to women's fates or to the moral fiber of remote country villages. Culture itself is suspect, for language inescapably offers characters ways of understanding the world that often become oversimplifying containers into which all experience must be poured. These cultural concepts correspond to what Bakhtin calls "centripetal forces" in language, tending to ideological uniformity, seeking to insure "a maximum of mutual understanding in all spheres of ideological life" (DN 271). They are forces which coexist with their opposite, the centrifugal forces of heteroglossia, or multi-languagedness, that may give rise to dialogism. In Austen's novels we see centripetal forces operating when characters spout social norms or conventional, axiomatic-sounding labels. Such labels and norms cover innumerable topics, from the need for young women to love flowers so they will go out and exercise, to the propriety of young women and men riding about the country in open carriages or the appearance of old abbeys in fictional narratives and the villainous character of their owners (*Northanger Abbey*); from the needs of single young men in possession of a good fortune or the requirements for a woman to deserve the title of "accomplished," to the proper parental attitude toward a daughter who lives with a young man before she marries him (*Pride and Prejudice*); from what constitutes the standard of perfection in young men, to the attraction men feel toward submissive women or the power of a person's virtue and superior ability to make inferior beings acknowledge superiority (*Emma*). The many ideological labels and norms put into play in the narrative are most often placed by Austen in an ironic light, shown to be homogenizing, stupefying clichés. As the few examples listed above suggest, these clichés are found both in "commonsense," everyday beliefs and in novelistic discourse.

Austen's ironic and satiric stance, then, was unique; her laughter was aimed at both the commonplace, commonsense ideology of "every body" and the literary traditions of her predecessors. Nevertheless, while Austen's delineation of plot and character often proceeds by satiric contrast to the fiction of her "sister authors," Austen's attitude is far from what Bakhtin calls "external and crude literary parody," with its flat condemnation of the parodied discourse. The subtlety and complexity of Austen's text can be compared to the "cunningly balanced dialogism of parodying discourse" Bakhtin finds in *Don Quixote* (DN, 413). Austen's parody is double, aimed at deflating *both* the view that contemporary novels are inferior to the classical solemnity of literary masters *and* the sentimental novel's convention of the pure, young, long-suffering heroine. By making a simultaneous attack on classical tenets and the modern feminine heroine, Austen's *Northanger Abbey*, as Julia Prewitt Brown puts it, "is challenging the Western tradition of heroism itself."[47] And the challenge, in this novel as in *Pride and Prejudice* and *Emma*, is made by laughter.

Neither from the viewpoint of genre nor from the perspective of her language is Austen's laughter easy to characterize. If we compare Austen's satire to the basic types recognized by traditional critics, the "mock-heroic," the "burlesque," and the "travesty," or even if we appeal to the concept of "menippea," we soon realize that none of them can be easily applied to her work. For Austen does not ridicule fools by contrasting them to admirable, superior models of heroism (mock-heroic), nor does she use bawdiness and obscenity to deal with a "presumed 'high' victim in a 'low' style" (burlesque) or indulge in "a deliberately inept imitation of a high style or manner"[48] in order to mock illiteracy or satirize pretentious or elevated literature (travesty). Superficially, her prose may seem closer to the mock-heroic for the syntactic elegance and elevated diction of her narratorial voices—if one dismisses the disruptive force of the characters' individual and collective voices. Upon closer examination, however, Austen's work may be closer to the basically subversive stance of travesties, burlesques, or menippean satires, in that her novels tend to undermine official literary ideology in general and martial or patriarchal heroism in particular.

Both menippean and Austenian satire subvert the notion of heroism while redefining and symbolically regenerating humankind by admitting that everyone is in some way deluded. In her juvenilia, for instance, Austen shows her reaction to two of the most important cultural sources of the idea of heroism in a young woman's education: history and sentimental and gothic novels. In "The History of England from the Reign of Henry the 4th to the Death of Charles the 1st," she parodies prejudiced historians who saw events as the actions of a few heroes and villains. As one critic, Brigid Brophy, suggests, the satiric tone of "The History" overcomes the common "childhood dream of inhabiting the gothic and absolutist splendor" of tales of great "ousted families and deposed monarchs."[49] In this short work and in other parodic pieces found in the juvenilia, including her mockery of sentimental novels, the reader can observe many of the traits Bakhtin points out in his discussion of "menippea" (PDP, 112-9, 121-47).

Eighteenth-century mock-heroic satire, on the other hand, was largely based on a conception of admirable greatness and ludicrous smallness corresponding to how characters and contemporary writers measured up to epic warriors and to the poets who sang of them.[50] As a satirist, Austen differs from Dryden, Swift or Pope in that she does not share the reverence they show toward the past. Nor does she adopt tactics similar to those used by Fielding, who, in the episode of the churchyard fight involving Molly Seagrim (*Tom Jones*, Book IV, Ch. 8), also plays on the contrast between "the Homeric style" and a violent brawl among low-class characters. This conventional type of satire, by upholding heroic and classical stature, indirectly serves to uphold the status quo and reinforce officialdom.

Austen's novels, on the contrary, do not use superior, flawless characters as foils for folly; Austen's heroes and heroines, from Catherine Morland to Mr George Knightley, grow by realizing their own delusion. (I believe the only exception is Anne Elliot, whose emotional growth involves not so much an improvement in perception and judgment as the recovery of hope for happiness.) When, in *Northanger Abbey*, *Pride and Prejudice* and *Emma*, characters experience the "brief epiphanic moments [that] often replace the continuous unfolding of an action" in feminine narratives of development,[51] the effect is often one of comic self-revelation. It is so, for instance, when "it darts through" Emma that if she fears that Harriet may be loved by Mr Knightley it is because he "must marry no one but herself!" (E, 408). Elizabeth Bennet herself makes fun of the growth of her own love for Darcy (a love made possible only by accepting how blindly prejudiced against him she has been) by telling Jane that it "has been coming on so gradually, that I hardly know when it began. But I believe I must date it from my first seeing his beautiful grounds at Pemberley" (PP, 373).[52] These characters' comic "moments of truth" involve their realizing that they, like everyone else, are liable to misconceptions.

Human blindness, then, is not a failing present only in the mob, nor are so-called "superior" beings exempt from it. On the contrary, the higher the degree of an Austen character's discernment, the greater its responsibility to become aware of its flawed perceptions. In this sense, we find satiric intent in Austen. According to Dryden, Horace's satire uses ridicule to "correct the vices and follies of his times."[53] Austen's novels, however, do not satirize through monological correction; rather, they lead the reader on a psychological investigation of generalized forms of comic delusion that have their roots in "vices and follies of her times."

Austen's satirical stance is more similar to the burlesque of Butler's *Hudibras* than to Dryden's, Swift's or Pope's satires, in the sense that Austen, like Butler, exhibits a radically skeptical attitude toward all forms of heroics. Both Austen and Butler distrust the mythification of war implied in hero-worhip: Austen, because it is based on a model of humanity that excludes women; Butler, because it appeals to an idealization of valor and self-sacrifice while it feeds on a pursuit of profits from which the lower classes are usually excluded. Both Austen and Butler were opposed to violent civil revolts, being too skeptical of political or religious convictions to justify destroying villages and human lives for their sake. In *Hudibras*, war becomes a collective madness incurred "When civil Fury first grew high/ And men fell out they knew not why."[54] Butler's is the laughter of a writer who sides with the common people, who stand to gain nothing from war: "Men venture *necks* to gain a fortune;/ The Soldier do's it every day/ (Eight to the week) for sixpence pay" (II, i, 512-4). The poem does not oppose "good," serious warriors or righteous heroes to the folly of the ones who created the revolt, but attacks the very justification of war by disclosing the mercenary motivations behind it.

Austen's work can be shown to be grounded on a similar (though implicit) irreverence toward the mythification of war, at least toward the idealization of the ability to participate in martial conflict as the definition of full humanity. For if the myth of glorious war is noxious to the common people, who die in battles that make others rich, it is no less so for women, whose exclusion from access to this glory diminishes them in patriarchal eyes.

Austen's narratives reveal an awareness of the symbolic pervasiveness of war and of the consequences of its idealization, for war appears in many comic episodes as an underlying metaphor for social contacts. In *Pride and Prejudice*, especially, the language of war is repeatedly employed; to name but a few examples, such language is used satirically to describe skirmishes between Miss Bingley and Elizabeth, "attacks" by Lydia on friends and neighbors and by Mrs Bennet on marriageable bachelors and on anyone whom she wants to bend to her opinions. The language of "the battle of the sexes" is used to refer to Elizabeth's attempts to "conquer" Wickham's heart; the very appearance of the conventional phrase is one signal to the reader that this relationship will not be good for Elizabeth. Such martial language is not used "heroically," but demoted to the level of ironic cliché. The bellicose terminology used to show characters conversing in prosaic settings on prosaic subjects serves both to uncover the hostility underlying social intercourse in an outwardly tranquil country village and to deride the idealization of war.

Austen and Butler may seem antithetical if, like traditional critics, we concentrate only on the latter's impudent and bawdy language and therefore dismiss it as verging on the "wantonly destructive."[55] If, on the contrary, we discover Butler's satiric undermining of martial heroism, we may begin to realize that Butler, like Austen, does not temper his consciousness "of the folly, hypocrisy and gullibility of men" with reverence for golden exceptions, realized in great heroes:

> What impressed [Butler] . . . was man's proneness to delusion. 'There are but few Truths in the world,' he said, 'but millions of Errors and falsities, which prevayle with the Opinion of the World.'[56]

Butler is aware of the generalized "fatal love" of human beings for "their own notions," their "confounding those 'Pictures of things in the Imagination' with 'their originals in Nature.'"[57] This is a realization that can be seen at work in Austen's work as well, for her fiction is a study of the different failings which can lead characters to misperceive what they experience. The human flaws blinding her characters include pride, prejudice (obviously, *Pride and Prejudice*), love (*Mansfield Park*), inexperience and the reading of gothic novels (*Northanger Abbey*), or of romantic novels and poetry (*Sense and Sensibility*), or idleness combined with "a disposition to think a little too well of herself" (*Emma*). *Emma*, especially, is a work that seems bent on placing doubt in the path of (almost) all anthropological certainties, all epistemological continuities.[58]

Austen's art is, like Butler's and, in another field, Hogarth's, "an outsider's art." In a work that contrasts Hogarth to Fielding in terms of "popular and polite art," Ronald Paulson has shown that Hogarth's work

[in Marcuse's terms] stimulates revolutionary consciousness, while Fielding. .
. remains on the side of the dominant society, even when he is aware of its
failings. [If Hogarth found less opposition than Paine it was] because there was
no French Revolution to . . . act as context for Hogarth's utterance; and because
Hogarth's language . . . placed on the periphery what Paine placed squarely in
the center. Moreover, Hogarth was never advocating overthrow; he was only
materializing a folklore [which took his art] back to lost sources of energy. Both
as politics and as aesthetics the subculture stimulated in Hogarth a nostalgia for
the past. . . : it sought a restoration of ancient liberties.[59]

While in much of Hogarth's work the placement of images of opulence in the
periphery suggested injustice by contrast to the grotesque central images of
poverty, in Austen's novels the placement of historical conflicts in marginal
position suggested women's limitations by contrast to the domestic scenes
shown in the center.

The great upheavals of her time, the Agrarian and Industrial Revolutions,
the French Revolution, the Napoleonic Wars, were actively present in her
narrative, yet ironically denied a place in the foreground. But the "large"
issues of national life were always there, lurking behind such commonplace
events as Sir William Lucas' mayoralty in Meryton and his knighthood after
an address to the king, Mr Gardiner's business in Cheapside, the commercial
origin of the Bingley fortune, the ——shire regiment and the whole campful
of soldiers near Brighton, Sir Thomas Bertram's colonial property in Antigua,
his seat in Parliament, General Tilney's "affairs of the nation" and Miss
Tilney's fear of riots for Captain Tilney's sake, the indigent gypsies that
frightened Harriet Smith, William Price's commission, Captain Wentworth's
ships and his fortune made at sea.[60] Almost invariably, Austen's attitude to
social mobility seems to be positive, while snobbery in members of any class
is condemned; as we shall see, injustice and slavery are indirectly decried.

Like Hogarth, both Butler and Austen exhibit a peculiar mixture of
radical social critique and conservatism, perhaps as a direct consequence of
their skepticism: since most individuals are in some sense deluded, in case of
doubt the safest course may be to follow tradition. It is Butler's blatant
skepticism about the glory of war and heroism, more than anything else, that
justifies Dryden's description of Butler's satire as "Varronian."[61] Varro, "one
of those writers . . . called *spoudogeloioi*, studious of laughter," considered his
own satires menippean,[62] for he shared Menippus' irreverent attitude to
Homer's epic presentation of heroes; Menippus, however, mocked the solemnity
of great classics with, in Dryden's own phrase, greater "cynical impudence and
obscenity."

The use of bawdiness and obscene language obviously separates Austen
from typically menippean satire. Austen's satire is far from the menippean
brand in that the former does not, even remotely, concern itself with

"grotesque images of the body" or "the material bodily lower stratum," or with billingsgate speech.[63] Nevertheless, Austen's work may be seen as closer to menippea than it at first appears, if we consider the reason why such language is used in the genre, and if we ask ourselves whether Austen may not seek to achieve similar ends through other means. One should take into account, when deciding whether to call a work menippean, the author's attitude vis à vis society and the reader, more than structural or other distinguishing marks. From this perspective, we find two essential ingredients in menippea in, first, an irreverent, sarcastic yet playful, anti-establishment attitude, assumed from the viewpoint of a social outsider, and second, a tendency to flaunt artistic and social conventions.[64]

On the other hand, it is doubtful whether sexual or scatological frankness and an attitude of opposition to the *status quo* will suffice for a work to qualify as menippean, if they appear in a joyless, negative, bitterly critical satire. Swift and Voltaire, for example, have often been regarded as examples "of misanthropy, of destructive mockery."[65] The former, brilliant as he is, often deserves Ian Watt's accusation: "Poised between the squalors of passion and the inoperancy of reason, Swift sat so long on the fence that the irony entered into his ... soul."[66] Of the latter, Bakhtin comments that his "laughter is reduced to bare mockery. ..., almost entirely deprived of the regenerating and renewing element" that is typical of carnival (RHW, 119).

Austen's works comply with the first condition, festive opposition to officialdom, in their ironic, decided resistance to all misogynist traditions in narrative. Her irony, of course, is much more subtle and complex than that of typical menippea. Partly for this reason, her novels do not fully meet the second condition, a flaunting of artistic and social conventions. Austen's fictional texts appear to remain within the bounds of novelistic and social tradition, while effectively undermining basic conventions. As Stuart Tave observes, "Jane Austen was unique, a cheerful wit, equally free of innocence and indecency."[67] Some Victorians, however, will later adopt forms of humor that seem to owe much to Austen's: Lewis Carroll and the Wilde of *The Importance of Being Earnest* exhibit, each in his own way, a type of anti-establishment irreverence disguised in respectable garments that allows them, to paraphrase Harding, to be read and enjoyed by the very people they gaily demolish. The people "demolished," however, are not those vulgar souls who do not know the dominant discourses, nor those hacks who are far below the intelligentsia, but those in power. And they are laughed at, not because they ignore the social or intellectual norm, but because they follow it. In a sense, it is social, intellectual, and ideological norms themselves that are under attack in Austen, Lewis Carroll and Wilde's *The Importance of Being Earnest.*

In *Northanger Abbey*, for example, Austen strove to undermine with laughter the exquisite pathos of persecuted virtue of protagonists of sentimental and Gothic novels and thus their established form of heroism. And she did so, not by opposing novels to classical epics, but precisely in recognition of the right of novelists to be ranked with "any other literary corporation in the world" (NA, 37). Paradoxically, she upheld the right of her "sister authors" to be taken seriously in order to attack them, not as ridiculously small, but as worthy of being assailed. The novelist makes this position clear in that famous passage at the end of Chapter V protesting the "general wish of decrying the capacity and undervaluing the labour of the novelist, and of slighting the performances which have only genius, wit, and taste to recommend them" (NA, 37-38).

This passage occurs, however, in a novel that is intended to mock the convention of the heroine as passive victim in both sentimental and gothic novels. Catherine Morland, Austen's "anti-heroine," is described throughout the entire narrative in ways that contrast her prosaic ordinariness to the unrealistic, improbable extraordinariness of "Cecilia, Camilla and Belinda." Austen insists, however, that she is not parodying such novels because she finds them wanting, but rather because she admires them as works "in which the most thorough knowledge of human nature, the happiest delineation of its varieties, the liveliest effusion of wit and humour are conveyed to the world in the best chosen language" (NA, 38).

In *Pride and Prejudice* and in *Emma*, Austen uses parody more sparingly. One form satire takes in these novels is the repeated humiliation of the heroine that is also present in *Northanger Abbey*. This humiliation does not occur because a hero's greatness dwarfs the heroine, but because heroism, male or female, is subverted. In addition, satire, in *Emma* even more than in *Pride and Prejudice*, is directed at the respective communities of Highbury and Meryton, at the relations among neighbors, their blindness and competitiveness, the conventionality of their language. Through all these means, these novels counter many received ideas of femininity and women and thus attack officialdom, undermining the status quo through laughter.

The most characteristic Austenian weapon against a culture that looks down on women is her irony. But she does not use it only for the defense of women. Through her ironic language she attacks the very presupposition that commonly held cultural views constitute the truth, assailing the generalized conceptions of reality that people trade back and forth, either in social interactions or in more academic uses of language. It is thus not surprising that Austen's typical use of irony may appear as the diametrical opposite of the dominant shape this trope took among satirical writers who preceded her and who constituted the literary establishment..

For while to the Augustans, according to Ian Watt, irony was a way to differentiate the élite from the mob,[68] for Austen it was often a route by which she found, in those who excelled in wit, judgment or "elegance of mind," similar failings to those found in ordinary people. Augustans saw themselves as a "righteous minority, ever battling for truth against every kind of deviation from the norm."[69] The Augustan understanding of irony, furthermore, was tied to a view of laughter as vulgar and reprehensible:[70] "the true gentleman, like Fontenelle, *'n'a jamais fait ha ha ha'*... and Swift's prose rigidly obeys the code of irony which, like that prescribed for Prussian officers, allows no more than *'ein kurzes militarische Lachen'*—a single, chilling `Ha!'"[71] Gentlemen, Lord Chesterfield informed his son, never laughed; of himself the nobleman said, "since I have had the full use of my reason, nobody has ever heard me laugh."[72] Although men such as Johnson found such strictures ridiculous, the third Lord Shaftesbury similarly observed that laughing befitted only "porters, carriers, clowns."[73] The controversy on laughter was old when Chesterfield's *Letters* were published in 1774, for in 1694 Congreve was already mocking the figure of Lord Froth, "a Solemn Coxcomb," who asserted that "nothing is more unbecoming a Man of Quality than to laugh; Jesu, 'tis such a vulgar expression of the Passion! every body can Laugh."[74]

Austen is far from agreeing with such condemnations of laughter. One need only remember that Darcy's witty refusal to dance at Sir William Lucas' house was couched in terms very similar to Lord Froth's: "Every savage can dance." Darcy's statement seems comparable to what Ronald Paulson calls "Chesterfield's distancing of the body," aimed at feeling superior to one's surroundings;[75] this aim is precisely Darcy's failing, as Elizabeth Bennet will tell him. In *Pride and Prejudice* we repeatedly find the heroine defending her right to laugh, affirming that she dearly loves to laugh, "laughing heartily," proposing to wait until Darcy learns to be laughed at (PP, 57, 174, 371). In *Northanger Abbey* Catherine Morland and Henry Tilney fall in love in conversations in which they make each other laugh. And in *Emma* the heroine not only makes others laugh, but mentally laughs at herself. Emma frequently jokes, in ways that can be subversive. For example, her joke supposing that Mr Knightley has mistaken Mr Martin's meaning ("It was not Harriet's hand he was certain of; it was the dimensions of some famous ox"—E, 473) undermines the solemn reliance on her future husband's perceptions that the contemporary ideological view of marriage would demand. In these novels, a certain type of laughter constitutes the saving grace by which haughtiness, pride and dogmatism are overcome.

Of course, laughter is not always positive in Austen. Lydia Bennet's is mindless, though by this same token it is used as a method of inversion by the author, for her giddiness is both the result of a social tendency to educate women irrationally and an avenue for disruption, a way for the unruliness of a "world-upside-down" mentality to infiltrate subtly Austen's narrative. Miss Bingley's laughter is often derisive, indeed Hobbsian. Elizabeth's and Emma's laughter, however, are often expressions of joy. Thus, Elizabeth proclaims that her happiness is greater than Jane's because "she only smiles, I laugh"

(PP, 383). And Emma, when her anxiety over Harriet's future is relieved after the latter accepts Mr Martin's new proposal, laughs, reflects, is serious, laughs again; in this and other cases, laughing is an expression of "a great pleasure" (E, 475). Again, such an attitude to laughter cannot be squared with the typical attitude of Augustan satirists.

On the other hand, neither romantic nor more recent accounts of irony seem really useful to explain Austen's humor. For Austenian irony is not, like Sterne's "new, romantic irony," a mixture of sentiment and satire[76] with a strong individualistic bent.[77] Nor do recent explanations seem more apt in dealing with Austen. Wayne C. Booth's account, for instance, in which irony, by contrast to romantic theories, is largely treated as finite, indeed most often "stable," fails to do justice to her complexity. Booth recognizes that many authors dwell in "local or infinite instabilities" and "ultimate ironic denial,"[78] but he places Austen and Chaucer, among others, on the side of stable irony, whose meaning is covert, but "fixed":

> In any given piece of stable irony, the central meaning of the word is fixed and univocal, regardless of how many peripheral and even contradictory significances different readers may add.[79]

The very first example offered in support of this view is Mr Bennet's remark to Elizabeth that "I admire all my three sons-in-law highly . . . . Wickham perhaps is my favourite, but I think I shall like *your* husband [Darcy] quite as well as Jane's." Booth comments, "Either Mr Bennet and Jane Austen are playing with irony or they are not; there are no two ways about it, and if you and I elect an ironic reading, we shall prove either both right or both wrong."[80] It is interesting that Booth never makes his "election" of meaning for the word "favourite" explicit. I believe, however, that a strong case can be made for an ambivalent "election"; Mr Bennet may be saying *both* that Wickham, a charming hypocrite, is the one son-in-law he disapproves of, *and*, simultaneously, that since Mr Bennet perversely enjoys savoring manifestations of human folly, he will find greater gratification in Wickham's company than in either Darcy's or Bingley's.

If we turn to the opening statement in *Pride and Prejudice*, we find its irony to be anything but "fixed." To cite only a few interpretations, the statement, "It is a truth universally acknowledged that a single man in possession of a good fortune, must be in want of a wife," has been seen by one critic to mean "its opposite—a single woman must be in want of a man with a good fortune";[81] by another, the "truth" in question is only such within the mental categories of the Mrs Bennets of her world, whose "narrowly female expectations of marriage as a self-justifying end are matched by and implicitly attributed to the male's proprietary view of women as possessions."[82] Recently one critic, Nancy Armstrong, has seen in the statement evidence that Austen's fiction was in easy agreement with "self-evident" social ideology.[83] And yet the elegantly phrased statement may be understood as reflecting the ironic conflict between the prototypical educated mind that could so express itself, and the common views of fortune-hunting women and their families.

Furthermore, the reference to universal acknowledgement of truths points the irony simultaneously in both directions, for it is aimed not only at the Mrs Bennets of this world, but also at the intellectual posture that so often relied on philosophical or gentlemanly consensus. In eighteenth-century argumentative prose Austen may have encountered many allusions to commonly acknowledged beliefs or truths; one appears in Dryden's essay on satire, dedicated in sycophantic, hyperbolic terms to the Earl of Dorset, whose beneficence and intelligence "is a truth so generally acknowledged that it needs no proof."[84] Similar allusions can be found in Berkeley's treatises and dialogues.[85] In a recent publication, Kenneth Moler has shown that the statement imitates both the language of proponents of moral self-examination and that "associated with Hume, Smith, and other prestigious philosophers of the day."[86]

In that famous sentence, then, Austen couples an allusion to a stylistic convention in contemporary prose and an idea suggested by the interest of parents of marriageable daughters: that any rich bachelor must get married. Thus she produces what should be an incongruent mixture of two particular stances vis à vis the world, two subjective positions in experiencing reality. The mixture, nevertheless, sounds authoritative, couched as it is in the language of educated people. Its fastidiousness (what I call its hyper-correction), should not obscure its double target. Austen's statement may be read as suggesting that conjectures are invested with the dignity of truths when it is in our interest to believe them to be true, whether for matrimonial, intellectual, or other purposes. Indeed, the fallacious argument that "everyone agrees" is no more illogical when used to substantiate the idea that a young man must get married because he is rich than it is when used in any other connection. In my reading, this opening statement attacks through narrative methods both the fictions posited as truths by intellectuals and those by which "respectable people" live. In doing so, it mocks both the eagerness of middle-class matrimonial aspirations and the self-serving character of many passages of authoritative prose.

And yet, the fictions Austen mocks may be simultaneously viewed as inescapable ways of approaching reality. In this sense, Austen's irony is not only complex in its allusions, but ambivalent. The "official" literary ideology regarding young women and marriage is both upheld and undermined in her work, in which major tenets of this ideology become tenable only after being reversed, so that Austen can simultaneously remain within orthodoxy and radically revise its meaning. This idiosyncratic position can be best understood in terms of essential elements of carnival present in her novels.

NOTES

1. It is a mistake to conceive carnival as opposed to the actual social structures of a given time; rather, what popular feasts opposed, in Bakhtin's view, were "oficial rituals." It was the myth created and celebrated in such rituals, that of monolithic truth, that carnival undermined. Politically, carnival was only indirectly a political statement; as a direct one, it would not have been tolerated.

2. Victor Turner and other anthropologist have described folk festivals and the rites of passage of many cultures in terms that bear striking similarities to Bakhtin's description of this "utopian realm." See Victor Turner, *The Ritual Process* (Chicago: Aldine, 1969), especially the chapters on liminality and *communitas.*

3. "The Place of Laughter in Tudor and Stuart England," pp. 77,78.

4. *Le Carnaval des Romans,* Paris, 1979, quoted in Dominick LaCapra, *Rethinking Intellectual History: Texts, Context, Language* (Ithaca: Cornell University Press, 1983), p. 295, n.10.

5. And yet, in spite of Rabelais' delight in the exuberance, freedom and generalized camarederie of folk festivals, Wayne C. Booth has pointed out the novelist's "Total obliviousness to the lot of the lower classes." This is one of the "ideological limitations" Booth finds in the portrayal of the utopian Abbey of Thélème, with its plentiful servants and "functionaries" laboring for the comfort of the monks and nuns (see Booth's "Freedom of Interpretation: Bakhtin and the Challenge of Feminist Criticism," *Critical Inquiry* 9 (September 1982), p.62).

6. The most famous summary of classical and patristic views of women remains the one penned by Simone de Beauvoir in *The Second Sex* (see pp. 113-28). For another excellent overview of misogyny in classical Greece and Rome, see Katherine M. Rogers' *The Troublesome Helpmate: A History of Misogyny in Literature* (Seattle: University of Washington Press, 1966), pp. 22-55. For an anthology of attacks on women from classical to modern times, see *Not in God's Image: Women in History from the Greeks to the Victorians,* eds. J. O'Faolain and L. Martines (New York: Harper & Row, 1963).

7. Park Honan, *Jane Austen: Her Life* (New York: St. Martin's Press, 1987), p. 17.

8. Claudia Johnson, *Jane Austen*, p. xviii.

9. See the views of her own niece, Fanny Knight Knatchbull, on Jane and Cassandra Austen's lack of refinement and cultivation in Park Honan, *Jane Austen: Her Life*, pp. 116-8.

10. Park Honan, *Jane Austen*, pp. 14 and 17-9.

11. In the critical literature, it is customary to retain Austen's misspelling in the title of this high-spirited parody, written when she was thirteen years old.

12. Virginia Woolf, "Jane Austen," in Ian Watt, ed., *Jane Austen: a Collection of Critical Essays*, p. 17.

13. Woolf, p. 17.

14. Howard S. Babb, *Jane Austen's Novels: The Fabric of Dialogue* (Columbus, Ohio: Ohio State University Press, 1962), p. 33.

15. Mary De Forest, "Review" (of Marilyn Butler's *Jane Austen and the War of Ideas* (Oxford: Oxford University Press, 1987)), *Eighteenth-Century Fiction* 1 (July 1989), p. 346.

16. *Vindication*, p. 166.

17. Paulson, *Popular and Polite Art*, p. 31.

18. Booth, "Freedom of Interpretation," p. 63, 64, 55.

19. Mary Russo, "Female Grotesques: Carnival and Theory," in *Feminist Studies/Critical Studies*, ed. Teresa de Lauretis (Bloomington, Indiana: Indiana University Press, 1986), p. 219.

20. For an interesting discussion of attitudes to the grotesque body from the viewpoint of male and female theoretics, see Mary Russo, "Female Grotesques: Carnival and Theory," in *Feminist Studies/Critical Studies*.

21. Of course I am not saying that any depiction of grotesquely hyperbolic or "obscene" bodily funtions in literature is necessarily sexist, any more than the portrayal of sexist characters constitutes sexism. I will invoke Booth's test: we may call a work bigoted if the prejudiced, biased or bigoted utterance, action or attitude of a character is not tempered with other reflections or occurrences that criticize or problematize such acts or attitudes (cf. "Freedom of Interpretation").

22. M. Foucault, *The History of Sexuality*, tr. Robert Hurley (New York: Vintage Books, 1980), pp. 17-49.

23. See, for instance, Mrs. Jennings' reference, in *Sense and Sensibility,* to her daughter Charlotte's "situation" and future confinement, while, to Lady Middleton's embarrassment, Mrs. Jennings points to her daughter, and, presumably, her large belly (SS 107).

24. See Margaret Kirkham, pp. 53-60.

25. Most of Austen's heroines are physically strong and active. Fanny Price, it is true, is frail, but fresh air and exercise (horseback riding) are all the more important to her, and even Fanny delights in her ball. Anne Elliot is barred from dancing, but she suffers from it. And walks in *Persuasion* seem to take up a large part of the narrative.

26. Natalie Zemon Davis, "Women on Top: Symbolic Sexual Inversion and Political Disorder in Early Modern Europe," in *The Reversible World: Symbolic Inversion in Art and Society,* ed. Barbara A. Babcock (Ithaca and London: Cornell University Press, 1978), pp. 156-8.

27. Natalie Zemon Davis, p. 149.

28. Davis, pp. 154, 163.

29. Davis, pp. 154-5.

30. Elizabeth Langland, *Society in the Novel* (Chapel Hill: University of North Carolina Press, 1984), p. 25.

31. Elizabeth Abel, Marianne Hirsch, and Elizabeth Langland, "Introduction," *The Voyage In: Fictions of Female Development*, eds. Abel, Hirsch and Langland (Hanover: University Press of New England, 1983), p. 6.

32. M. Bakhtin, "Forms of Time and of the Chronotope in the Novel," *The Dialogic Imagination*, p. 106. Further references to this work will be market FTCN and included in the text.

33. See M.M. Bakhtin, "The Bildungsroman," in *Speech Genres and Other Late Essays*, tr. Vern Mc Gee, eds. Caryl Emerson and Michael Holquist (Austin, Texas: University of Texas Press, 1986), p. 23.

34. Michel Focault, *Discipline and Punish: The Birth of the Prison*, tr. Alan Sheridan (New York: Random House, 1979), pp. 136-7.

35. Michel Focault, *Discipline and Punish*, p. 184.

36. Nancy Armstrong, *Desire and Domestic Fiction: A Political History of The Novel*, Chapter 2.

37. A lengthier version of this argument appears in my book, *¿Por Qué Somos el Segundo Sexo?* (Cali, Colombia: Universidad del Valle, 1991).

38. J. M. S. Tompkins, *The Popular Novel in England: 1770-1800* (Lincoln, Nebraska: University of Nebraska Press, 1961), p. 89.

39. There is a suggestion in Armstrong's reading of the novel that, although Pamela does not feel sexual desire, she nevertheless implicitly desires a domestic, wifely, bourgeois situation. As Armstrong points out, the young girl's rejection of Mr. B's advances is contrasted to Mrs Jewkes' "verdict of common sense", according to which it is "natural for a gentleman to love a pretty woman" (Armstrong, p. 116). But in neither of the two attitudes is there any recognition of Pamela's own sexual desire; in Mrs Jewkes' speech, acceptable conduct is dictated by the need to satisfy gentlemen's feelings, not those of pretty women, and Pamela is only considering the question of morality. If Pamela does act motivated by a desire to become her master's wife rather than lover (which seems very plausible, in spite of the text's rhetoric), she nevertheless appears to have no awarenes of her own sexual needs, but only of moral and social considerations.

40. Samuel Richardson, *The History of Sir Charles Grandison*, ed. Jocelyn Harris (London: Oxford University Press, 1972), Part 2, Vol III, Letter X, p. 316. All further references to this novel will be included in the text.

41. J.M.S.Tompkins, pp. 88-89. (Tompkins is quoting from Burney's *Camilla*, Vol. I, Chapter i).

42. Fanny Burney, *Camilla, a Picture of Youth* (London: Oxford Univerity Press, 1972), p. 9.

43. Claudia Johnson, pp. 20-21.

44. Judy Simons, *Fanny Burney* (Totowa, N.J.: Barnes & Noble, 1987), p. 37.

45. Wollstonecraft, *The Wrongs of Woman, or Maria,* in William Godwin, ed. *Posthumous Works of the Author of a Vindication of the Rights of Woman* (Clifton, N.J.: Augustus M. Kelley, 1972), Vol. I, p. 39 (First published in 1798).

46. Foucault, *Discipline and Punish,* p. 164.

47. Julia Prewitt Brown, *Jane Austen's Novels: Social Change and Literary Form* (Cambridge, Mass.: Harvard University Press, 1979), p. 2.

48. D.C. Muecke, *The Compass of Irony* (London: Methuen, 1969), p. 79.

49. Brigid Brophy, "Jane Austen and the Stuarts," in *Critical Essays on Jane Austen,* pp. 24-36.

50. Cf. Ian Jack, *Augustan Satire: Intention and Idiom in English Poetry 1660-1750* (Oxford: Clarendon Press, 1952), pp. 43-52, and 77-96.

51. Elizabeth Abel, Marianne Hirsch, and Elizabeth Langland, "Introduction," *The Voyage In: Fictions of Female Development,* eds. Abel, Hirsch and Langland (Hanover: Univerity Press of New England, 1983), p. 12.

52. Those who have found in this speech ground for holding that Elizabeth is fooling herself into believing she loves Darcy because she has been dazzled by his wealth and power, fail to realize the "distrust of the serius tone" in *Pride and Prejudice.* In this novel, more than in any other, Austen has an attitude akin to what Bakhtin has described as the understanding "that hypocrisy and lies never laugh but wear a serius mask" (RHW, 95).

53. John Dryden, "A Discourse Concerning the Original and Progress of Satire," *Essays of John Dryden,* ed. W.P. Kerr (New York: Russell & Russell, 1961), Vol. II, p. 79.

54. Samuel Butler, *Hudribas,* ed. John Wilders (Oxford: Clarendon Press, 1967), p. 1. Further references to this work will be included in the text.

55. Cf. Muecke, *Compass of Irony*, p. 79.

56. John Wilders, "Introduction," Samuel Butler's *Hudibras*, ed. Wilders, pp. xxi-ii.

57. From Butler's "Characters," quoted in "Introduction," Hugh de Quehen, Samuel Butler's *Prose Observations*, ed. Hugh de Quehen (Oxford: Clarendon Press, 1979), p. xxi.

58. I use these terms in the Foucauldian sense (cf. *The Archaeology of Knowledge*, tr. A.M. Sheridan Smith (New York: Pantheon Books, 1972)).

59. Ronald Paulson, *Popular and Polite Art in the Culture of Hogarth and Fielding* (Notre Dame, Ind.: University of Notre Dame Press, 1979) p. 23.

60. For another, more thorough list of episodes and allusions to British social history in Austen's fiction, see Raymond Williams, *The English Novel*, pp. 19-21.

61. John Dryden, "A Discourse Concerning... Satire," p. 105.

62. For Bakhtinian discussions of "menippea," see *Rabelais and His World*, *Dostoevski's Poetics*, and "Forms of Time and of the Chronotope in the novel" in *The Dialogic Imagination*. For useful comments on, and a compilation of, menippea through the ages, see Eugene P. Kirk, *Menippean Satire: An Annotated Catalogue of Texts and Criticism* (N. Y. and London: Garland, 1980). Kirk apparently bases his remarks on Northrop Frye's sketch of the genre in *Anatomy of Criticism*. He also invokes Wittgenstein's concept of "family resemblances" to outline some common traits among menippean texts: their "unconventional diction," their use of the structure of a medley, outlandish topics and the theme of "right meaning or right learning" (p. xi).

63. These are categories discussed by Bakhtin in *Rabelais and his World*; see pp. 303-474.

64. This approach to the description of menippea is based on the Bakhtinian circle's view of art, according to which "Definite forms of social intercourse are constituent to the meaning of the works of art themselves." Within this perspective, literary genres and works are defined in relation to "the living interactions of concrete social and historical life." (M. M. Bakhtin/P. N. Medvedev, *The Formal Method in Literary Scholarship: A Critical Introduction to Sociological Poetics*, tr. Albert J. Wehrle (Baltimore and London: The Johns Hopkins University Press, 1978), pp. 11, 37.)

65. Tave, p. 31.

66. Ian Watt, "The Ironic Tradition in Augustan Prose from Swift to Johnson," *Restoration and Augustan Prose* (Papers Delivered at the Third Clark Library Seminar (Los Angeles: William Andrews Clark Memorial Library, 1956), p. 38.

67. Stuart M. Tave, p. 147.

68. However, the term "mob" itself was an undesirable neologism for Augustans (cf. Ian Watt, "The Ironic Tradition," p. 20).

69. Watt, "The Ironic Tradition," pp. 21-27.

70. Such views may have been based partly on gentlemen's desire to distance themselves from a human expression that many ancient and Renaissance philosophers believed was derived from malicious rejoicing in the misfortunes of others; "The best known formulation of the concept of laughter as a mean, scornful expression of superiority to a deformed thing was in Hobbes." (Stuart M. Tave, *The Amiable Humorist*, p. 46).

71. Watt, "The Ironic Tradition," p. 24.

72. Quoted in Ronald Paulson, *Popular and Polite Art*, p. 67.

73. Quoted in B. Sprague Allen, *Tides in English Taste* (Cambridge, Mass.: Harvard University Press, 1973), Vol. I, p. 94.

74. William Congreve, *The Double-Dealer*. A Solar Press Facsimile (London: Scholar Press, 1973). Act I, Scene 1, p. 7. Lord Froth adds that he goes to comedies only "To distinguish myself from the Commonality and mortify the Poets" (p. 8).

75. Paulson, *Popular and Polite Art.* p. 81.

76. Ian Watt, "The Ironic Tradition," pp. 38-39.

77. Indeed, the individualism of Sterne's laughter makes it a precursor of Kierkegaard's existentialist irony, grounded on "the paradox ... of the individual — continually being yet always becoming" (Ronald Schleifer, "Irony and the Literary Past: On *The Concept of Irony* and *The Mill on the Floss*," in *Kierkegaard and Literature: Irony, Repetition and Criticism*, eds. Ronald Schleifer and Robert Markley (Norman, Oklahoma: University

of Oklahoma Press, 1984), pp. 186-88). Similarly, "For Schlegel the basic [irony] of man is that he is a finite being striving to comprehend an infinite hence incomprehensible reality" (Muecke, *Irony and the Ironic*, p. 23).

78. Wayne C. Booth, *A Rhetoric of Irony* (Chicago and London: The University of Chicago Press, 1974), p. 233-77.

79. Booth, *Rhetoric of Irony*, p. 91.

80. Booth, *Rhetoric of Irony* p. 16.

81. Dorothy Van Ghent, "On *Pride and Prejudice*," in *Pride and Prejudice*, ed. Donald J. Gray, Norton Critical Edition (New York: Norton, 1966), p. 364.

82. Lloyd W. Brown, "Jane Austen and the Feminist Tradition," *Nineteenth - Century Fictions* 28 (1973), p. 337.

83. Nancy Armstrong, p. 135.

84. John Dryden, *Essays of John Dryden*, ed. W. P. Kerr (New York: Russell & Russell, 1961), Vol. II, p. 16.

85. Cf. George Berkeley, "A Treatise Concerning the Principles of Human Knowledge," and "Three Dialogues between Phylas and Philonous, in Opposition to Sceptics and Atheists," in *The Empiricists* (New York: Anchor Books, 1974), pp. 138, 151, 152, 160.

86. Moler, *"Pride and Prejudice": A Study in Artistic Economy*, p. 34.

Chapter 3
"Northanger Abbey":
Catherine, or the Strength
of the Ordinary

This novel, the most explicitly parodic of Austen's mature works, is also the most playful. It probably owes much of its ludic quality to its heroine, Catherine Morland, one of the youngest and certainly the most cheerful of Austenian protagonists. Lurking mischievously behind its fun, however, there is scathing social criticism, especially of contemporary attitudes to and treatment of young girls. This complexity is partly due to the fact that *Northanger Abbey* joins the insouciance of youth to the critical depth of maturity. It contains what are probably some of the earliest chunks of material found in any of Austen's mature novels, as well as successive layers of revisions, the last of which dates from 1816, less than a year before her death.[1]

Some critics distinguish the main plot from the parodic chapters (I-II, XX-XXV), which they recognize as "a brilliant commentary on Catherine's general character and behavior," but which they consider "detachable units" perhaps introduced later into the original story.[2] The novel has appeared flawed to some because of the separation they establish between the "novel's satiric element" and its "main concern—the story of Catherine Morland's development from girlhood to comparative intellectual and emotional maturity."[3] On the contrary, I will argue that the satire of fiction in *Northanger*

Abbey does not "interfere with more important business,"[4] but effectively illuminates the story of her development to maturity. These chapters, whether written early or late, constitute a key to the understanding of the novel as a whole. Furthermore, the parody is integrated with other carnivalesque devices, such as characters acting as fools, clowns and rakes, to invite laughter and to underscore Catherine's sentimental and moral education.

The parodic style achieved in *Northanger Abbey* is highly original. The novel's burlesque passages, more than a subplot, can be seen as an "Ur-novel," a composite of all the improbabilities and exaggerations contained in the fictions Austen had read and wished to satirize. The plot of *Northanger Abbey* itself may be considered as an inversion, a positive picture developed from an original negative impression. I employ the words "negative" and "positive" advisedly, for the Ur-novel has a feminine protagonist who can be characterized as an innocent victim of continual adversity, while Catherine Morland's fictional life is nothing if not an affirmation. This statement might seem paradoxical, for Catherine is from the initial paragraph presented, through a series of negations, as an anti-heroine:

No one who had ever seen Catherine Morland in her infancy would have supposed her born to be an heroine. Her situation in life, the character of her father and mother, her own person and disposition, were all equally against her. Her father was a clergyman, without being neglected, or poor, and a very respectable man, though his name was Richard—and he had never been handsome. He had a considerable independence, besides two good livings—and he was not in the least addicted to locking up his daughters. Her mother was a woman of useful plain sense, with a good temper, and, what is more remarkable, with a good constitution. She had three sons before Catherine was born; and instead of dying in bringing the latter into the world, as any body might expect, she still lived on—lived to have six children more—to see them growing up around her, and to enjoy excellent health herself. A family of ten children will be always called a fine family, where there are heads and arms and legs enough for the number; but the Morlands had little other right to the word, for they were in general very plain, and Catherine, for many years of her life, as plain as any. She had a thin awkward figure, a sallow skin without any colour, dark lank hair, and strong features;—so much for her person;—and not less unpropitious for heroism seemed her mind. She was fond of all boys' plays, and greatly preferred cricket not merely to dolls, but to the more heroic enjoyments of infancy, nursing a dormouse, feeding a canary-bird, or watering a rosebush. Indeed she had no taste for a garden; and if she gathered flowers at all, it was chiefly for the pleasure of mischief—at least so it was conjectured from her always preferring those which she was forbidden to take. Such were her propensities—her abilities were quite as extraordinary. She never could learn or understand any thing before she was taught; and sometimes not even then, for she was often inattentive, and occasionally stupid. (NA, 13-14)

Thus the novel immediately establishes that its protagonist is unlike other heroines—and the reader discovers that this is a novel unlike others, since it compares itself to other novels.

What makes Catherine different from other heroines is precisely what makes her much like "ordinary" people, for she and her family are middle-class, plain, and unremarkable, as are "her propensities" and "her abilities." In this way this novel reverses the meanings of ordinary and extraordinary: within this narrative, to be like the average, "middling" group of people will be counted as extra-ordinary. For, it is implied, a novel is a fiction whose protagonists must be extraordinary, the opposite of an ordinary, "real-life" young woman. If a heroine follows the extra-fictional, ordinary norm, she must be seen as eccentric by novelistic standards, i.e. opposed to an opposition, and thus extraordinary *qua* heroine. This particular novel will be about an atypical heroine; its whole narrative world will be related to the real world, not as its representation, but as the reverse of an inverse copy.

It must be stressed that this chain of representations does not proceed in a direct line starting from a reflection of "reality." As Susan Stewart suggests, realistic works are based on symbolic constructions as much as carnivalesque ones; the two types simply operate as different "domains of meaning" and communicative modes. While realism "partakes of . . . the ideology and the rhetoric of the everyday lifeworld," carnival is one type of metafiction which "traverses and manipulates not only the domain of common sense, but the domains of other kinds of fictions as well." This "fiction about fictions" takes place "in nonsense context" and foregrounds "the cultural nature of signification," exposing "systems of interpretation as systems."[5]

Northanger Abbey is indeed a "fiction about fictions," although the fictional domain it mocks and imitates differs from full-fledged realism; the sentimental novels parodied are still dominated by a desire to surpass and transcend what in *Northanger Abbey* Austen will call "the common feelings of common life" (NA, 19). Within the bounds of the typical sentimental novel, the world of ordinary people was self-evident, and therefore insufficient, insatisfactory, boring. Such is the inescapable conclusion one derives from the fictions, not only of Richardson and Burney, but of Rousseau and Goethe as well. It was this disillusionment with ordinary reality as too bland that led them to create such extraordinarily sensitive beings as their heroes and heroines. A passage such as the following is typical of novelistic accounts of the exquisite virtues of such heroines:

But though thus largely indebted to fortune, to nature [Cecilia] had yet greater obligations: her form was elegant, her heart was liberal; her countenance announced the intelligence of her mind, her complexion varied with every emotion of her soul, and her eyes, the heralds of her speech, now beamed with understanding and now glistened with sensibility.[6]

Such a heroine Catherine Morland was not, and so this novel announces from the beginning, comparing its protagonist to the typical, sublimely sensitive heroine.

The extraordinariness of the typical protagonists of sentimental fiction, however, does not exempt them from falling into stereotype. Their exceptionality itself becomes a cliché, as certain characters are described as the epitome of perfection while others appear as unredeemably evil. It was Austen's most characteristic impulse to mock such fictional stereotyping, for we find it already as the butt of some jokes in Austen's *Juvenilia*. It is satirized, for instance, in the description of Lady Williams in a piece written, according to Chapman, sometime between Austen's twelfth and her fifteenth year:

> In Lady Williams every virtue met. She was a widow with a handsome Jointure
> & the remains of a very handsome face. Tho' Benevolent & Candid, she was
> Generous & Sincere; tho' Pious & Good, she was Religious & Amiable, and tho'
> Elegant & Agreeable, she was Polished & Entertaining. ("Jack and Alice," MW,
> 13)

The last three clauses obviously satirize rhetorical devices that may be more Euphuistic than Johnsonian. If we observe the first two sentences, however, it becomes clear that the absurdity is not limited to the use of the adversative ("tho'") to contrast adjectives not usually considered as opposite to each other (benevolent and generous, candid and sincere). Rather, the nonsensical quality of the passage extends to all the qualities of Lady Williams as a fictional character: her property and her once-handsome face count as virtues. Thus the passage implies that, since Lady Williams is a literary type, "a gracious and virtuous lady," she will of course conform to the requisites of fortune and appearance.

In Chapter I of *Northanger Abbey* we find a similar parody of literary stereotyping when we are told that, although Catherine "never could learn or understand anything before she was taught," and even though "she shirked her lessons . . . whenever she could,"

> with all these symptoms of profligacy at ten years old, she had neither a bad heart
> nor a bad temper; was seldom stubborn, scarcely ever quarrelsome, and very kind
> to the little ones, with few interruptions of tyranny; she was moreover noisy and
> wild, hated confinement and cleanliness, and loved nothing so well in the world
> as rolling down the green slope at the back of the house. (NA, 14)

Because she is both mischievous and good-tempered, Catherine is termed "strange and unaccountable"; thus it is hinted that characters who are not angelic in childhood must be preparing to grow up as villains. Catherine, however, is neither saintly nor satanic, but prosaically inclined to prefer idleness to schoolwork and to love noise and dirt.

By laughing at fictional conventions, Austen was effectively "scoffing at the deity" (RHW, 6) that rules over novels, and thus profaning their seriousness and solemnity. Such an act constitutes a most carnivalesque use of reversal, of the world turned upside down—only the world reversed is a fictional world, which itself is an inversion of what novelists think they know about reality. (Austen, of course, is also a novelist, and so she cannot escape the pitfalls of her metier; of this fact she is clearly aware, and she makes it part of the carnivalesque fun of *Northanger Abbey*.) In this sense *Northanger Abbey* achieves what Bakhtin considers the effect of works of grotesque realism: "to degrade, bring down to earth, turn their subject into flesh" (RHW, 20). It is not the flesh of "the lower bodily stratum," but it is, nevertheless, the too-tangible flesh that bears warts and breathes through evident, sometimes unsightly, pores.

It is important to understand the role of this reversal, this interest in profanation, at the core of *Northanger Abbey*, for Catherine Morland's growth as a woman must be seen against the background of the satirical allusions we have called *Northanger Abbey*'s Ur-novel. The very first line, as we have seen, already poses the problem of the relation between art and life. The relation between text and text, or intertextuality, is approached through a satire on the use of literary quotations in novels. Accordingly, we are told that, in spite of her inauspicious beginning, Catherine Morland "from fifteen to seventeen was in training for a heroine; she read all such works as heroines must read to supply their memories with those quotations that are so serviceable and so soothing in the vicissitudes of their eventful lives" (NA, 15). This passage has been taken as a parody of *Emmeline*, "a good representative of the type" of heroine of which Catherine seems to be a deliberate inversion.[7] The choice of quotations Catherine is supplied with is indeed "precisely in Mrs Smith's manner."[8] However, Emmeline is only one of the many characters alluded to in Austen's satire; as Mary Lascelles observed, "there is a great similarity among the heroines of that age."[9] It is precisely this sameness that provides the basis for the satire.

Through the parody, a particular image appears, a stereotypical image of young womanhood these novels love to draw from literature. Together, the quotations Austen chooses as examples of Catherine's reading paint a picture of feminine youth as helpless, delicate, dependent and victimized (cf. NA, 15-16). The first three quotations are significant for the titles of the works they come from as much as for their content: Pope's "To the Memory of an Unfortunate Lady," Gray's "Elegy," and Thomson's "Spring." The three from

Shakespeare (from *Othello*, *Measure for Measure* and *Twelfth Night* respectively)
deal with women in love as victims, with pain and death, and emphasize
smallness and suffering.

This picture is in keeping with the general tendency of sentimental
novels to exaggerate the sufferings of the protagonist as much as her qualities.
If the typical heroine of novels is exceptionally beautiful, sensitive and
intelligent, her fate is no less extraordinary, for she is the victim of many
"vicissitudes." These two characteristics, extraordinary qualities and
extraordinary sufferings, seem to be the predominant motifs in all the
allusions, running throughout *Northanger Abbey*, to the ways in which
Catherine Morland and her actions depart from novelistic norm.

These allusions are in fact so often repeated that in the view of one critic
these passages exhibit an "obssessive concern" on the part of the author.[10] I
believe the reiteration, more than an obsession, shows the narrator's delight
in what Bakhtin calls "carnivalistic parodies on sacred texts" (PDP, 123), in
this case the sacrosanct purity of heroines of sentimental novels. The reader
who can be moved to respond to many of the best sentimental novels of the
late eighteenth and early nineteenth centuries, but who at the same time
recognizes their absurdities, will never tire of the varied ways in which the
narrator's wit will oppose the high-flown style of sentimental and Gothic
fiction to prosaic details of "ordinary life."

If we string together all the allusions to what does *not* happen to
Catherine, turning the statements of her "strangeness" as a heroine (of what
she, being unheroical, is not and does not) into statements of what the typical
heroine *is*, we obtain a story which illuminates, by inversion, the story of
Catherine's growth as a woman. In this implicit or "negative" story of a
prototypical heroine we may also discover some of the likely sources for each
episode among the novels by Austen's predecessors and contemporaries.

Starting from the opening paragraph, *Northanger Abbey*'s Ur-novel begins
with a heroine in her childhood. Her father is a tyrant, given to "locking up his
daughters," (cf. Richardson's *Clarissa*,[11] Fielding's *Tom Jones*)[12] while the mother
has died after giving birth to her (cf. Fanny Burney's *Evelina*,[13] Charlotte Smith's
Emmeline);[14] the young woman has no siblings (NA, 13). The protagonist of this
supposed novel (we will call this hypothetical, prototypical protagonist "Heroine"),
from whom Catherine is repeatedly said to be so different, is "a beauty from her
cradle" (NA, 15). She is also delicately sensitive, and prefers picking flowers,
feeding birds, and nursing small animals to any physical activity (as did Monimia
in Charlotte Smith's *The Old Manor House*[15] and Mary in Wollstonecraft's *Mary,
a Fiction*;[16] NA, 13). Heroine is also exceptionally intelligent (cf. Mary Hays'
Memoirs of Emma Courtnay, Burney's *Camilla*, Charlotte Smith's
Emmeline), learning many things without being taught (cf. Smith's *Emmeline*),[17]
and showing talents for sonnet-writing (the protagonist in Mary Wollstonecraft's
Mary, a Fiction wrote poetry from childhood),[18] drawing (*Emmeline*)[19]

and music (*Clarissa*,[20] *Emmeline*;[21] NA, 14).

As soon as she reaches young womanhood, Heroine inspires many passions in a variety of men, among whom there are titled characters (as was the case of the admirers of Harriet Byron in Richardson's *Sir Charles Grandison*, [22] and of the protagonist in Maria Edgeworth's *Belinda*),[23] as well as a young man of unknown origin (cf. Fielding's *Tom Jones*; NA, 16). When Heroine leaves her home, she encounters frightful events: one nobleman forces her "away to some remote farm house" (cf. Richardson's *Sir Charles Grandison*;[24] NA, 18). During one journey she is robbed, and a lucky overturn introduces the hero (cf. Goldsmith's *The Vicar of Wakefield*,[25] Mary Hays' *Memoirs of Emma Courtney*;[26] NA, 19). She appears in society with a chaperon, who will contribute to reduce Heroine "to all the desperate wretchedness of which a last volume is capable" (NA, 20). This chaperon will intercept her letters, ruin her character and turn her out of doors (NA, 20). (Among the possible candidates for the original chaperon we have *Evelina*'s Mme. Duval, *Emmeline*'s Mrs. Ashwood, Madame Cheron in Anne Radcliffe's *The Mysteries of Udolpho*, Madame Laronne in Eleanor Sleath's *The Orphan of the Rhine*, and Mrs Margland in Camilla.) When Heroine attends a ball, all men present start "with rapturous wonder on beholding her" and call her "a divinity" (cf. *Sir Charles Grandison*; NA, 23). Sonnets are written to her "in celebration of her charms" (*Evelina*;[27] NA, 24).

Heroine meets a widow who relates to her (in "three or four chapters") all her "past adventures and sufferings," which serve as evidence of "the worthlessness of lords and attorneys" (cf. Eliza Parsons' *The Castle of Wolfenbach*;[28] NA, 34.) Then, Heroine herself suffers at the hands of villains, becoming "disgraced in the eyes of the world," appearing to be infamous "while the heart is all purity" (cf. Richardson's Clarissa, Smith's *Emmeline*, Burney's *Evelina*, *Cecilia* and *Camilla*; NA, 53.) She also suffers a misapprehension when, seeing the man she loves with another woman (his sister), she considers him "lost to her forever, by being married already" (Augustus, the man Emma Courtney loves, turns out to be married; NA, 53.) After suffering reverses, Heroine retires "to a pillow strewed with thorns and wet with tears" (all the heroines mentioned above). Just when she is preparing for a much-expected meeting with her lover, some difficulty arises, some "sudden recollection," "unexpected summons," or "impertinent intrusion" intervenes (as it happens repeatedly in Burney's *Camilla*,[29] and in Smith's *Emmeline*;[30] NA, 106). Heroine's friend and confidante talks to her about her relationship with her lover, full of "arch penetration and affectionate sympathy" for Heroine's sentiments (as Kenneth Moler suggests, we find such a confidante in Miss Mirvan, a character in Burney's *Evelina*;[31] NA, 71, 117-9). In the course of one of these conversations, a young lady expresses the determination of proving that, if she had millions, even then her lover would be "her only choice" (cf. Virginia St Pierre's utterance, wishing to be very rich while Mr Hervey was poor, "that I might make him rich," *in Belinda*;[32] NA, 119).

At one point, Heroine is persecuted by "three villains in horsemen's great coats, by whom she will be forced into a travelling chaise and four, which will drive off with incredible speed" (Sir Hargrave Pollexfen in *Sir Charles Grandison*[33] and Theodore in *Horrid Mysteries*[34] instigate such abductions of the heroine; NA, 131). On another occasion, Heroine sees one gentleman whispering to her lover, and imagines that she is being slandered (in Burney's *Evelina, Cecilia* and *Camilla* the heroine's honesty is often apparently compromised, suspected, and/or she is slandered).

So far the Ur-novel has been building up through the narrator's comments on what is happening to Catherine in contrast to typical heroines. At a certain point, however, Henry Tilney, the young man who will eventually marry Catherine, takes over the telling of the Ur-novel—except that his is not a story of what usually happens to heroines that we may infer from what does *not* happen to Catherine, but a story of what purportedly *may* happen to her. As he drives this young lady to Northanger Abbey, his home, where she will stay as a guest, he tells her a mock-horror story of what may befall her at such an old abbey, in her imagination as romantic as a Gothic castle. (I will call the heroine of his parodic narrative "Catherine"; he tells the story in second person, using "you" for the subject of his utterances.) "Catherine" will be lodged, he says, in rooms "apart from the rest of the family" (NA, 158). After narrating a few circumstances that create a frightful atmosphere (a portrait of a knight, a sullen old housekeeper—called Dorothy, like the housekeeper in *Udolpho*, a room without a lock on the door), Henry tells her that, on the third night, "Catherine" will be frightened by a violent storm. While it rages she will notice a wall-hanging concealing a door, leading to a small vaulted room. "Catherine" will there discover an old ebony cabinet, in whose secret compartment she will find many sheets of manuscript. When she is about to read it, her lamp will "suddenly expire in the socket," leaving her "in total darkness;"[35] NA, 160). The story ends there, for Henry is so amused by Catherine's naive, horrified interest in his story that he cannot go on.

Catherine will continue the story herself in her imagination, however. While staying at the Abbey, on three separate occasions she will believe she is on the verge of discovering some long-buried secret. Each time she will have to conclude that she has only been foolishly indulging her fancy. The Ur-novel is not continued until Catherine returns home after her ignominious expulsion from Northanger Abbey. At that point we find her contrasted to our Ur-novel's Heroine, who purportedly returns, "at the close of her career, to her native village, in all the triumph of recovered reputation, and all the dignity of a countess" (NA, 232). (Thus, for example, does Emmeline return to Mowbray Castle, not as a countess, but as its mistress, and is received "with transport" by Mrs Stafford and "numberless tenants and dependents.")[36]

The passage about Heroine's return marks the end of *Northanger Abbey*'s Ur-novel. Having thus pieced it together, we can now analyze the story of Heroine. This fictional young lady is remarkable for her lack of response to the many plots against her; her languid demeanor is coupled with her unusually contemplative interests. Heroine thus appears as the embodiment of ethereal spirit in a world governed by the too solid, lurid flesh. She is always threatened by the sinfulness of others, usually in the form of concupiscence, which strives to defame, defile, destroy her. While engulfed by raging lasciviousness and greed, she remains helpless. Unlike the heroes of traditional romances, who overcome temptation through the strength of their virtue, Heroine is never tempted to fall into sin. But she is also, again unlike male romantic protagonists, unable to exert the slightest force in order to extricate herself from her many painful predicaments. The slightest occurrence, such as seeing her beloved with his sister, seriously threatens her peace of mind. She is so far from ever taking any initiative, that she does not even inquire about the identity of her presumed rival. Heroine represents, therefore, a spirit of beauty that is, more than merely disembodied, utterly devoid of any energy but that which may be devoted to the enjoyment of exquisite suffering (or to placing herself in needless, but apparently unsurmountable, paralyzing danger).

From a narrative viewpoint, furthermore, Heroine's story seems to exist on a level of Platonic ideals. Each episode seems to be a schema untouched by time or change; each leads only to a repetition of similar episodes, without any progression. This lack of progression or movement is not surprising, since the Ur-novel is not told as a continuous, self-sufficient narrative, but as a running commentary on the story of Catherine Morland. What is more significant is that, within each of the episodes, there is no possible advancement toward an object sought, simply because there is never any quest. At any given point of the narrative, Heroine is no closer to achieving a goal than she is at any other point, simply because she has no quest, no capabilities for action, no desire. Heroine's story presents the paradoxical characteristic of being untouched by the "delusions" of becoming. Not only do we find that time does not touch the protagonist, who remains essentially unchanged throughout the course of her "vicissitudes"; time does not even affect the story itself. In this sense, Heroine is even more drastically outside time than the heroes of Greek romances Bakhtin describes as acting

> in adventure-time—they escape, defend themselves, engage in battle, save themselves—but they act, as it were, as merely physical persons, and the initiative does not belong to them. . . . In this time, persons are forever having things happen to them. . .; a purely adventuristic person is a person of chance. (FTCN, 95)

Heroine, on the contrary, is not "merely physical" but merely emotional; while heroes placed in "Greek adventure-time" re-act rather than act, she does neither, for she can only feel. Her bondage to chance is even greater than that of heroes of Greek romances. It is therefore not surprising that her story should stop abruptly, unmotivatedly. When the narrative, capriciously interrupted, is resumed by a new narrator (Henry Tilney), it is left unresolved. His "Catherine," who moves only to place herself in unnecessary danger, thus remains forever suspended in her vaulted room, quaking with mortal terror in the darkness. If we can speak of a chronotope of Heroine's story, it must be one of endless repetition in suspended time and space.

Similarly, Catherine's own efforts at imagining stories lead nowhere. Her fanciful narrative of a wife's imprisonment does not evolve, but merely vanishes when confronted with everyday reality. And then Heroine reappears, as whimsically as she had vanished from the novel, by recourse to the device of narrating another "Platonic type" of episode,[37] that of her triumphant return to her native village. When the narrator decides that it is time to end the story, then, Heroine leaps from her state of suspended animation to a finale of fairy-tale happiness.

Being everything Catherine Morland is not, Heroine serves to underline the fact that Catherine is an active, affirmative protagonist in sharp contrast to the passive, dependent, hysterical young women at the center of many sentimental novels. Thus *Northanger Abbey* both exaggerated and satirized an image of the novelistic heroine based on an ideological position regarding women that, with some variations, was common to most novels by women. As Claudia Johnson, among others, has shown, Austen can be placed in a feminine tradition she both continued and altered in her dialogic response to the novelistic ideology found in the works of her "sister authors."

It is interesting to note that the novels satirized in the Ur-novel already contain some elements of feminist protest. In contrast to Heroine's vaporous saintliness, other characters in the Ur-novel are gripped by highly charged passions. While chaperons are often disagreeable old ladies, the source of most of the malevolence is male: fathers and suitors are most often the persecutors, though lords and attorneys also intervene. The Ur-novel, therefore, points to a tendency in sentimental and Gothic novels to idealize the feminine protagonist, contrasting male iniquity to the young woman's innocence.

At least one eighteenth-century novel contains allusions to novelistic stereotypes as possible incitements to resistance. One heroine (Geraldine Verney of Charlotte Smith's *Desmond*) in a letter to her sister specifically links Gothic stories to the unveiling of male victimization of women. Claudia Johnson interprets this passage as evidence of the way in which "reform-minded novelists" like Charlotte Smith, who "combined politics and gothicism most regularly," used Gothic as a background of feudal injustice to politicize the heroine's persecution as a symbol of both class and gender oppression.[38] Unfortunately, Geraldine comes to read such fiction too late, when she is already a victim of a greedy family and an even greedier and more heartless husband, who is planning to sell her to a rich duke. Nevertheless, her summary of the typical plot of Gothic novels is useful, as is her description of her own reactions as a reader:

> I ran through [novels] with extreme avidity . . . and devoured with an eager appetite the mawkish pages that told of damsels, most exquisitely beautiful, confined by a cruel father, and escaping to a heroic lover, while a wicked Lord laid in wait to tear her from him, and carried her off to some remote castle— Those delighted me most that ended miserably; and having tortured me through the last volume with impossible distress, ended in the funeral of the heroine. Had the imagination of a young person been liable to be much affected by these sort of histories, mine would, probably, have taken a romantic turn, and at eighteen, when I was married, I should have hesitated whether I should obey my friends' directions, or have waited till the hero appeared. . . . But, far from doing so, I was, you see, "obedient—very obedient."[39]

It is true that Gothic tales appear to Geraldine as incitations to rebel against patriarchal injustice. And yet, we see her "delighting" in those tales where the heroines meet the most miserable ends. The masochistic pleasure of the reader is ironically underlined; both reader and heroine are, quite unlike reader and heroine in *Northanger Abbey*, extremely passive. Ultimately, in spite of Smith's irony, the novels Geraldine has read only serve to romanticize feminine passivity before male persecution.

For all her progressive political sympathies, Charlotte Smith is not far in her feminist protest from the more conservative Ann Radcliffe. Both present male figures as the fictional saviors and protectors of young women who often merely wait to be released from bondage. It is true that Smith protests patriarchal abuses while Radcliffe recommends respect for established authority. Nevertheless, Radcliffe unconsciously paints a picture of male tyranny that may equally well serve as a rebuke to dark despots and benevolent patriarchs. As Claudia Johnson observes, in spite of the Burkean strain of paternalism in *The Mysteries of Udolpho*, when Radcliffe has the villain Montoni force Emily into marriage to consolidate his wealth, she "is describing what patriarchal society daily permits as a matter of course"; in consequence, "protectors of order and agents of tyranny can look alarmingly alike."[40]

The typical heroine's morbid passivity, furthermore, can be seen as an unconscious response to women's grotesquely constricting situation. As Daniel Cottom has shown, the feminine body in Radcliffe's fiction is governed by neurasthenic reactions, "swoons, syncopes and trances." Even when these fictional young women are neither being forcibly carried away, unconscious, or paralyzed by fear, they "frequently find their bodies beyond their control." In a quivering lip, a lowered eyelid or a blushing cheek, the heroines of Radcliffe's novels "find their bodies betraying them . . ., speaking for them when they desire to be secretive or, in the more extreme situations of paralysis and unconsciousness, stealing from them all power of response." This uncontrollable body is rebelling against an immense "pressure for decorous behavior," expressing "an otherwise insurmountable conflict between the desire for expression and the fear of impropriety."[41]

The heroine's typical predicament in Radcliffean fiction is of course a symptom of and a response to contemporary social situations. In this sense Anne Radcliffe's novels meaningfully interact with patriarchy; they might even be said to bear witness to the depth of its misogyny. Nevertheless, the glorification of the neurasthenic body and the sadomasochistic reveling in victimization are politically self-defeating postures. As Cottom observes, a heroine's suffering confirms her delicacy, for "the fineness of [her] character is measured by how rude the world appears in contrast to it."[42] This criterion of "delicacy" not only poses impossibly high and rarefied standards for feminine conduct, it also binds women to total passivity.

Though so far we have been referring exclusively to Gothic fictions, a similar ambiguity regarding feminist issues can be observed in sentimental novels, again on both sides of the political divide. Of many of Burney's narratives, for instance, we could say, paraphrasing *Northanger Abbey*'s concluding statement, that it is uncertain whether their tendency be altogether to recommend the hero's tyranny or reward the heroine's disobedience (cf. NA, 252). In *Camilla*, for instance, the protagonist's virtue is constantly suspected by the excessively preachy, repressive hero, Edgar Mandlebert. Thus, for instance, he objects to her pursuing Mrs Arlberry's acquaintance, whom he thinks too witty and lively, although she is "a woman of reputation as well as fashion," who is moreover kind and charitable.[43] He also objects to her accepting her friend Mrs Berlington's invitation, and repeatedly appears "agonised by suspence and doubt." This attitude, however, only serves to provoke rebelliousness in the heroine, who tends to do the opposite of what he advises, "for her wounded spirit panted to prove its independence and dignity."[44] There is a suggestion that what Edgar Mandlebert objects to in Mrs Arlberry is her satirical intelligence and independent spirit, which makes her regale Camilla, an intelligent young lady, with such dangerous feminist remarks as the following:

> [Men] are always enchanted with something that is both pretty and silly; because they can so easily please and so soon disconcert it; and when they have made the little blooming fools blush and look down, they feel nobly superior and pride themselves in victory. Dear creatures! I delight in their taste; for it brings them a plentiful harvest of repentance, when it is their connubial criterion; the

pretty flies off, and the silly remains, and a man has a choice companion for life left on his hands![45]

(Austen will allude to this passage in connection with Catherine's attractiveness for Henry Tilney due to her ignorance of "the picturesque;" Mrs Arlberry's remarks also obviously constitute one of the fictional sources for the relationship between Mr and Mrs Bennet in *Pride and Prejudice*.)

All of Burney's heroines are eventually placed, through no fault of their own, in compromising positions that give rise to doubts of their virtue. Even Cecilia, one of the most mature and self-possessed of Burney's heroines, is slandered by Mr Monckton and suspected of being "impure" by her father-in-law and even her husband. This loving young man must see her deranged and near death before he will repent, calling himself "the wretch who for an instant could doubt the purity of a mind so seraphic." Of course she forgives him, but not before he kneels before her, in an agony of self-abasement.[46]

While *Camilla* and *Cecilia* dwell on feminine resentment against the too scrupulous moral demands males make of their chastity and obedience, *Evelina* puts the heroine in constant jeopardy due to men's lasciviousness. Nevertheless, while denouncing some males' "libertinism towards women,"[47] the novel itself suggests the propriety of young women's clinging to male protection, rather than their seeking independence. In contrast to the many assaults on these heroines' virtue and reputation, Catherine Morland stands in a placid situation, almost neglected and ignored by men. Again paraphrasing the narrator in *Northanger Abbey*, we may observe that such circumstances, though "dreadfully derogatory of an heroine's dignity" (cf. NA, 273), do resemble the "common life" of young ladies more than the typical heroine's predicament.

If we move from conservative authors such as Burney to progressive women writers of sentimental novels, we encounter a very similar ambivalence towards women's situation. We have already seen how Charlotte Smith uses Gothic elements in her depiction of male tyranny and passive heroines. In *Emmeline* we see the novelist repeating the pattern. Delamere, son of Lord Montreville and heir apparent to Mowbray Castle, persecutes her with the dark determination of a Montoni and the fire of a Werther. Emmeline is said to be spirited and talented, a young woman of uncommon "native firmness" and superior "understanding."[48] Indeed, she shows her mettle in a confrontation with Lady Montreville[49] that, as we shall see, seems a precursor of the meeting between Elizabeth Bennet and Lady Catherine (PP, Vol. III, Ch. xiv). And yet when males torment her she acts very much like a "helpless orphan." Whether she is persecuted along the dark passages of Mowbray Castle by night, or in Mrs Ashwood's garden in broad daylight, her responses to all adverse circumstances are similar: she trembles, she pleads, she sobs or she faints. (Let us remember that when John Thorpe succeeds in coaxing Catherine into his carriage under false pretenses, his boorish behavior has no more dangerous aim than forcing her to go on an insipid outing; her reaction, once she discovers the hoax, is immediate and lively: she protests repeatedly, asking him to to stop in order to jump out. Though she is prevented, her emotional response is not fear or sadness; rather, she becomes "angry and vexed" —NA, 87.) When Emmeline finds herself in especially dire circumstances, as when she is abducted by Delamere, she falls into "an access of fever."[50] She is finally to accept the tutelage of Godolphin; as soon as she admits to him that she loves him, he acquires authority over her: "Emmeline seemed to be happier since she had confessed to Godolphin his influence over her mind, and since she had made him in some measure the director of her actions."[51]

Even those novels where women do not assume a posture of subjection to male authority insist on presenting women as helpless victims. Such is the case of Mary Wollstonecraft's *Maria or the Wrongs of Woman*, written, as the title suggests, in protest against the plight of women. Woman is presented as a weak victim, a "fragile flower," cruelly "suffered to adorn a world exposed to the inroad of . . . stormy elements."[52] This novel reiterates the claims made in *A Vindication of the Rights of Woman* that society corrupts women. By allowing them "but one way of rising in the world, the fostering the libertinism of men, society makes monsters of [women], and then their ignoble vices are brought forward as a proof of inferiority of intellect."[53] Thus the worst aspect of the victimization of women is the fact that they are degraded "so far below their oppressors, as almost to justify their tyranny."[54]

Mary Hays would also insist that women were "rendered feeble and delicate by bodily constraint, and fastidious by artificial refinement."[55] Her heroine, Emma Courtney, in a dialogue with her mentor and friend, Mr Francis, will claim her sex has made her more vulnerable:

> "I thought you contemned the plea of *sex*, as a sanction for weakness!" [said Mr Francis.]
> "Though I disallow it as a natural, I admit it as an artificial, plea . . . : the customs of society . . . have enslaved, enervated and degraded woman."[56]

In spite of her "weakness," Emma will determinedly court Augustus Hartley, both in person and through letters. Her independence and originality, however, appear to be limited to her obsessive pursuit of her lover; they are not carried to the point where she, faced with his reiterated repulses, can conceive of living without him. Her feeling of worthlessness when she cannot hope to be loved in return painfully represents woman's stunted self. In the end, however, Emma will be neither a rebellious Werther nor a sorrowful, nostalgic Julia, Rousseau's heroine, to whom she compares herself. Struggling to break loose from vitiated femininity, she clings to the judgment passed on women as monstrous products of society. The result is that she is left in a void; rebellious, but helpless, she can only lash out resentfully against those who would help her. When Mr Francis exhorts her to independence, Emma replies:

> Why call woman, miserable, oppressed, and impotent woman—*crushed, and then insulted*— why call her to *independence*—which . . . the barbarous and accursed laws of society, have denied her? *This is mockery!*[57]

Is this all that women could choose from in the eighteenth century? Were those who aspired to act as moral beings condemned to be either scrupulous to the point of being paralyzed like Radcliffe's heroines, partly subservient to males like Camilla, Cecilia or Emmeline, or crushed and without hope like Emma Courtney?

Northanger Abbey can be seen as a response, not only to Radcliffe or Burney, but to Wollstonecraft and Hays as well, indeed to the whole ideology of the young heroine we have been discussing. It is an ideology we can call quasi-official for two reasons: First, because it was generalized and dominant,[58] in the sense that it had become conventional in the novels of Austen's contemporaries. Second, because, in spite of its feminist protest, this ideology of the young novelistic heroine shared with the viewpoints of officialdom a sense of women's moral inferiority to men based on contempt toward the typical moral and psychological structure of young women. Northanger Abbey both undermines the anti-feminism of this quasi-official position and carries much further the incipient protest of Austen's "sister authors." The novel responds to that bitter denunciation of "barbarous society" found in some of their works, decrying patriarchy through very different means: carnivalesque laughter and a new conception of women's development and growth.

In Northanger Abbey, Austen chose to undermine the validity of the novelistic image of ethereal, victimized femininity by a movement toward diminishing the stature of both the male tyrant and his saintly victim. Both monsters and angels are reduced by a debasing transposition from a mythical to a quotidian realm, contrasting their fictional idealization to the prosaic reality of middle-class society and individuals. Indeed, if we must describe a struggle between young womanhood and powerful patriarchs in the early nineteeth century, we need not look to remote mountainous settings and medieval times and relationships; a contemporary English village would provide less lurid but more representative examples.

This novel translates the struggle between feminine innocence and patriarchal depravity to more mundane and contemporary settings and circumstances. Instead of a Montoni who locks up the heroine and commands armies of bandits, we have General Tilney, a selfish man who sets a monetary price for every human relationship, bullies everyone, and rudely evicts the heroine from his home, where she was a guest, because she turns out not to be a great heiress. Instead of being courted by noblemen and assailed by men driven mad by her beauty, our heroine will only receive the oblique hints of

John Thorpe, a stout, ungraceful and greedy young man who only wants her because he thinks she is rich. Instead of an angelic, brilliant heroine like Emmeline, Cecilia or Camilla, we have Catherine Morland, an ordinary young lady, who is energetic, even lusty, where her predecessors have been languid and listless.

By switching the emphasis to everyday events and situations, the novelist obeyed an impulse she shared with menippean satirists, whose interest lay in current events, trends and topical issues, in "the great and small directions in the developments of everyday life" (PDP, 118). That *Northanger Abbey*, specifically, was meant to reflect what was current and in vogue is shown by the "Advertisement By the Authoress." This note, appended to the novel in 1816, apologized for "those parts of the work which thirteen years have made comparatively obsolete"; it suggests that Austen's original intention was to allude to "places, manners, books and opinions" that were in fashion at the time of her first writing, trends and issues that had "undergone considerable changes" since 1803 (NA, 12). Evidently, "the authoress" meant her work to enter into ironic dialogue with trends and issues of her times (cf. PDP, 118).

Finally, *Northanger Abbey* not only updates the typical Gothic conflict; it also applies "the bodily and popular corrective of laughter" (RHW, 22) to the extreme spirituality of contemporary novelistic heroines. Hilarity in this novel can be shown to share in all the essential features of carnival laughter: first, it is "the laughter of all the people"; second, it is "universal in scope"; and third, it is ambivalent in that "it is gay, triumphant, and at the same time mocking, deriding. It asserts and denies, buries and revives" (RHW, 11-12).

Before proceeding any further, some marginal comments on the phrases "laughter of *all* the people" and "*universal* in scope" are in order. It may be, in part, because of a misinterpretation of such terms that Aaron Fogel, comparing Bakhtin's notion of anacrisis as "ingenious strategies of pressure to speak" to a scene of violent coercion to speak in Conrad's *Nostromo*, concludes that the scene is "more radical and critical, and less innocent than Bakhtin."[59] The image of the benevolent, naive Bakhtin may also be based on some of the interpretations he has received. As Ken Hirschkop observes, for some of Bakhtin's commentators dialogism appears as

> the promise of a coherent and peaceful society, in which individual voices are
> ultimately reconciled because they 'take into account' each other's opinions.
> This is a far cry from the condition of fierce social struggle outlined by Bakhtin
> in "Discourse in the Novel." ... It is likewise remote from the carnival culture
> described in the study of François Rabelais, which takes its internally dialogical
> form from its function as an oppositional and subversive culture.[60]

If we understand Bakhtin, with Hirschkop, as far from "a dialogism which both recognizes and defuses difference," we must interpret the generalizing terms "all the people" and "universal" as part of the fiction of carnivalesque laughter. The "point of view of the whole world" (RHW, 12), in a discourse that rises by opposition to the ritual seriousness of official feasts can only be a mask, not an actual unity, a tranquil concord achieved by individuals. The "whole world" represents, not a melting of all differences into peaceful communion, but a negation of a negation, the mocking, all-including contestation to the exclusion of the common people by the solemnity of official rites. This "universal" laughter is still an utterance which, to borrow Susan Stewart's phrase, "stands in tension or conflict with the utterances of others."[61]

In this sense, carnival laughter in *Northanger Abbey*, as befits the rejoicing of an anti-Ur-novel, is anti-exclusive in its celebration of the heroine's ordinariness, her lack of heroic qualities. In the face of all the claims to exceptionality of the typical novelistic heroine, Catherine Morland stands as a resolutely unexceptional young woman. For instance, she and her family uniformly behave, in the novel's narrator's ironic words, "with a degree of moderation and composure, which seemed rather consistent with the common feelings of common life, than with the refined susceptibilities, the tender emotions" of a heroine *comme il faut* (NA, 19). Nevertheless, although Catherine is not poor, she belongs to one most severely despised underclass, from an intellectual and moral standpoint: young womanhood. Thus her story is "popular" in the sense in which "common people" is synonymous with "underdog."

This novel's laughter is universal because, like festive laughter, it is "directed at all and everyone, including the carnival's participants" (RHW, 12) in the sense of anti-exclusion we have been discussing. The most obvious and common butt of the laughter is the heroine herself, whose mind is, we are told from the very beginning, "as ignorant and uninformed as the female mind at seventeen usually is" (NA, 18). Furthermore, not only do we find laughter at the expense of fashionable manners and people and contemporary fiction, but also laughter aimed at him whom many critics have taken to be the narrator's surrogate, Henry Tilney, and at the narrator herself. Again, this posture of self-mockery is not an abject individualistic attitude or a gesture of naive goodwill. Rather, self-directed laughter is a form of opposition to the ritual self-glorification typical of dominant groups, who celebrate their hegemony through the solemn proclamation of official truths. By laughing at themselves, carnival participants are not renouncing power, but denouncing self-worship as a sham.

In this vein, Henry, the hero, appears as a high-spirited young man with a penchant for satire, poking fun at many things, from typical ballroom conversation and fashionable flirting manners to the Gothic exaggerations of the novels he admittedly admires. He is much given to parody; when he first meets Catherine he wins her (and the reader's) interest by mimicking the affectations and "simpering air" of smirking "fops" addressing young ladies on a Bath dancing floor (NA, 26). He pretends to share commonly held views, in order to ridicule them; in this capacity he plays the role of clown, a role also played by the novel's own narrator.

Indeed, the narrator can show affinity with her hero and at the same time laugh at him, as indeed she laughs at herself. For instance, while Henry indulges both his penchant for mockery and his passion for linguistic precision he is himself laughed at by his sister: Catherine Morland has used the word "nice" to describe *Udolpho*. Henry derides this usage of a word which "originally . . . was applied only to . . . neatness, propriety, delicacy or refinement," but which now is incorrectly used to comprise "every commendation on every subject." To this fussiness his sister counters that the word nice in its original meaning "ought only to be applied to you, without any commendation at all. You are more nice than wise." She then dismisses his fault-finding remarks as irrelevant:

> "Come, Miss Morland, let us leave him to meditate over our faults in the utmost propriety of diction, while we praise Udolpho in whatever terms we like best." (NA, 108)

By laughing at Henry for being a stickler for precise diction, *Northanger Abbey* subverts the "propriety" of its own, very well-spoken narrator. This movement is continued in the many instances where characters' utterances are reported indirectly, for many of these utterances are faulty in logic or syntax or both, and yet they appear embedded in one of the narrator's impeccable sentences. Her correction, however, cannot defuse the unruliness of the characters' utterances. Such is the case, for instance, when Catherine asks Maria Thorpe for details about their outing the day before:

> Maria desired no greater pleasure than to speak of it; and Catherine immediately learnt that it had been altogether the most delightful scheme in the world; that nobody could imagine how charming it had been, and that it had been more delightful than any body could conceive. (NA, 116)

The narrator's hypotactic style imposes a superficial order on the young lady's paratactic effusions, but the latter's hyperbolic, repetitive and trite gushings stand intact.

The narrator does not reserve for herself the prerogative of infallibility, any more than she attributes it to Henry Tilney. From the beginning the narrating voice created by Austen refuses to adopt the manner of the authoritarian, monologic narrator. Far from solemnly appearing to know all, the narrator ironically pretends to be surprised by the "strangeness" of Catherine's "ordinariness" ("What a strange, unaccountable character!" (NA, 14); "This was strange indeed!" (NA, 16.)) The customary dignity of the fictional narrator is also undermined in this novel by means of the many instances where she refers ironically to her own performance. In one such reference, "And now may I dismiss my heroine to the sleepless couch, . . . the true heroine's portion" (NA, 90.), the storyteller employs a meta-narrative device, narrating *by* giving herself permission to make a narrative decision. Thus, in parodying contemporary fiction she is directing the irony at her own narrating function.

As was to be expected, the reader does not escape being laughed at in the course of the narration. Julia Prewitt Brown has pointed out that the novel satirizes the exaggerated fancy of naive readers who expect fiction to show an extravagant world.[62] But the irreverent spirit animating the novel will not respect even the reader who can claim some sophistication. Thus the narrator plays games with her audience, unexpectedly introducing, in a suspenseful moment, a teasing statement that changes its apparent meaning as one reads on: Catherine Morland explores the abbey on her own, looking for confirmation of her fancies regarding Mrs Tilney's imprisonment; she finally comes to the late Mrs Tilney's room:

> The lock yielded to her hand, and, luckily, with no sullen sound that could alarm a human being. On tip-toe she entered; the room was before her; but it was some minutes before she could advance another step. *She beheld what fixed her to the spot and agitated every feature.*— She saw a large, well-proportioned appartment, an handsome dimity bed, arranged as unoccupied with an housemaid's care, a bright Bath stove, mahogany wardrobes and neatly-painted chairs, on which the warm beams of a western sun gaily poured through two sash windows! (NA, 193—emphasis added)

The underlined statement seems mischievously ambiguous, as though the narrator were playing a joke on the reader: Catherine is dumbfounded not due to any extraordinary sighting, but precisely *because*, having worked herself up to breathless expectation, she sees nothing out of the ordinary, and is shocked by the contrast to her imaginations. But the reader first encountering the statement may interpret it by reference to the horror-story schema which Catherine is trying to live out, a schema well-known to most readers. Just as Catherine "expected to have her feelings worked," we, Austen's audience, may have also slipped into such an expectation under the manipulation of the author, who did "work" our feelings.

Laughter in this novel, then, is alternately aimed at subject spoken of, speaker and audience. The examples above also show that the novel's festive attitude complies with the third characteristic of carnival laughter as defined by Bakhtin, by being simultaneously mocking and gay, and thus "regenerative." In the words of Julia Prewitt Brown, the purpose of Austen's humor "is corrective, not malicious."[63]

Northanger Abbey corrects, or better, regenerates because it liberates us from what Bakhtin called "the great interior censor" (RHW, 94), in the sense that it frees us from the sexist severity that dismisses young women impatiently as fools. Many people, male and female, have at some point been rebuked with the charge of feminine puerility. Such taunts inevitably turn into unconscious fears that threaten to lower our self-esteem, and that in time give rise to defensive urges to throw the accusation at others. This novel embraces that charge and turns the despised figure of the foolish schoolgirl into a symbol of renewal.

Catherine Morland is "ignorant and uninformed" (NA, 18), but she is not feeble; rather, from childhood, she is an "unruly" or "disorderly" woman:[64] she revels in dirt, dislikes study, loves mischief, and enjoys physical activity in blissful ignorance of conduct books, which warned girls that men would interpret rambunctiousness as a symptom of "sexual susceptibility."[65] The sources of this young woman's unconscious resistance to patriarchy can be found both in the literary figure of the fool and in the ideology of an unlikely group: schoolgirls. Austen, who had herself been a student at two boarding schools, knew well the jargon and the attitudes of schoolgirls, which she associated with disruptive laughter. In one of her earliest recorded letters, Austen reacts with enthusiasm to the style of Cassandra's corespondence, calling her sister "the finest comic writer of the present age," and commenting, "I could have died of laughter at [Cassandra's letter], as they used to say at school."[66]

Although Catherine's unruly tendencies in childhood "mend" as she grows to young womanhood, her "training for a heroine" is radically altered when she meets Isabella Thorpe. This character, a fortune-hunting, shallow, hypocritical young lady, functions as an unruly carnivalesque influence that subverts the lofty code of the best novelistic heroism. For, although she continually applies to her current situation a series of novelistic clichés she would like to live up to, she often behaves with the profane resolution of a schoolgirl who has escaped surveillance.

Indeed, Isabella uses several styles of discourses with equal disingenuousness. From novels, she borrows sentimental rant regarding love; from earlier romances, she imitates the courtly ideology of female independence;[67] from conduct books she may have acquired her high moral tone regarding friendship and disinterest. But she is also an expert at a less lofty type of discourse: the one related to the confidences and discourses of young women. Isabella will introduce Catherine to such practices of a young woman's subculture as talking about novels and even reading them together, teasing each other about the men they like, eyeing and slyly commenting on the young men they meet at public places, and even following them around town (cf. NA, 41-43). In these conversations and in this pursuit Isabella and Catherine give evidence of an interest in sexuality both unorthodox and commonplace (for orthodox ideas of what is common in everyday life are often entirely mythical); an interest, by the way, which is genuine in Isabella in spite of her duplicity and mercenary spirit.

In addition to serving as romantic confidante for Catherine, Isabella introduces her to Gothic fiction and so prepares her for her humiliation or "uncrowning." As Catherine applies to her experience the fictions of Gothic novels, she both acquires greater independence in judgment and is humbled by the results. On the other hand, her naive incomprehension of what is expected of a sentimental heroine and of an ideologically up to date young lady serves to underline the "lie of pathos" (cf. DN, 401) of fashionable sentimentality. Catherine Morland is, in spite of the inexperience and ignorance to which society condemns her sex, an intelligent and morally alert human being. She is so in the typical ways open to a young girl in the late eighteenth and the beginning of the nineteenth century, for she tends to be superficially compliant and gullible. She is determined to learn and to do "what is right" for a young girl; by both temperament and education, she is open to persuasion and tolerant. But for all her initial willingness to yield to the judgment of others, once Catherine makes up her mind she is firm and steady in her beliefs, and at every point she is more aggressive than her lover.

If Isabella provides the occasion for an acknowledgement of young women's interest in handsome strangers, Catherine improves upon her boldness, since she does not wait for her young man to woo her, as sentimental pathos dictates. She is attracted to Henry Tilney before he has ever given her a thought, a circumstance that allows the narrator to laugh at the sentimental convention dictating that the lady must be assiduously courted before she responds.[68] After their first meeting, Henry and Catherine part "on the lady's side, at least, with a strong inclination for continuing the acquaintance":

> Whether she thought of him so much, while she drank her warm wine and water, and prepared herself for bed, as to dream of him when there, cannot be ascertained; but I hope it was no more than in a slight slumber, or a morning doze at most; for if it be true, as a celebrated writer [Richardson] has maintained, that no young lady can be justified in falling in love before the gentleman's love is declared, it must be very improper that a young lady should dream of a gentleman before the gentleman is first known to have dreamt of her. (NA, 29-30)

Catherine is so far from minding such doctrines by "celebrated writers" that, when Henry finally "solicits" Catherine's "heart," he cannot truthfully employ the commonplace of expressing anxiety regarding her reply, for both, admits the narrator, are aware she loved him. Indeed, the narrator "must confess" that although he now "truly loved her society,. . . a persuasion of her partiality for him had been the only cause of giving her a serious thought" (NA, 243). The narrator's ironic apology for her "wild imagination" in introducing this "new circumstance in romance," strongly suggests such a situation is not "new in common life," where women's sexuality is more active than novels will admit. And yet the impropriety of this situation, "dreadfully derogatory of an heroine's dignity," makes Catherine an anomalous heroine.

Catherine's complete ignorance of the need to conceal her admiration for the hero indeed appears to be new in romances. Even in *Tom Jones*, where Sophia Western loves the title character for months before he gives her a thought, she will not "betray herself" until her concern for his safety overcomes her maidenly reticence. Her charms only impress him when she shows she loves him, which she cannot avoid doing after he rescues her and breaks a bone restraining her runaway horse: "His heart now brought forth the full secret, at the same time that it assured him the adorable object returned his affection."[69] Tom Jones, then, has the double advantage of being spared any anxiety as a lover and of not giving up an atom of masculine supremacy over "the timid sex."

Very different is the case of Catherine Morland's love for Henry Tilney. It is not the heroine's trembling adoration or the hero's exploits that provides the grounds for their attraction. Catherine is instantly attracted to Henry for the irreverence of his wit. He notices her because she shows her interest in him, and then finds her naive frankness amusing, her ignorance flattering and her level-headedness refreshing. Their mutual appeal would perhaps not have led to a lasting relationship had not Catherine been so resolute. As she tells him herself, when a misunderstanding arises between them, if she had not been prevented by Mr Thorpe's callousness, "I would have jumped out and run after you" (NA, 94). Thus, her ingenuousness exempts her from the requisite coyness. She has not a clue that she is being improper; nevertheless, the figure of a girl running after a man is a common image in the carnivalesque inversion of the "women on top" variety.[70]

Indeed, it is Catherine who actively seeks the Tilneys: she goes to their lodgings to apologize after John Thorpe has tricked her into breaking her engagement to go for a walk with Eleanor and Henry; accidentally meeting Henry in the theater, she openly declares herself "wild" in her desire to make her apologies. Later she will run down the streets of Bath to break into the Tilneys' drawing room, breathless and unannounced, when John Thorpe once more tries to trick her into being rude to Eleanor and Henry Tilney. Such forwardness may have been disorderly and unlady-like; and yet, the narrator suggests that it is not extraordinary. Catherine is presented as an ordinary young lady who, though she has to suffer under her share of male arrogance and patriarchal contempt, takes great advantage of even slightly propitious situations to achieve her goals as best she can. Catherine may or may not represent a type of "Everygirl"; her case may or may not be altogether typical. Nevertheless, there is a strong suggestion that she is not exceptional. There is, then, a contradiction between what is expected of young women and supposed to be normal behavior among them, on the one hand, and what often takes place, on the other. Therefore, this novel reverses both certain fictions about young women in novels and some tenets of the "common" ideology of everyday life.

In addition to the inversion of sex roles as Catherine actively courts her young man, a prominent use of reversal in this novel occurs in the presentation of both Catherine and Mrs Allen as wise fools, of Frederick Tilney as rogue, and of Henry Tilney as clown. In the speech of these characters the novel provides interesting material for the analysis of the ways in which the meaning of words depends on the speaker's characteristics and situation. Through its clowns and fools, this work simultaneously undermines certain conventional and novelistic discourses on friendship, love and the spurious feminism of romances.

Clowns and fools, Bakhtin tells us, have been associated with carnival since the inception of the medieval culture of humor (RHW, 8). In the novel, furthermore, the image of the fool has had enormous significance:

> The naiveté of a simpleton who does not understand pathos (or who understands it in a distorted way. . .) is counterposed to a false pathos, which together with gay deception has the effect of "making strange" any pretensions to lofty reality a discourse of pathos might have. (DN, 402)

This statement is clearly applicable to Catherine Morland, who, time and again, fails to understand the role she is expected to play as confidante to Isabella Thorpe. The latter wishes to appear as interesting as a novelistic heroine; unfortunately Catherine does not cooperate. Not only does she fail to see through Isabella's machinations; she does not even know the lofty discourse of pathos to which Isabella aspires.

The narrator herself clownishly mimics Isabella's sentimental discourse, commenting on the young ladies' delight in becoming acquainted by producing an aphorism: "Friendship is certainly the finest balm for the pangs of disappointed love." (NA, 33). "Love" and "friendship" are hyperbolic terms for the circumstances, for, although Catherine had been feeling disappointment at not seeing Henry Tilney in the Pump-room, she had seen Henry only once before, and known Isabella Thorpe only for a few minutes.

As soon as they meet, Isabella, four years older, assumes the lead. Her "decided advantage" over Catherine, however, is confined to knowledge of fashions and an ability to recognize flirtations. The narrator pretends to be taken in by Isabella's airs of worldliness: "These powers received due admiration from Catherine, to whom they were entirely new;" indeed Catherine might have been overwhelmed by them, but Isabella's friendly familiarity "softened down every feeling of awe, and left nothing but tender affection" (NA, 33-4). Again, the irony in this characteristic passage profanes a novelistic canon of elevated sentiment by applying it to a ludicrously inappropriate situation.

The malleable Catherine proves to be a very useful companion for Isabella, who has set her sights on marrying Catherine's brother, James Morland, a clergyman. Catherine does not, however, understand Isabella's calculated hints, nor her affected emotion, presented ironically by the narrator in the language of sentimental pathos ("something like a sigh escaped [Isabella] as she said," in referring to a clergyman, that she was "very partial to the profession"). The narrator's discourse goes on to mock the sentimental ideology of the "finesse of love" and "duties of friendship" by ironically excusing Catherine for not "demanding the cause of that gentle emotion," and for failing to produce the "delicate raillery" that was "properly called for" (NA, 36).

Time and again, Isabella makes similar claims on Catherine's fulfilling the "duties of friendship," with similar results. Catherine inevitably fails to understand Isabella's hints, and so she cannot tease her, or make her blush prettily. Thus, Isabella's pretensions to novelistic pathos are foiled by Catherine's naiveté, and the code of sentimentality itself is comically exposed. As Bakhtin says, what lies at the heart of such incomprehension in a novel is

> a polemical failure to understand someone else's discourse, someone else's pathos-charged lie that has appropriated the world and aspires to conceptualize it, a polemical failure to understand generally accepted, canonized, inveterately false languages with their lofty labels for things and events. (DN, 403)

Isabella Thorpe is a character who seems to need to assign false labels to the events of her life and the emotions they elicit in her. She often uses fictionalizations, casting herself in the self-aggrandizing role of novelistic heroine. No better description of Isabella could be found than Mary Wollstonecraft's strictures on the repulsive results of most female education: "[women] are made to assume an artificial character before their faculties have acquired any strength;" "In short, the whole tenor of female education (the education of society) tends to render the best disposed romantic and inconstant and the remainder vain and mean."[71] Nevertheless, Austen is more optimistic than Wollstonecraft, for if Isabellas are produced by society, so are Catherines, ignorant and naive, yet sturdy and authentic.

In the final chapter in the novel's first volume, for example, having achieved her goal of securing James Morland, Isabella is ready to live out the schema of full sentimental disclosure. She thus sends for Catherine, and, praising her "arch eye" and penetration, begs her to "compose" herself, as though they were both overcome by emotion. Catherine, however, can only respond "by a look of wondering ignorance." For three pages Isabella acts out the role of the happy heroine, casting Catherine in the part of the penetrating friend. Finally, Catherine "dared no longer . . . refuse to have been as full of arch penetration and affectionate sympathy as Isabella chose to consider her" (NA, 119).

Catherine's artlessness and gullibility provide the perfect foil for Isabella's hypocrisy; the dialogic contrast becomes, in Bakhtinian terms, a controversy in which the "lofty pseudo-intelligence" of sentimental pathos is unmasked (cf. DN, 403). In the present case, the mask torn away reveals the deepest motive behind Isabella's deception, greed. Isabella, the reader will later find, set out to conquer James' affection because she was deceived as to the extent of his father's wealth.

Isabella is used to uttering "grand ideas" in support of her self-praise. Two of her most common themes are the strength of her emotional relationships, both as friend and as lover ("My attachments are always excessively strong" —NA, 40) and the exaltation of her feminine independence ("I make it a rule never to mind what [men] say. . . They are the most conceited creatures in the world!" —NA, 42). Catherine's unwordly ignorance of the conventional code Isabella is handling serves to point up its artificiality. Isabella's pretended feminism is one more stratagem to use in engineering her pose, for Isabella's first object is to make males worship her. Men are, therefore, the center of her life, as surely as they would be if she acted submissively toward them. Her "feminism" can be regarded as a pose through which the novelist reveals a flaw at the core of her "sister author's" presentations of women characters whose only interest and glory lies in being adored by the hero. Isabella's tendency to evaluate every circumstance in terms of whether or not it will allow her to seem more alluring leads her to see even virtues as occasions to look well in the eyes of others. As she tells Catherine,

> "Modesty, and all that, is very well in its way, but really a little common honesty is sometimes quite as becoming." (NA, 144)

"Modesty," for her, is, like "honesty," a ploy to be used when it seems "becoming" to do so.

Evidently, Isabella adapts her values and beliefs to her needs to a greater degree than do others in the novel. The extent to which characters are willing to twist what they consider to be true to fit their convenience may be a dividing line between principled and unprincipled characters in this narrative.

And yet the handling of discourse by all characters in this narrative is relativistic enough to justify comparing *Northanger Abbey* to what Bakhtin called "satiric-realistic folk novellas and other low parodic genres associated with jokesters." This similarity is not, of course, due to any coarseness in language or images, but to this novel's "philosophy of discourse." Indeed, in *Northanger Abbey*, just as in the "novellas" to which Bakhtin refers, "Every discourse has its own selfish and biased proprietor; there are no words with meanings shared by all, no words 'belonging to no one.'" Therefore the conditions surrounding an utterance are part of "what determines the word's actual meaning" (DN, 401).

The characters who people *Northanger Abbey* are comically willing to adapt words to fit their wishes in a given situation. Thus Catherine, for instance, as she anxiously watches the weather one rainy morning, hoping that her projected walk with the Tilneys will not have to be postponed, forgets that she has outgrown her childhood love of dirt,[72] that she has grown "clean as she grew smart" (NA, 15). It is this wish to go out with the Tilneys that moves her, when Mrs Allen observes that after the rain it will be too dirty for a walk, to answer, "Oh! that will not signify; I never mind dirt" (NA, 82). At another moment, Catherine, disappointed in her hopes of seeing the charming Mr Tilney again, surveys the crowds of people passing in and out of the Pump-room, "people whom nobody cared about, and nobody wanted to see; [while] he only was absent" (NA, 31). Under different circumstances Catherine would have been willing to admit that somebody else might care about those people who were not Henry Tilney.

Other characters similarly exhibit discourse that adapts itself to harmless untruth, acquiescing, for instance, in an interpretation of events that undeservedly flatters them. So does James Morland, who has come to Bath hoping to see Isabella Thorpe again, when he receives his sister's delighted welcome:

> "(How) good it is of you to come so far on purpose to see *me*."

> James accepted this tribute of gratitude, and qualified his conscience for accepting it too, by saying with perfect sincerity, "Indeed, Catherine, I love you dearly." (NA, 51)

Nevertheless, there is a profound difference between the discourse of such characters, willing mildly to accommodate truth to their current needs, and that handled by such manipulators as Isabella and John Thorpe or General Tilney, who care not how others will be hurt by their lies. A further difference has to do with the latters' pretense that what they say is an "unmediated," universally applicable, almost eternal truth. While Isabella invokes senti-mental wisdom as dogma, her brother, "a rattle" led by "the excess of vanity," uses exclamations, oaths and outrageous fabrications to bully his interlocutor into accepting his "many idle assertions and impudent falsehoods" (NA, 65). General Tilney, on the other hand, appeals to the "timeless" language of gallantry to hide his tyrannical rule over his household and to flatter Catherine, whom he mistakenly considers heiress to Mr Allen's estate.

In a world where self-interest plays a crucial (through not exclusive) part in determining meaning, Isabella mouths her clichés, affixing to whatever suits her needs her "lofty pathos-charged labels" as though they were axiomatic. To oppose her, Austen creates a character Bakhtin would call a "gay deceiver," capable of offering a "verbal and effective response to the lie of pathos":

> Opposed to the *lie of pathos* . . . there is not straightforward truth (pathos of the same kind) but rather a gay and intelligent deception, a *lie* justified because it is directed precisely to *liars*. (DN, 401)

The "gay deceiver" or "merry rogue" in this novel is Captain Frederick Tilney, who can match and excell Isabella at her own game. Thus we see him parrying with Isabella in the most fashionable language of coquetry (cf. NA, 147), playing the gallant to Isabella's damsel. His language deftly parodies Isabella's flirting style; it "parodically reprocesses" her false pathos, allowing us to apply to him Bakhtin's words, for Frederick bandies about this pathos

> in such a way as to rob it of its power to harm, "distanc[ing] it from the mouth" as it were, by means of a smile or a deception, mock[ing] its falsity and thus turn[ing] what was a lie into gay deception. Falsehood is illuminated by ironic consciousness and in the mouth of the happy rogue parodies itself. (DN, 402)

Frederick's actions would be inexcusable in a serious moral discourse; the fact that Henry attempts to justify them is further evidence that Frederick is acting as a "pícaro," a deceiver of deceivers, and thus as a figure beyond moral judgement. When Frederick's flirt with Isabella leads to James' unhappiness, Catherine thinks Frederick very wicked. At first she resists Henry's arguments to the contrary, naïvely attributing them to his "standing by his brother." However, she is "complimented out of further bitterness" by Henry, who simply makes light of the issue. Again, relativity wins the day, for Catherine feels that "Frederick could not be so unpardonably guilty, while Henry made himself so agreeable" (NA, 219).

The episode in which they discuss Frederick's actions is only one of many where Henry and Catherine are counterposed in that functional "coupling of incomprehension with comprehension, simplicity and naiveté with intellect" that Bakhtin considers a "highly typical phenomenon in novelistic prose" (DN, 403). But our heroine does not only play the role of fool through her inability to understand. She also often acts a positive role, in similar vein to what Bakhtin calls the "ambivalent—serio-comical—image of the 'wise fool'" (PDP, 150). Time after time she weighs "social conventionality" against her experience, and finds that the latter, scant though it is, will refuse to uphold the former. Her commonsense responses to Henry's badinage evidence an ingenuous level-headedness that charms him. For instance, when Henry mouths the cliché regarding "time [spent] so much more rationally in the country" than in Bath, Catherine disagrees; when Henry argues that at Bath she is "in pursuit only of amusement all day long," she replies,

> "And so I am at home—only I do not find so much of it. I walk about here, and so I do there;—but here I see a variety of people in every street, and there I can only go and call on Mrs Allen."

> Mr. Tilney was very much amused. "Only go and call on Mrs Allen!" he repeated. "What a picture of intellectual poverty!" (NA, 79)

Catherine Morland achieves perspicacity through her lack of pretensions and through her ignorance of conventional, worldly "wisdom". Thus, when Henry marvels somewhat cryptically at her candor and honesty, her unworldly confidence that everyone is as straightforward as herself, she replies,

> "I do not understand you."

> "Then we are on very unequal terms, for I understand you perfectly well."

> "Me?—yes; I cannot speak well enough to be unintelligible."

> "Bravo! an excellent satire on modern language." (NA, 132-3)

As "wise fool," Catherine Morland is a character whose ignorance and inexperience allow her to question conventional "truths," what "everyone knows." She constitutes, therefore, a comic counterpart to Dostoevski's "ridiculous man," who, says Bakhtin, "is *alone* in his knowledge of the truth and . . . is therefore ridiculed by everyone else" (PDP, 151). In this capacity she delivers herself of some deceptively candid but actually scathing criticisms of history both as discourse and as ideological record, and incidentally of the prevailing system of instructing small children. Naively marveling that Miss Tilney could like to read history, she confesses it only either vexes her or wearies her:

> "The quarrels of popes and kings, with wars or pestilences, on every page; the men all so good for nothing, and hardly any women at all—it is very tiresome;

and yet I often think that it could be so dull, for a great deal of it must be invention. The speeches that are put into the heroes' mouths, their thoughts and designs—the chief of all this must be invention, and invention is what delights me in other books." (NA, 108)

As a record of the evolution of culture and ideology, of the way human beings live, history is sorely deficient, implies Catherine, since it has traditionally focused almost exclusively on disasters and on power seen from the viewpoint of the dominant. As discourse it is not much better, for it strains the credulity of the reader without delighting her imagination. When Miss Tilney, a more mature, more adult young woman, defends history, Catherine again expresses her wonder that so many people in her acquaintance should like it:[73]

"At this rate I shall not pity the writers of history any longer. If people like to read their books, it is all very well, but to be at so much trouble in filling great volumes, which, as I used to think, nobody would willingly ever look into, to be labouring only for the torment of little boys and girls, always struck me as a hard fate; and though I know it is all very right and necessary, I have often wondered at the person's courage that could sit down on purpose to do it." (NA, 109)

Right on cue, Henry Tilney seizes the opportunity to laugh at her for using "to torment" as synonymous of "to instruct." In her reply, Catherine shows once more her unorthodox, far-reaching vision by criticizing contemporary methods of instruction that employed history books as early readers:

"You think me foolish to call instruction a torment, but if you had been as much used as myself to hear poor little children first learning their letters and then learning to spell, if you had ever seen how stupid they can be for a whole morning together, and how tired my poor mother is at the end of it, as I am in the habit of seeing almost every day of my life at home, you would allow that to *torment* and to *instruct* might sometimes be used as synonymous words." (NA, 109-10)

Her views on education, of course, are at variance with what was then the norm, and they are as likely to be held in contempt as the views of dominated groups (in this case schoolchildren) usually are. Catherine's critique gives voice to two socially ignored groups of people: women and the young. In this episode, as usual, Henry Tilney seems to have the last word: he patronizingly lectures her on the need to teach reading or "Mrs Radcliffe had written in vain" (Catherine is at the moment quite charmed by Mrs Radcliffe's novels). But of course what is at issue here is not whether or not children should learn to read, but *how* they should be taught,[74] and Henry's argument simply sidesteps that issue.

Another character who occasionally acts as a wise fool is the ineffably dull Mrs Allen. No one could seem farther from wisdom than this lady, described in very unflattering terms as "one of that numerous class of females" who invite "surprise at there being any men in the world who could like them well enough to marry them. She had neither beauty, genius, accomplishment, nor manner." The lady is good-tempered and indolent; her only passion is dress (NA, 20).[75] The reader will later get a clue as to what Mr Allen could possibly have seen in her. Mrs Allen, it appears, being placidly unconcerned about anything other than her own apparel, was so far from ever contradicting her husband that she generally "thought his expressions quite good enough to be immediately made use of again by herself" (NA, 237). With Mrs Allen for wife, Mr Allen may safely expect never to have his wishes contradicted or his word doubted. Mrs Allen's reaction to whatever her husband says, even when it runs counter to opinions she has just expressed, is likely to be, "That is just what I was going to say" (NA, 105). To certain men, the text appears to be saying, being constantly flattered by bland assent, rather than stimulated and occasionally challenged by genuine dialogue, is more attractive than beauty or charm.

And yet Mrs Allen's tendency to acquiesce in her husband's opinions does not prevent her from holding more liberal and enlightened views than his own, as becomes evident when Mr Allen considers Catherine's outing to Clifton with the Thorpes as an improper scheme, on the grounds that "it has an odd appearance, if young ladies are frequently driven about [in open carriages] by young men, to whom they are not even related." Mrs Allen immediately assents, "Yes, my dear, a very odd appearance indeed." However, when Catherine asks "why did you not tell me so before? . . . I always hoped you would tell me, if you thought I was doing wrong," Mrs Allen replies, "And so I should, my dear. . . But one must not be over particular. Young people *will* be young people, as your good mother says herself" (NA, 104-5). Mrs Allen thus dismisses the question of impropriety, leading the reader to surmise that the kindly Mr Allen may have been more concerned about his own image as Catherine's temporary guardian than zealous in protecting her reputation. Catherine will later find that General Tilney, in his eagerness to promote her intimacy with his son, finds no breach of manners in allowing her to be driven by Henry in an open carriage. Proper conduct for young women, it appears, is often relative to male self-interest.

If Catherine and Mrs Allen play the roles of different kinds of fools, and occasionally even act as wise ones, Henry's function in the novel can be analyzed in terms of a composite figure posited by Bakhtin, that of the clown:

Between the rogue [who lies to liars] and the fool [who fails to understand lies]
there emerges, as a unique coupling of the two, the image of the *clown*. He is
a rogue who dons the mask of a fool in order to motivate distortions and
shufflings of languages and labels, thus unmasking them by not understanding
them. (DN, 404-5)

Indeed, during the scene when Henry first appears in the novel he
performs his most outrageous clowning, reversing and distorting gender roles
as he converses with Mrs Allen on the merits of different muslins. During this
conversation he gravely mirrors Mrs Allen's concerns and opinions, making
this sartorially obsessed lady feel "quite struck by his genius" (NA, 28).
Catherine, who witnesses the scene, begins to fear "that he indulged himself
a little too much with the foibles of others"; but she finally yields to his charm,
his compliments and witticisms (NA, 29).

Again in his capacity as clown, the young man pretends to misinterpret
a harmless conversation between John Thorpe and Catherine, while she
dances with Henry, as an intrusion on his rights: "I consider a country-dance
as an emblem of marriage. Fidelity and complaisance are the principal duties
of both; and those men who do not chuse to dance or marry themselves, have
no business with the partners or wives of their neighbours." In this manner,
Henry "distorts" the proprietary airs jealous men assume, by exhibiting them
on an inappropriate occasion. Catherine, however, cannot see the similarity
between marriage and dancing: "People that marry can never part," says she,
"but must go and keep house together. People that dance only stand opposite
each other in a long room for half an hour." Thus, quite unaware of what is
expected of a witty female in such a setting, she exhibits her homely common
sense. When Henry continues to make ingenious analogies, Catherine allows
"all this sounds very well," but she cannot bring herself to agree. He then plays
the devil's advocate, supplying what should have been her witty objections to
his comparisons, but Catherine will not even cooperate by allowing that he
has represented her arguments correctly. Henry ironically declares himself
"quite at a loss" to understand what objections she could possibly have to his
analogy (NA, 76-7).

Henry's clowning, in this and other instances, constitutes a "shuffling
of languages and labels" having to do mostly with gender relations and
women's social roles. It is ironically significant that one of his mock-serious
arguments likening marriage to dancing involves the conventional view that
"man has the advantage of choice, woman only the power of refusal"; in this
novel, there is no doubt that it is the female who has first made the choice.

It is the ambivalence and "joyful relativity" of Henry's humor that give
rise to such widely diverging readings of his role in the novel as those we find,
for instance, in A. Walton Litz and Lloyd Brown, on the one hand, and Claudia
Johnson on the other. Brown holds that Henry, as "the most penetrating

character in the novel," does almost the author's own job: "In effect, [Henry] is the parodist who mimics Catherine's language (words like 'torment,' for example) and intellectual values in order to demonstrate their limitations vis-a-vis the complexities of experience."[76] Litz goes even further, assuming that Austen has given up so much of her authority to this character that she has lost any right to criticize him: "Henry's attitudes merge with those of his creator on so many occasions that we are disturbed when she speaks to us directly, or when Henry is suddenly subjected to her irony."[77] Johnson, on the other hand, is so impressed by Henry's occasional displays of male arrogance that she portrays him as a flippant, self-serving, smug conversationalist, who often "will with magisterial conmplacence lay down the law." As an overbearing brother, Henry is only different from John Thorpe in being less boorish:

> [The] cool possession of privilege entitles [both males] to disparaging banter, not the less corrosive for being entirely in the normal course of things. On most occasions, however, Tilney's bullying is more polished. A self-proclaimed expert on matters feminine, . . . Tilney simply believes that he knows women's minds better than they do, and he dismisses any "no" to the contrary as unreal.[78]

In my reading, Henry is neither the author's unquestionable alter ego nor a representative of male oppressors. Nevertheless, both sides on the matter of Henry Tilney's worthiness and credibility adduce strong arguments in support of their position. The reason for these two conflicting bodies of evidence can be understood when we see the novel from the Bakhtinian perspective of "a radical scepticism toward any unmediated discourse and any straightforward seriousness" (DN, 401).

If this is indeed a novel where laughter is "universal in scope," then Henry cannot escape being laughed at. As a male member of the gentry living in turn-of-century England, Henry is liable to the arrogance that, it is implied, will color the viewpoint of even the most enlightened men. Such is the conclusion one draws from the narration of a fascinating conversation among Henry, Eleanor Tilney and Catherine during their walk round Beechen Cliff. In this episode Henry and Catherine interact as fool and clown, while only Eleanor plays a "straight" role. As they talk, we see Henry and Catherine advancing in their mutual admiration; Henry is sanctioned as worthy of being her lover both through the narrator's and his sister's authority, though in terms that strongly contrast with those habitual in sentimental novels. Far from being alluded to as "worthiest of males," a frequent appellation given, for instance, to Godolphin, the hero in Charlotte Smith's *Emmeline*, Henry is referred to very ironically. The narrator's mocking tone ceases to seem incompatible with her use of Henry as the "intelligent" pole in his dialogues with Catherine, cast as the "simpleton" (as some critics have seen it), when we place the narrator's discourse in the context of the novel's relativism and its polemic intention.

Our hero is enthroned as Catherine's lover after she expresses shame for her ignorance of drawing, an avocation for both Henry and Eleanor, and of the canons of the picturesque. The two Tilneys, however, will not think less of her, observes the narrator ironically; the narrator's remarks about the vanity of people in general then lead to highly-charged comments on men's attitudes toward women:

> Where people wish to attach, they should always be ignorant. To come with a well-informed mind, is to come with an inability of administering to the vanity of others, which a sensible person would always wish to avoid. A woman, especially, if she have the misfortune of knowing anything, should conceal it as well as she can.[79]

> The advantages of natural folly in a beautiful girl have been already set forth by the capital pen of a sister author;—and to her treatment of the subject I will only add in justice to men, that though to the larger and more trifling part of the sex, imbecility in females is a great enhancement of their personal charms, there is a portion of them too reasonable and too well informed themselves to desire any thing more in woman than ignorance. (NA, 110-1)

The passage by "a sister author" alluded to here is an utterance by Mrs Arlberry in Fanny Burney's *Camilla* we already quoted above. The narrator ironically implies that the highest form of enlightenment we can expect in men is their being satisfied with female ignorance rather than outright imbecility. She also classes Henry among the enlightened few, since he "became perfectly satisfied of [Catherine's] having a great deal of natural taste". . . but only after she "began to see beauty in everything admired by him."

Later on during the same episode, we see Henry acting as clown "who has the right to speak in otherwise unacceptable languages and the right to maliciously distort languages that *are* acceptable" (DN, 405). Henry moderates in a misunderstanding between Catherine and his sister when the latter interprets the former's remarks about a forthcoming horror novel as news about an impending London riot. The confusion is caused by Catherine's tendency to speak of fiction as though it were fact, to dwell in a world highly colored by schemas common in the sentimental and Gothic novels she has been reading. On this occasion, Henry distorts the language of male contempt for females by addressing his feminine interlocutors with utterances abusive of women that may be more common among men alone, or when more ironically disguised. Our hero intervenes to clarify the misunderstanding between Catherine and his sister in an ironically condescending tone, professing to have

"no patience with such of my sex as disdain to let themselves sometimes down
to the comprehension of yours. Perhaps the abilities of women are neither sound
nor acute—neither vigorous nor keen. Perhaps they may want observation,
discernment, judgment, fire, genius and wit." (NA, 112)

Such blatant presumptuousness can be seen as a merry pose, an instance
of hyperbolic self-parody showing Henry's awareness of the ludicrous
presumption of superiority that often characterizes the language used by
heroes to instruct the tender heroine. Being apparently in the mood for high
comedy, he proceeds to explain their mutual error, begging Catherine to
forgive Eleanor's stupidity. Eleanor's apprehension that her other brother,
Captain Frederick Tilney, could be endangered by acting to quell the
rebellion, have added "the fears of the sister" to "the weakness of the woman;
for she is by no means a simpleton in general" (NA, 113).

As many critics have pointed out, the details Henry uses to depict the
riot Eleanor must have been imagining are drawn from recent political events;
and yet, since these critics interpret Henry's derogation of his sister (and of
women in general) literally, they do not see in Henry's allusions to real
political events his awareness that Eleanors' fears are plausible, and not a mark
of the simpleton. Henry, they hold, undercuts his own argument when he
laughs at his sister for fearing what is quite likely to happen.[80] But why would
Henry do this? Must we conclude he is a simpleton himself? On the contrary,
Henry is not expecting to be taken literally when he accuses his sister of
weakness and excessive sensibility. Eleanor, who knows him better than
anyone else, immediately interprets his words as a jest. First, she dismisses his
disparagement of women in general without showing the slightest offense by
turning to Catherine, "Miss Morland, do not mind what he says—but have
the goodness to satisfy me as to this dreadful riot" (NA, 112). Then, when
Henry explains that Catherine has not been speaking of a riot but of a new
publication, when he apparently insults his sister, Eleanor's reaction is very
different from Catherine's. The latter apparently believes he is serious and
seems to blame him, for she "looked grave." Eleanor, for her part, only seems
worried that Catherine will not understand; she is afraid that "[Miss Morland
will] think you intolerably rude to your sister, and a great brute in your
opinion of women in general. Miss Morland is not used to your odd ways"
(NA, 113).

Are we, indeed, to think Henry a great misogynous brute? His actions
and speeches in other episodes cannot justify such a conclusion. Although
Henry sometimes boasts of his superior knowledge (as when he tells Catherine
that he "had entered on [his] studies at Oxford while [she was] a good little
girl working [her] sampler at home!"—NA, 107), his mild young-male
arrogance is offset by his explicit confidence in the equality of the sexes as far
as intellectual and artistic powers are concerned ("In every power of which

taste is the foundation, excellence is pretty fairly divided between the sexes",
he says to Catherine while discussing women's writing ability—NA, 28). The
best alternative when deciding how to view Henry's disparagement of women
in this episode is to follow Eleanor's lead in interpreting Henry's remarks as
clowning. For Eleanor knows that her brother *does* "think very highly of the
understanding of women," although when she tries to get him to acknowledge
it before Catherine Morland he persists in spouting the anti-feminist drivel
he is parodying. Treating her brother as she would a mischievous child,
Eleanor explains to Catherine, in Henry's presence, that he "is not in a sober
mood. But I do assure you that he must be entirely misunderstood, if he can
ever appear to say an unjust thing of any woman at all, or an unkind one of
me" (NA, 114). Thus is Henry instated and sanctioned as Catherine's
romantic interest, in spite of the fact that she cannot fully understand his "odd
ways," his role as clown.

It may be argued that Miss Tilney and Miss Morland are both too
indulgent, that Henry enjoys his jest a bit too much. However, Eleanor's
humoring her brother, and Catherine's faith that this marvelous man must be
in the right, may be read as ironic comments by the narrator on women's
excessive mildness; if men's folly leads them to arrogance, she seems to be
saying, some women may act as accomplices of their own oppression. After
all, Catherine's tendency to acquiesce in male opinion has already been the
butt of irony during that memorable ride in which we are introduced to John
Thorpe:

> [John Thorpe's] discourse now sunk from its hitherto animated pitch, to
> nothing more than a short decisive sentence of praise or condemnation on the
> face of every woman they met; and Catherine, after listening and agreeing as long
> as she could, with all the civility and deference of the youthful female mind,
> fearful of hazarding an opinion of its own in opposition to that of a self-assured
> man, especially where the beauty of her own sex is concerned, ventured at length
> to vary the subject. (NA, 48)

In contrast to the typical sentimental novel, where the heroine is a victim and
certain male figures embody evil power, while the hero can do no wrong,
Northanger Abbey ridicules misogynous discourse and laughs at the heroine's
general subservience before males and her specific admiration for the hero.
Catherine's fear of challenging any male opinion is utterly ludicrous when the
male is John Thorpe; when it is Henry Tilney's utterances that are in question,
her need to be wary seems less evident. And yet Catherine's development will
lead her to recognize that Henry, also, can be wrong.

Northanger Abbey is the story of Catherine's growth from her original
docility to a higher level of independence. Her coming of age, however, does
not follow the serious process of mastering her difficulties that is characteristic

of male novelistic *Bildung*. Rather, through a series of crownings and uncrownings, Catherine is led to a narrative Utopia, which can be seen as amenable to her needs only from the peculiar perspective of carnival laughter.

This novel traces her development through the process of courtship; the reason for the lovers' mutual attraction is related to their growth. In other words, we can understand what attracts them to each other by analyzing what it is they need to learn, and vice versa. What pulls Catherine and Henry together is their common delight in pitting conventional ideas from different sources against evidence drawn from their own experience. Each needs to learn how far to rely on certain available ideologies in order to assess people, events, circumstances. Furthermore, both this process of growth and the one by which they fall in love are animated by carnivalesque logic, by the gay relativity that challenges the absolutism of prevailing truths and authorities. As a female of nearly school age, Catherine Morland remains outside most spheres of power; as the son of a tyrannical and greedy father, Henry Tilney finds his affective life played on in ways he cannot control. These circumstances pit them, in some senses, against certain official ideologies, which are so often challenged that this novel can be said to be governed by carnivalesque logic: "the peculiar logic of the 'inside out' (*a l'envers*), of the 'turnabout,' of a continual shifting from top to bottom, from front to rear, of numerous parodies and travesties, humiliations, profanations, comic crownings and uncrownings" (RHW, 11).

From the beginning, Catherine's story is one of confrontations with ideologies, many of which are new to her. When there are no significant practical consequences involved, she can often dismiss an ideological "truth" as incompatible with her own experience. But *Northanger Abbey* does not oppose a ready-made ideology to the conventional wisdom it often challenges, nor does it exalt a wise heroine capable of opposing official error. Rather, the reader is never allowed to forget that she is an ignorant schoolgirl, and that her placement in the position of heroine is itself a form of unruliness.

In this sense, Catherine can be seen as a figure of the "carnival king," instituting a radically different approach to power and truth. The crowning of a carnival king, or king of fools, or Lord of Misrule, does not simply substitute a member of the underprivileged classes for the official, traditional rulers, nor does it merely raise a new anti-dogma in place of the old official creed. In carnival's "living sense of the world," the crowning of a mock-king is neither "absolute negation and destruction" of an old order, nor absolute affirmation of an alternative one; both absolutes are alien to carnival. As the festival of renewal, carnival crowns a king in order to decrown it:

> Crowning/decrowning is a dualistic ambivalent ritual, expressing the inevitability and at the same time the creative power of the shift-and-renewal, the *joyful relativity* of all structure and order, of all authority and all (hierarchical) position.

Crowning already contains the idea of imminent decrowning: it is ambivalent from the very start . . .—From the very beginning, a decrowning glimmers through the crowning. (PDP, 124-5)

Catherine's learning process presents this dualistic, two-leveled character. She is crowned the central character, but she is humbled repeatedly. At Bath Catherine will find her old assumptions severely shaken, so much so that even the ways in which she has been accustomed to look at landscapes are challenged. It appears she must even relearn how to see, and how to talk about what she sees; as she listens to Henry and Eleanor Tilney discuss the prospect from Beechen Hill as an object for a drawing, she finds she cannot even understand their language:

The little which she could understand, however, appeared to contradict the very few notions she had entertained on the matter before. It seemed as if a good view were no longer to be taken from the top of an high hill, and that a clear blue sky was no longer a proof of a fine day. She was heartily ashamed of her ignorance. (NA, 110)

It is characteristic of this novel that we are not then presented by the narrator with the "right" way of seeing the landscape. Rather, Catherine's old-hat notions are simply and sensibly stated, so that Henry and Eleanor's newfangled ideas of "the picturesque" seem to deserve as much irony or gentle mockery as Catherine's old-fashioned views. The passage, then, is imbued with "joyful relativity," with the attitude that believing often shapes seeing.

As we have seen, Henry Tilney will only like Catherine better for her ignorance. He will often seriously counter some of her ideas, such as the notion that men do not like novels: "The person, be it gentleman or lady, who has not pleasure in a good novel, must be intolerably stupid," explains Henry (NA, 106). Under his tutelage, and faced with Isabella's example, she will begin to question her received views about love, including the adage that, "A woman in love with one man cannot flirt with another," to which Henry replies, "It is probable that she will neither love so well, nor flirt so well, as she might do either singly. The gentlemen must each give up a little" (NA, 151). But by far the greatest revolution Catherine's thinking must undergo is related to her awareness of evil, the realization that quite ordinary people might harbor rather reprehensible feelings and be animated by vicious motives. This realization, in turn, is related to her daring to question patriarchal authority.

A first stage of this momentous process in Catherine's personal development is facilitated by her reading Gothic novels, to which Isabella introduces her. Influenced by these readings, and by Henry's parody of a Gothic episode,[81] she views Northanger Abbey as a place such as "one reads about," and comes to suspect that its owner is the perpetrator of Gothic horrors. Her three attempts to "read" the old abbey as a novelistic setting end in humiliating confrontations with prosaic reality, but these attempts must not be regarded, following the critical commonplace, only as unfortunate mistakes. Just as at Beechen Hill she finds she must learn to see anew, at Northanger Abbey she needs to discover, through her ludicrous attempts to uncover buried secrets, how far she can trust appearances of respectability. Having started out from a position of utter gullibility and blind trust, she will go to extremes of suspicion, and then through humbling self-reproach, until she learns to question patriarchal authority on more plausible grounds.

Initially, she is tempted, it is true, by the siren song of novelistic "extraordinariness"; in time she will learn that a seemingly upstanding citizen such as General Tilney can be suspect, but not of unusual or extraordinary crimes. Nevertheless, in hunting for old secrets, under the influence of her Gothic reading, Catherine is taking crucial steps towards independence by making bold to question façades, to test the validity of the "monolithically serious" male authority she has been trained to respect. She has also been preparing for her suspicions of General Tilney as a murderer or his wife's jailor through her own observations.

The first time she spends some time with the Tilneys in the General's company Catherine is puzzled by the fact that, in spite of his "great civilities to her ... it had been a release to get away from him." At this point, however, she cannot yet give up the preconception that, being "tall and handsome and Henry's father," the General must be blameless (NA, 129). As the General's guest at the abbey, Catherine encounters evidence of his disregard for his daughter's feelings, his egotism, his hypocrisy, his apparent indifference to his late wife's memory. In consequence, "what had been terror and dislike before" becomes "absolute aversion." This new feeling has the advantage of allowing her to rebel against two patriarchs under whose roof Catherine has lived, for in believing the General to have been odious to his wife Catherine finds reason to prove Mr Allen wrong: "She had often read of such characters [as General Tilney]; characters, which Mr Allen had been used to call unnatural and overdrawn; but here was proof positive to the contrary" (NA, 181). Her reading Gothic novels, then, becomes a form of crowning by which she has acquired a new, ambivalent authority.

Her new ability to suspect, to doubt the positions of her old authority figures, is for the "well-read Catherine" a "two-leveled" power of judgment (in the Bakhtinian sense of "crowning and uncrowning"), since it shows her independence but leads her to a kind of reverse authoritarianism, a naive belief that she has now "proof positive" of her improbable ideas. Having decided that the General is as wicked as a Radcliffean villain, Catherine begins to doubt his every word. His "magnificent compliments" can no longer impose on her: "There must be some deeper cause" even for his seemingly trifling actions than he is willing to admit (NA, 187). Ironically, Catherine does not suspect the prosaic truth of the General's greedy designs on what he thinks is Catherine's great fortune; far from deducing what his real vices are, she makes up an improbable tale of his being his wife's murderer or jailor. However, these gruesome suspicions will prove fortunate from the viewpoint of Catherine's *Bildung*, for she will become less trusting and pliable, and come to rely less on the benevolence of male authority figures.

Her challenge to patriarchal authority takes the form of a fact-finding tour of Mrs Tilney's apartment which, as we have seen, ends in fiasco. Her challenge is then in turn challenged by Henry, who discovers her as she slinks around a passage, and soon gets her to acknowledge the reason. He reacts with shock:

> "If I understand you rightly, you had formed a surmise of such horror as I have hardly words to—Dear Miss Morland, consider the dreadful nature of the suspicions you have entertained.... Remember the country and the age in which we live. Remember that we are English, that we are Christians.... Could [such atrocities] be perpetrated without being known, in a country like this ... where every man is surrounded by a neighbourhood of voluntary spies, and where roads and newspapers lay every thing open? Dearest Miss Morland, what ideas have you been admitting?" (NA, 197-8)

This speech at first sight seems to resolutely affirm English superiority and respectability. And yet, since D. W. Harding's commentary on this text,[82] it has been often interpreted as a shrewd reflection on what we could call the policing function of neighbors, those "voluntary spies," as the real source of English virtue. If Catherine's "surmise" is "of such horror" that it fragments the glib Henry's sentences, it seems he is too little disposed to reflect on his own admission that the "dreadful" act is improbable, not because it is horrible, but because the neighbors' voluntary surveillance would prevent it.

Having suffered what Bakhtin would call a "comic uncrowning," Catherine, full of remorse, indulges in hyperbolic self-abuse; for one day "She hated herself more than she could express." She has now learned that in spite of those "charming works" of Mrs Radcliffe and her imitators, at least "in the midland counties of England," people and their habits showed "a general though unequal mixture of good and bad" (NA, 199-200).

Though most critics consider this episode as climactic, Catherine must yet undergo the most important phase of her growth. What she has learned is important, but she is in danger of admiring Henry's "astonishing generosity and nobleness of conduct" a bit too much, when he so patronizingly endeavors to make her feel comfortable again (NA, 201). And she has yet to learn to discern between what people say about themselves and what they are. As "the anxieties of common life ... succeed to the alarms of romance," Catherine must find that even people she thinks she knows well can lie about important things. She must first discover that Isabella loves neither James Morland nor Frederick Tilney, and finally that the General, though not a murderer, is nearly as bad as she had thought him, and, in spite of his frequent protestations to the contrary, very much interested in money.

Catherine has greatly advanced in her development from the time when she dared not doubt John Thorpe's judgment; she can now suppose Henry and Eleanor must be mistaken when they think General Tilney will object to Isabella's marrying Frederick Tilney because she is portionless. Having once been humbled for suspecting the General's character, Catherine now trusts his word; therefore, remembering his frequent "most generous and disinterested sentiments on the subject of money," she concludes that "his disposition in such matters [was] misunderstood by his children" (NA, 208). However, she will soon realize the General habitually professes not to want to give trouble to others, when actually he expects to be treated most handsomely. This inconsistency will thoroughly puzzle Catherine: "why he should say one thing so positively and mean another all the while was most unaccountable! How were people, at that rate, to be understood?" (NA, 211).

The General's pointed chivalry to Catherine is suddenly at an end when he discovers that the reports of her fortune are false. The contrast between his former complaisance and the wrath he now feels is great. As a result, Catherine suffers the direst uncrowning the novel contains, when she is peremptorily ordered to leave Northanger Abbey in a few hours, without even being allowed time to inform her family or provided with a servant to accompany her. And yet, much as Catherine suffers, her family's plain common sense will downplay the seriousness of the affair, so that her role as victim is ironically diminished.

Nevertheless, Catherine's uncrowning is not the last one to be found in the novel. Henry Tilney must undergo the humiliating experience of accepting that he has been partly wrong in his self-righteous preaching to Catherine, and the even more humbling one of discovering to what lengths his father's greed and selfishness will lead him. Such an unexpected discovery must be particularly painful to a young man who had so much assurance in his own good judgment, who has so blithely passed judgment on everyone. Ironically, Henry Tilney, for all his young-male arrogance, has been wooed by Catherine and obedient to his father's whims until the latter's patriarchal dominance finally becomes intolerable. And yet, though his pain in "having such things to relate of his father" to Catherine makes him "pitiable," the result is salutary, since it finally makes him rebel. Although the General has demanded military obedience of everyone, though he has been "accustomed on every ordinary occasion to give the law in his family," this time "his anger, though it must shock, could not intimidate Henry" (NA, 427).

Catherine Morland and Henry Tilney, therefore, both come of age at the same time and in similar ways. Her personal growth takes the form of a final, now fully justified challenge to patriarchal authority. She feels, when Henry reveals the General's motives in turning her from his house, "that in suspecting General Tilney of either murdering or shutting up his wife, she had scarcely sinned against his character or magnified his cruelty" (NA, 247). Once more, the ironic tone of this statement makes it carnivalesque and ambivalent, for it laughs at the hyperbolic terms in which her anger is expressed, while at the same time it supports her right to be very angry.

In contrast to the General's character, Catherine's honesty and ability to love make her admirable. Nevertheless, she is not enthroned as so angelic as to be her lover's superior, as Fanny Burney's Cecilia, for instance, had been. Although Henry's pride is leveled, we do not find Catherine's dignity rising until she towers above him. Rather, in a typically carnivalesque suspension of "all hierarchical precedence" with regard to gender relations, *Northanger Abbey* installs a new, feminist utopia, in the sense that oppressive patriarchal barriers are dissolved and the two genders appear "so to speak, reborn for new, purely human relations" (RHW, 10).

The installation of this new utopia is reflected through both the description of the relations among characters and narrative technique. In four short pages, the narrator proceeds to remove all obstacles to a satisfactory conclusion, providing the best possible end for every sympathetically portrayed character. Furthermore, the narrator openly and gaily refers to this adjustment of narrative circumstances to fit human desires of perfect justice, as the narrating voice hints that such utopian aspirations are part of novelistic convention. Therefore we are told that Catherine's parents' decision not to sanction her engagement until the General consents to the marriage will not frighten the readers, "who will see in the tell-tale compression of the pages that we are all hastening together to perfect felicity" (NA, 250). The number of pages left in a volume, then, is itself capable of conveying meaning to a reader. This ironic pointing to the materiality of the reading process constitutes a carnivalesque inversion of those fictional conventions that idealize and absolutize the truth-telling powers of the narratorial voice. Thus this novel achieves much the same effect of what Bakhtin calls the "removal of footlights" in a medieval French drama which abandoned illusion-creating conventions to present "many features of real life" (RHW, 257).

Similarly, the novel's final chapter returns to the playful hints of the fictional character of the story that were contained in its initial statement, "No one who had ever seen Catherine Morland in her infancy would have supposed her born to be an heroine." By means of this ambiguous reference to her birth, the opening combines the customary fictional pretense that the protagonist was born and lived through actual stages of life with the admission that she was born *to be* a heroine, i.e., as a fictional creation of the author. The ambivalent "as if" character of all fictional narrative is thus avowed and brought to the fore.

In the novel's conclusion we find a similar meta-narrative or self-referential phenomenon in the allusion to "the rules of composition" for novels. This reference occurs in the passage relating how the obstacle to the protagonists' marriage was removed when the General, in a moment of euphoria caused by Eleanor's marriage to a peer, gives Henry permission "to be a fool if he liked it!" Literary rules, admits the narrator, "forbid the introduction of a character not connected with my fable"; she then mockingly justifies herself by revealing that this peer "was the very gentleman whose negligent servant left behind him that collection of washing-bills, resulting from a long visit at Northanger, by which my heroine was involved in one of her most alarming adventures" (NA, 251).

Finally, the utopian character of the ending allows the narrating voice to ironically stress the novel's subversive tendency. Since every conflict is so happily resolved, and since the General's cruelty and "unjust interference" leads to the characters' beginning "perfect happiness at the respective ages of twenty-six and eighteen," the narrator finds a propitious occasion to end on a carnivalesque note. Therefore, she leaves "it to be settled by whomsoever it may concern, whether the tendency of this work be altogether to recommend parental tyranny, or reward filial disobedience" (NA, 252).

One of the characteristics of utopia as a genre is its implicit disparagement of actual conditions, its unspoken admission that real-life conditions are not as good as utopia describes. This conclusion is clearly warranted by this novel's utopian ending; its narrator has throughout the narrative given too much evidence of her merry skepticism to allow us to take seriously her assurances that all deserving characters will attain to "perfect felicity." Paradoxically, however, *Northanger Abbey*'s carnivalesque utopia at the same time presents a more affirmative, more positive view of society. For this is a novel written against the idea that women are best seen as victims, that they are inescapably malformed by a sexist culture, that their development is invariably thwarted and their moral and intellectual capacities ineluctably stunted in patriarchy. While obviously Catherine is the product of a sexist culture where women are kept ignorant and subservient to men, she is not a submissive victim. Without being extraordinary or tragic, our heroine often acts as an unconscious subversive. She thinks of herself as dutiful, and yet she obeys the norms of conduct for young ladies only in what is inconsequential. In what is crucial, she disobeys without ever being aware of it, for she not only has sexual feelings but acts upon them, taking the initiative and naively courting her young man. Although a member of a subordinate group, her no—nonsense determination to pursue her happiness allows her to confront the most powerful patriarch in her world and ultimately win.

This novel thus qualifies one ideological position regarding women in the eighteenth and nineteenth centuries. According to both Wollstonecraft and

Hays, men enjoy all the comparative moral and intellectual advantages, being deformed by society only in their sexual habits. Early feminists typically decried male presumptions of superiority as cruelly injurious to women, not as masculine defect. In *Northager Abbey,* on the contrary, both males and females show signs of cultural deformation. While, typically, women are kept ignorant and trained for complaisance, men harbor lucicrously inflated ideas of their own worth and judgment. All culture forms and deforms; in a society where there is gender–subordination, both sexes will exhibit deformities.

By carnavilesque means, however, such deformities are fictionally healed. *Northanger Abbey* tranforms the official ideology and generates, reforms, the institutions of love and marriage, making them amenable to both men and women. Thus, while Catherine at first believes Henry nearly infallible, she learns the limitations of his views and reinforces her faith in her own perceptions when she suffers from his father's very real shortcomings. Furthermore, the merry optimism of the final chapter dismisses our young couple to a life of financial "independence and comfort." Thus Henry and Catherine are transported to their utopia, or "no-place" (so unlike the culture the novel has been portraying), where not only are women strong, but their husbands will stand by them and learn with them. Their happiness will be perfect and enduring. When they marry, Henry and Catherine enter a relationship characterized by "freedom, equality and abundance," three of the qualities of the "utopian realm" (RHW, 11) which, according to Bakhtin, characterized the world of festive traditions, the world of carnival.

NOTES

1. Critics disagree on the chronology for this and the other novels, but they generally accept that *Northanger Abbey* underwent a series of revisions. According to tradition Jane Austen wrote her novels during two well-defined periods of her life; on the other hand, according to Q.D. Leavis, Austen revised her works incessantly, covering older material with new layers of revisions. Nevertheless, in spite of B. C. Southam's criticism of Mrs Leavis' teories, both writers consider *Northanger Abbey* an early work that was revised as late as 1816. (Cf. Q.D. Leavis, "A Critical Theory of Jane Austen's Writings," *Scrutiny*, 10 (October and January 1941 and 1942), 114-42, 272-94; and B.C. Southam, "Introduction", *Jane Austen, Northanger Abbey and Persuasion: A Casebook* (London: Macmillan Press, 1976), pp. 11-38). For a good summary of the traditional opinion that Jane Austen's writing career falls into two periods divided by the time she lived at Bath and Southamptom (1801-1809), see A. Walton Litz, "Chronology of Composition," *The Jane Austen Companion.*

2. See, for instance, A.Walton Litz, *Jane Austen: A Study of Her Artistic Development* (New York: Oxford University Press, 1965), p. 59.

3. Kenneth L. Moler, *Jane Austen's Art of Allusion* (Lincoln, Nebraska: University of Nebraska Press, 1968), p. 19.

4. Moler, *Jane Austen's Art of Allusion*, p. 21.

5. Susan Stewart, *Nonsense: Aspects of Intertextuality in Folklore and Literature* (Baltimore: Johns Hopkins University Press, 1979).

6. Fanny Burney, *Cecilia* (London: George Bell & Sons, 1906), p. 2.

7. Cf. Mary Lascelles, *Jane Austen and Her Art*, p. 60, n. 1.

8. Anne Henry Ehrenpreis, "Introduction," in Charlotte Smith's *Emmeline: The Orphan of the Castle* (London: Oxford University Press, 1971), p. xiii.

9. Lascelles, *Jane Austen and Her Art*, p. 60, n. 1.

10. Jan Fergus, *Jane Austen and the Didactic Novel* (London: The Macmillan Press, 1983), p. 22.

11. See Samuel Richardson, *Clarissa, or the History of a Young Lady* (London: Dent & Sons, 1962).

12. Henry Fielding, *The History of Tom Jones, A Foundling* (New York: Random House, 1948), p. 259.

13. *Evelina, or the History of a Young Lady's Entrance into the World* (London: Oxford University Press, 1968) Vol. I, Letter II, p. 13.

14. *Emmeline*, Vol. I, Ch. i, p. 2.

15. *The Old Manor House* (London: Oxford University Press, 1969), p. 13.

16. *Mary, a Fiction* (London: Oxford University Press, 1976), p. 5.

17. Cf. the following passage from *Emmeline:* "Sensible of the defects of her education, she applied incessantly to her books; for of every useful and ornamental feminine employment she had long since made herself mistress without any instruction" (London: Oxford University Press, 1971, p. 41).

18. *Mary, a Fiction*, p. 11.

19. Another passage from *Northanger Abbey* comments on Catherine's deficiencies as a heroine in having no notion of drawing—not enough even to attempt a sketch of her lover's profile, that she might be detected in the design (Na, 16). Cf. Delamere's discovery of a drawing of himself inside Emmeline's music book— *Emmeline*, p. 115.

20. *Clarissa*, Vol. I, p. 274.

21. Vol. I, Ch. xiv, p. 103.

22. Cf. Harriet Byron's suitor, Sir Hargrave Pollexfen, *Sir Charles Grandison*, Part I, Vol. 1.

23. Cf. Sir Philip Baddley's proposal, Edgeworth's *Belinda* (London: J.M. Dent & Co., 1893), Vol. I, xxii, pp. 178-81.

24. *Sir Charles Grandison*, Vol. I, p. 136.

25. In *Vicar of Wakefield* Sophia is thrown from her horse and saved by Mr. Burchell, who will later marry her, (New York: J.H. Sears & Co.) p. 19.

26. *Memoirs of Emma Courtney* (New York: Garland Publishing Inc., 1974), p. 121.

27. *Evelina*, Vol. III, Letter XI, p. 33.

28. *The Castle of Wolfenbach*, D.P. Varma, ed. *The Northanger Set of Jane Austen Horrid Novels* (London: The Folio Press, 1968). pp. 80-88.

29. In this novel, Camilla is repeatedly shown as she is about to explain her conduct to Edgar Mandlebert, who first suspects her of flirting with Major Cerwood, and later of wishing to marry Lord Valhurst; some sudden recollection often prevents her from doing so. In one typical passage, offended by Edgar's suspicions, she decides not to risk such another mark of his cold superiority; she therefore accepts Mrs Berlington's invitation *because* she knows Edgar dislikes this acquaintance. This decision of course retards the clarification of her acts to Edgar—Book VII, Ch. x, p. 582.

30. Emmeline treats the man she loves, Godolphin, with coldness and reserve, even after all serious obstacles to their union have been removed. She continues to hold back, it is said, from a series of qualms and fears stemming from her delicacy (*Emmeline*, Vol. IV, Ch viii, pp. 428-429).

31. Kenneth L. Moler, *Jane Austen's Art of Allusion*, p. 2.

32. *Belinda*, Vol. II, Ch. xxvii, p. 215.

33. Samuel Richardson, *Sir Charles Grandison*, Vol. I, Letter xxiii, pp. 116-9.

34. *Horrid Mysteries*, tr. from the German of the Marquis of Grosse by Peter Will (London: Folio Press, 1968), pp. 48-9.

35. The heroine who is hunted along the dark rooms of a castle is so common in Gothic fiction that it seems futile to attempt a list of predecessors of Henrys Catherine; Emily St. Aubert in *Udolpho* goes through similar experiences, as does Emmeline in Charlotte Smith's novel. As Anne Ehrenpreis points out, however, the earliest occurrence of such an episode in literature is found in Isabella's nocturnal flight in Walpole's *The Castle of Otranto (1964);* Isabella's candle goes out in a sudden gust of wind while she runs aways from an unwelcome lover ("Introduction," *Emmeline*, p. xi). On the other hand, incidents of young ladies persecuted along passages of Gothic castles occur in all the horrid novels Isabella Thorpe recommends to Catherine Morland. These novels (*The Castle of Wolfenbach, Clermont, The Mysterious Warning, Necromancer of the Black Forest, Midnight Bell, Orphan of the Rhine, and Horrid Mysteries*) were for a long time

supposed to have been mere titles invented by Austen. It was not until 1917 that Montague Summers, in an article in *The Times Literary Supplement,* identified six of the seven novels; an American reader provided news of the remaining one (D. P. Varma, "Introduction," *The Castle of Wolfenbach,* ed. D.P. Varma, The Northanger Set of Jane Austen Horrid Novels (London: The Folio Press, 1968), pp. xvi-xviii).

36. *Emmeline,* p. 527.

37. These stereotyped episodes are curiously similar to the functions Propp found to make up one basic matrix for the folktale (cf. Vladimir Propp, *Morphology of the Folktale ,* tr. Laurence Scott (Austin: University of Texas Press, 1968).

38. Claudia Johnson, *Jane Austen,* pp. 32-3.

39. Charlotte Smith, *Desmond* (New York: Garland Publishing Co.), vol. II, p. 174.

40. Johnson, *Jane Austen's,* pp. 33-4.

41. Daniel Cottom, *The Civilized Imagination: A Study of Anne Radcliffe, Jane Austen and Sir Walter Scott* (Cambridge: Cambridge University Press, 1985), pp. 52-53.

42. Cottom, pp. 53-54.

43. Fanny Burney, *Camilla,* Book III, Ch. xiii, p. 257.

44. *Camilla,* Book VII, Ch. x, p. 582.

45. *Camilla,* Book II, Ch. xii, p. 254.

46. Fanny Burney, *Cecilia* (London: George Bell and Sons, 1906). Vol. II. Ch. x, p. 458.

47. Cf. Burney, *Evelina,* pp. 11 and 113.

48. Charlotte Smith, *Emmeline,* Vol. I, Ch. i, p. 6.

49. *Emmeline,* Vol. II, Ch. ii, pp. 132-5.

50. *Emmeline,* Vol. II, Ch. vi, p. 167.

51. *Emmeline*, Vol. IV, Ch. X, p. 457.

52. Wollstonecraft, *The Wrongs of Woman, or Maria, in Posthumous Works of the Autor of "A Vindication of the Rights of Woman"* (Clifton, N.J. Augustus M. Kelley, 1972), Vol. I, p. 39. (First published in 1798).

53. *Vindication*, p, 176.

54. *Maria*, Vol. II, p. 108.

55. Mary Hays, *Memoirs of Emma Courtney* (New York: Garland Publishing Inc., 1974), Vol. I, p. 55.

56. Mary Hays, Vol. I, pp. 70-1.

57. Mary Hays, Vol. II, p. 107. Emphasis in the original.

58. I am using the term dominant in a sense analogous to Descombes' conception of dominant discourse as an established language even the opposition must use in attacking the official viewpoint (see Richard Terdiman, *Discourse/Counter Discourse* (Ithaca: Cornell University Press, 1985), p. 62).

59. Aaron Fogel, "Coerced Speech and the Oedipus Dialogue Complex," *Rethinking Bakhtin: Extensions and Challenges*, eds. Gary Saul Morson and Caryl Emerson (Evanston, Illinois: Northwestern University Press, 1989), p. 188.

60. Ken Hirschkop, "A Response to the Forum on Mikhail Bakhtin," in *Bakhtin: Essays and Dialogues on His Work,* ed. Gary Saul Morson (Chicago and London: The University of Chicago Press, 1986), p. 74.

61. Susan Stewart, "Bakhtin's Anti-Linguistics," in *Bakhtin: Essays and Dialogues on His Work,* p. 46.

62. *Jane Austen's Novels*, p. 52.

63. Brown, *Jane Austen's Novels*, p. 53.

64. As we discussed above (see section on "Women on Top," Chapter 2 of this study), Natalie Zemon Davis offers a fascinating wiew of women as queens of May festivals and as officers during other occasions of festive misrule in her article, referred to above, "Women on Top: Symbolic

Sexual Inversion and Political Disorder in Early Modern Europe," in *The Reversible World*, pp. 166-71. .

65. Catherine's love of exercise and lively spirits would seem to be a response to Mary Wollstonecraft's cry, "In the name of truth and common sense, why should not one woman acknowledge that she can take more exercise than another? or, in other words, that she has a sound constitution; and why, to damp innocent vivacity, is she darkly told [by Dr. Gregory's *A Father's Legacy to His Daughters*] that men will draw conclusions that she little thinks of?" (*A Vindication of the Rights of Woman*, p. 55).

66. *Letters*, p. 8.

67. Indeed, Andreas Capellanus made it clear that the courtly lover's correct attitude before his lady was one of humility and submission (*The Art of Courtly Love*, tr. J.J. Parry (New York: Frederich Ungar,1975). Some critics have seen the lady's predominance as a shallow convention, barely masking her subservience. However, Joan Kelly has shown, I believe conclusively, that the ideology of courtly love, in which the knight assumed the posture of a spiritual vassal to his lady, stemmed from the relative independence many aristocratic women had gained by the twelfth century (see "Did women Have a Renaissance?" in *Women, History and Theory: The Essays of Joan Kelly* (Chicago: University of Chicago Press, 1984).

68. In a note to the Oxford University Press edition of *Northanger Abbey*, Chapman refers the reader to a letter from Mr Richardson, No. 97, vol. ii, *Rambler*, in which this author holds that feminine love cannot be modest if it springs unsolicited.

69. Fielding, *Tom Jones*, p. 167.

70. In addition to Natalie Davis' article, "Women on Top," see David Kunzle's account of such images in sixteenth to nineteenth century broadsheets, (both in *The Reversible World*). Such images appear to have played an ambivalent role, serving to denounce female forwardness and yet having a potentially subversive character.

71. *A Vindication of the Rights of Woman*, pp. 81 and 133.

72. Allusions to dirt, it has been noted, are part of those "creative negations which remind us of the need to reinvest the clean with the filthy, the rational with the animalistic, the ceremonial with the carnivalesque in

order to maintain cultural vitality. And they confirm the endless potentiality of dirt and the pure possibility of liminality" (Barbara Babcock, "Introduction," in B. A. Babcok, ed, *The Reversible World: Symbolic Inversion in Art and Society*, p. 32). This anthropological perspective, in spite of its many obvious parallels to Bakhtin's, differs substantially from his in orientation, in its emphasis on carnival and rites collaborating to "maintain cultural vitality," where Bakhtin would emphasize the radical difference between popular and official festivities.

73. Again, in this regard Austen may have based her satire on Wollstonecraft's discussion of women, who, says Wollstonecratf, in their ignorance, often slight as insipid the sober dignity and matronly graces of history (*A Vindication*, p.325). Austen, however, goes beyond Wollstonecraft's feminism, since Austen suggests that the patriarchal bias of traditional history may also be responsible for feminine distaste for it.

74. It is significant that Mary Wollstonecraft, apparently aware of the educational plight of young children, wrote a primer for her daughter that graded both the topic and the difficulty of the material through several levels (cf. "Lessons," *Posthumous Works by the Author of "A Vindication"*).

75. Compare Mrs Allen's obsession with being fine to Wollstonecraft's discussion of feminine concern with dress: "Men order their clothes to be made, and have done with the subject; women make their own clothes, necessary or ornamental, and are continually talking about them; and their thoughts follow their hands. It is not the making of necessaries that weakens the mind, but the frippery of dress" (*A Vindication*, p. 134). Even more obvious is the similarity between the passage on Mrs Allen's preparations for her appearance at Bath, and Wollstonecraft on feminine travel: "A man, when he undertakes a journey, has in general the end in view; woman thinks more of the incidental occurrences, the strange things that may occur on the road; the impression she may make on her fellow-travelers; and above all, she is anxiously intent on the care of the finery that she carries with her when, to use an apt French turn of expression, she is going to produce a sensation" (*Vindication*, p. 108).

76. Lloyd W. Brown, *Bits of Ivory*, p. 174.

77. A. Walton Litz, *Jane Austen: A Study of Her Artistic Development*, p. 69.

78. Claudia Johnson, *Jane Austen: Women, Politics and the Novel*, p. 37.

79. Austen is here probably parodying Dr. Gregory's advice to his daughters: "But if you happen to have any learning, keep it a profound secret, especially from the men, who generally look with a jealous and malignant eye on a woman of great parts, and a cultivated understanding." This passage is quoted by Wollstonecraft in *A Vindication of the Rights of Woman*; the author counters, "If men of real merit, as [Gregory] afterwards observes, are superior to this meanness, where is the necessity that the behavior of the whole sex should be modulated to please fools?" (p. 174).

80. See, for instance, Litz, *Jane Austen*, p. 64.

81. Through Henry's remarks on novels, Austen seems to be basing her satire on ideas, if not taken from Wollstonecraft, at least compatible with hers. In the passages where he parodies sentimental and Gothic fiction, Henry Tilney appears to be using ridicule, the method Wollstonecraft recomended in order to correct a fondness for novels in young women; she also counsels pointing out by tone and apt comparisons the disparity between reality and romantic sentiments *(A Vindication*, p. 325). Nevertheless, Austen, through Henry's defense of novels, defends her own metier.

82. See "Regulated Hatred", pp. 347-8.

Chapter 4
"Pride and Prejudice":
Elizabeth, or Merry War

Jane Austen's most widely known novel, probably the best loved of her works, is also one of the most carnivalesque, although in a very different vein from *Northanger Abbey*. In the carnival images and philosophy of *Pride and Prejudice* we encounter a more complex, more deeply ambivalent attitude. Thus, for instance, while carnivalesque parody is more explicit in *Northanger Abbey* than in *Pride and Prejudice*, there is in the latter both a greater emphasis on mésalliances, and fools that appear more absurd and grotesque than those found in the former. Thematically, while *Northanger Abbey* concentrated on the problem of women's education and moral choices, *Pride and Prejudice* makes the social context for this issue more explicit, directing the reader's attention to the concept of community and interpersonal bonds. Therefore, there is much greater insistence on the theme of merry war through everyday social contact and interpersonal ties. In carnivalesque literature, the term "merry war" may be used to refer to beatings, bloody yet comic battles, dismemberments, insults and other forms of violent conflict which are nevertheless "regenerative," since the victim survives and laughs, and as a result the new order is engendered (see RHW, Ch. 3). In Austen, of course, merry war is not physical; rather, it is found in hostile interpersonal and social relations as well as in discourse, both that of narrative passages and dialogue.

In addition, utopia is more complex, less carefree, in the ending of *Pride and Prejudice*, and yet it is present from the inception of its fictional world.

Given these differences in carnivalesque atmosphere between the two novels, it is not surprising that the story of their protagonists should differ, that Elizabeth Bennet's development should diverge deeply from Catherine Morland's. (Of course, this divergence is also to be expected because Elizabeth Bennet is a remarkably intelligent young woman, and older than Catherine.) Elizabeth's growth is marked by an uncrowning readers share, rather than by one we witness, as was the case in Catherine's development. The reader tends to identify with Elizabeth's process because the narrator in *Pride and Prejudice* does not ironize the protagonist's behavior and speech as often as was the case in *Northanger Abbey*.

And yet Elizabeth is in no sense idealized. On the contrary, the first time we encounter her name it is spoken by her father, who refers to her in a way sadly lacking in the deference usually shown to a heroine. This reference occurs in the first chapter, in which we may discover, at least in germ, many of the elements that will be of central importance in the novel. A close reading of this chapter will provide a good avenue into the two interrelated issues of carnival and Elizabeth's development in *Pride and Prejudice*, as well as into the common ground between them, the novel's conception of community.

The chapter holds, of course, one of the most famous opening sentences in English literature: "It is a truth universally acknowledged that a single man in possession of a good fortune must be in want of a wife" (PP, 3). As remarked earlier (see Chapter 2), this statement ironically combines the viewpoint of fortune-hunting parents of marriageable women and the language of the prototypical educated mind of Austen's times.

In this case, since the sentence serves as introduction to a dialogue between Mr and Mrs Bennet, we are led to see it as superimposing their viewpoints; Mr Bennet would appear as representative of the educated individual, while Mrs Bennet would embody the attitudes of the "neighbourhood's surrounding families," who see any rich bachelor as "the rightful property of some one or other of their daughters." Mr Bennet, on the other hand, evidently considers such an attitude absurd.

Indeed, the entire chapter is a verbal battle between the spouses, with Mr Bennet repeatedly pretending to ignore social conventions and Mrs Bennet insisting on his adhering to them. Mrs Bennet tries to convince her husband that he must visit Mr Bingley, the rich, single newcomer to the neighborhood, since convention dictates that the head of the household must pay his respects to new neighbors. Women cannot initiate social relationships: "Indeed you must go, for it will be impossible for *us* to visit him, if you do not." Mr Bennet's reply is that of the clown who, pretending not to understand conventions, unmasks them (cf. DN 402-6): "You are overscrupulous surely. I dare say Mr Bingley will be very glad to see you; and

I will send a few lines by you to assure him of my hearty consent to his marrying which ever he chuses of the girls" (PP, 4). The lady, therefore, acts as the champion of society's claims, while the gentleman mocks them, avowing openly that the business of getting daughters married is a goal underlying many social mores. And yet Mr Bennet, for all his show of eccentricity, *will* visit Bingley; this attitude is in keeping with the figure of the clown, who will distort and expose "official" social languages without individualistically opposing them. As we shall see, Mr Bennet's character is ambivalent, since he both acts as an eccentric individualist and performs the role of clown, whose utterances serve the readers as signals pointing to the need to examine, to reflect upon, certain social codes and languages.

The social language exposed here, then, is that of sanctioned, accepted customs within the marriage market forcing women to parade themselves before males (as Miss Bingley will later do before Darcy (PP, 56)) in the hopes that one man will "chuse" them. The concern with women's situation is also evident in this chapter in Mr Bennet's sardonic comments about his daughters, who, he says, "are all silly and ignorant like other girls," although he makes the very modest claim regarding Lizzy that she "has something more of quickness than her sisters" (PP, 5). Elizabeth (Lizzy to her parents) will later be shown to possess an intelligence only Darcy and her father can match; Mr Bennet's comment seems to be another distortion aimed at exposing both anti-feminist prejudice about women's mental powers and a social and educational situation that often tended to produce the giddiness and vapidity of a Kitty and a Lydia. It also stands in ironic contrast to the rapturous introductions fictional heroines are usually given.

The entire dialogue in this chapter, furthermore, exposes the fierce competition among families striving to "get their daughters married," a competition going on *sub rosa* through shows of neighborly friendliness and solidarity. Thus Mrs Bennet fears that Sir William and Lady Lucas will seek Mr Bingley's friendship with a view toward securing "an establishment" for one of their daughters. (In Chapter II Mrs Bennet calls Mrs Long "selfish and hypocritical" for no worse reason than her having "two nieces of her own," who will probably be pushed toward Mr Bingley; Mrs Bennet believes Mrs Long, who must think of her own nieces, will in the end forfeit her promise to introduce Bingley to Mrs Bennet and her daughters.) A community, then, is governed by mores by which a surface fellowship is preserved while actually generalized war is going on, with social standing and a high yearly income as its prizes.

Hostilities, however, do not only exist among a neighborhood's families; they are also prevalent within a single family, even between husband and wife. Verbal struggle, as it appears in the following exchange, is one of the forms war takes:

"My dear Mr Bennet," said his lady to him one day, "have you heard that Netherfield is let at last?"

Mr Bennet replied that he had not.

"But it is," returned she; "for Mrs Long has just been here, and she told me all about it."

Mr Bennet made no answer.

"Do not you want to know who has taken it?" cried his wife impatiently.

"*You* want to tell me, and I have no objection to hearing it."

This was invitation enough. (PP, 1)

What we witness here is a battle in which information and showing interest in acquiring that information are the weapons. The interlocutors, then, are not only warriors but hagglers: Mr Bennet pretends not to care enough about the data to be acquired to make any effort to obtain it, while Mrs Bennet wishes her husband to admit he is interested before she will provide the data. There are two superimposed models at work in this communicative interchange: one a martial, the other a commercial one.

When Mr Bennet rather perversely refuses to show the proper attitude toward Mrs Bennet's information, when he even refuses to admit that he will visit Bingley, Mrs Bennet introduces a new weapon: her nerves. But in this novel, as we shall see, disease and death are sources of merriment; they do not threaten or provoke fear. Thus her husband will steadfastly refuse to be intimidated by her fancied illness. He has an apt answer ready for her every move, proving himself an abler player than she is. The underlying metaphor in this case is "games," with war as a deeper substratum.

In spite of this constant sparring between the two interlocutors, the battle we witness is a merry one. The attitude the text seems to call for is one of gay confidence that there are no malevolent intentions involved, and that, even in the presence of malice, these verbal thrashings and discursive triumphs and defeats will leave the participants unscathed. In this sense we may see the verbal beating in *Pride and Prejudice* as "a feast of death and regeneration in the comic aspect" (RHW, 205). Indeed, Mrs Bennet, no matter how severely beaten, will rise from each encounter with renewed energy to pursue her goals. And no matter how often she makes a fool of herself in the course of the novel, she will find new and surprising ways to display her grotesque absurdity.

The chapter ends with an apparently authoritative comment on the part of the narrator, characterizing Mr Bennet as an odd "mixture of quick parts, sarcastic humour, reserve, and caprice," and Mrs Bennet, his wife of twenty-three years, as a silly, ignorant, moody woman who did not understand her husband (PP, 5). As Julia Prewitt Brown observes, this seemingly conclusive trivialization of Mrs Bennet's powers is contradicted by the novel itself. The more we see Mrs Bennet in action, the more we are required

> to acknowledge the audacity, the variety and complexity of this woman's "mean understanding." The cadence of moral rationalism, the abstract, judgmental sensibility revealed in such statements as "mean understanding, little information, and uncertain temper," are always checked by action and dialogue.[1]

Even without proceeding to observe Mrs Bennet in later episodes, we find already, in this very chapter, subtle indications that this evaluative, seemingly monologic statement evaluating Mrs Bennet is not to be interpreted too literally. Its mock-authoritative tone will neither allow us to despise (as, for instance, Miss Bingley will) these people who see their community as the universe nor to share their ideological position unquestioningly. The opening statement, while laughing at common ideology, also parodies the language of enlightened individuals who seek stable, generally accepted truths; we cannot safely assume that the rationalistic judgment passed on Mr and Mrs Bennet in the first chapter's concluding paragraph is to be taken at face value.

This chapter, then, sets the gaily relativistic tone that will characterize the entire novel. This relativism can be described, borrowing F. Anne Payne's words regarding "a commonplace of Menippean satire," as the belief that, in spite of attempts to achieve universal truths, "there is ... no accurate standard, no recognized true answer, which mortals can use to guide their lives and assess their thinking."[2] This opening chapter can be read as a festive introduction into the carnivalesque fictional world that will frame the story of Elizabeth Bennet's personal growth, a world in which a close-knit community (or "neighbourhood") demands from its members an observance of manners that seems to obliterate the underlying belligerence.

Among the most striking carnivalesque characteristics in *Pride and Prejudice* we find its fools, clowns and disorderly women and the characters' diverse mésalliances. Through these devices the novel effects a reversal of and laughs at conventional views on love and women, unmasking the unfair paucity of their means of support and their inappropriate education. It also adopts an attitude of irreverence that mocks the grimness of sin and death, and laughs at both war and society, viewing the bonds of community as both inescapable and tinged by merry hostility.

The two notorious fools in this novel are of course Mrs Bennet and Collins. Mrs Bennet, and to a higher degree Lydia, her youngest and giddiest daughter, act also as disorderly women whose conduct subverts decorum.

These characters' speech and action serve an important function, unmasking ludicrous aspects of social customs and languages. The three appear as caricatures, as grotesquely exaggerated yet convincing portraits of a rather generalized vulgarity. Mrs Bennet, for instance, when speaking to the man she hopes will marry her eldest daughter, Jane, shamelessly and obviously advertises the young woman's beauty. Thus she praises Jane, not only at the expense of her neighbors and "particular friends" ("You must own [Charlotte Lucas] is very plain," she tells Bingley) but even putting down her own younger daughters while praising Jane: "I often tell my other girls they are nothing to *her*" (PP, 42-44). Throughout the novel Mrs Bennet's ignorance, her inability to conduct the business of getting her daughters married with any subtlety or finesse, serves to reveal the vulgarity of the process itself of, as Lydia puts it, "getting husbands," for oneself or for one's daughters. The very worldly-conscious Miss Bingley, for instance, would never commit any of the *gaffes* Mrs Bennet is guilty of, and yet her relentless pursuit of Darcy is as determinedly mercenary as any husband-hunting behavior in the novel.

Lydia Bennet herself often plays a role similar to her mother's, for her exaggerated, vulgar flirting merely underscores the crass behavior to which sexual attraction may lead. Seeing herself in Lydia for a moment, Elizabeth comes to realize that her infatuation with Wickham has momentarily gotten the best of her judgment; thus, when Lydia exclaims that Wickham could not possibly have been in love with Mary King, "such a nasty little freckled thing," Elizabeth "was shocked to think that, however incapable of such coarseness of *expression* herself, the coarseness of the *sentiment* was little other than her own breast had formerly harboured and fancied liberal!" (PP, 220).

Similarly, Collins' absurd references to "the violence of my affection," his recourse to romantic clichés when proposing to Elizabeth, whom he neither loves nor really knows, show the ridiculousness of certain conventions of love (cf. PP, 104-9).[3] By his own admision, Collins has been ordered by Lady Catherine, his patroness, to marry. Her "advice" was given to Collins "the very Saturday night before I left Hunsford--between our pools at quadrille;" his "violent" love for Elizabeth was thus born at this card table, before he ever saw her, and will soon be transferred to Charlotte Lucas. What makes his behavior laughable is not his ignorance of the conventions of love, but his failure to achieve any degree of plausibility in following them.

In a sense, Austen uses these fools much as she used Catherine Morland in *Northanger Abbey*, to "interact dialogically" with "a lofty pseudo-intelligence" that posits a "pathos-charged lie," the whole elaborate code of "poetic," romantic love. However, there is a marked difference between our attitude as readers toward Catherine and the one the text seems to call for toward Mrs Bennet, Lydia and Collins. The latter do not appear in as positive a light as Catherine Morland, for they are clearly mercenary while Catherine was guileless; also, our sympathies lie with Elizabeth Bennet, whose happiness often seems threatened by their actions. And yet the novel also dwells on the several ways in which these fools breach decorum so repeatedly and hilariously that we as readers seem to be invited to revel in their impropriety. Austen's handling of these characters can be exactly described in Bakhtin's words:

> A fool introduced by the author for purposes of "making strange" the world of conventional pathos may himself, as a fool, be the object of the author's scorn. The author need not necessarily express a complete solidarity with such a character. Mocking these figures as fools may even become paramount. But the author needs the fool: by his very uncomprehending presence he makes strange the world of social conventionality. By representing stupidity, the novel teaches prose intelligence, prose wisdom. Regarding fools . . . the novelist's eye is taught a sort of prose vision, the vision of a world confused by conventions of pathos and by falsity. (DN, 404)

By engaging her fools in dialogue with the "poetry" of conventions of love, Austen creates her "prose vision" which allows her "to expose and structure images" of this "social language," that of romance (DN, 404). The function of these "fools" in the novel, then, is one of desecration, of profanation of a social code. What appears to be lofty spiritual love is shown to be ludicrous, a travesty by which a crass commercial exchange is hidden from view, and by means of which individuals are led deeper into self-delusion. The foolish behavior of Mrs Bennet, Mr Collins, and Lydia acts as a mirror in which distortion leads to revelation, for it is through hyperbolic exaggeration that we may unmask a widespread social ideology that usually appears enmeshed in a web of sophistry.

In addition to their function as fools, however, both Mrs Bennet and Lydia are women who "make spectacles of themselves," female grotesques who seem unaware of codes of feminine decorum, who flout them, and who therefore introduce threatening but, for women, beneficent disorder in social relationships that tend to severely constrain them.[4] Their unruliness is beneficent, from a feminist viewpoint, because it subverts such codes and relationships.

Of course, from a serious, rationalistic perspective, Mrs Bennet can be seen as a sobering reflection of what a faulty feminine education will produce. Her ignorance and frivolousness, her inconsiderate, unfeeling obsession with getting her daughters married, her warped values, contribute to make the Bennet home an uncomfortable place, a site of folly and vulgarity.[5] Nevertheless, Mrs Bennet's folly is itself a form of disorder within the novel that subverts traditional portraits of ludicrous matrons as obedient creatures under their husbands' tutelage.[6]

Also, as a mother, Mrs Bennet is very defective. She has contributed to the moral vacuousness and intellectual vapidity of her two youngest daughters.

And she continually hurts her two eldest. Mrs Bennet, it must remembered, does not only press Elizabeth to marry Collins; she also unfeelingly adds to Jane's misery. While Jane is trying to bear her disappointment, her mother demands "Jane to confess that if [Bingley] did not come back she should think herself very ill used. It needed all Jane's steady mildness to bear these attacks with tolerable tranquillity" (PP, 129). The clearer it becomes that Bingley is not coming back, the longer flow Mrs Bennet's expressions of irritation "about Netherfield and its master"; in the end, even patient, sweet Jane complains to Elizabeth that their mother has "no idea of the pain she gives me by her continual reflections on him" (PP, 134). And yet all her ludicrously inappropriate efforts to get her daughters married constitute a carnivalesque caricature of a mother's care for her marriageable daughters. In the end, her maladroit efforts do not bring about painful results for her daughters, and thus readers can laugh at her folly without being saddened by any adverse consequences. As Bakhtin puts it,

> Folly is . . . deeply ambivalent. It has the negative element of debasement and destruction . . . and the positive element of renewal and truth. Folly is the opposite of wisdom- inverted wisdom, inverted truth . . . Folly is a form of gay festive wisdom, free from all laws and restrictions, as well as from preoccupations and seriousness. (RHW, 260)

As a fool, disorderly Mrs Bennet helps to subvert "official laws and conventions" which she either flouts or attempts to follow so ineptly as to make a mockery of them.

If Mrs Bennet subverts conjugal decorum and makes a mockery of motherly love, Lydia is a character designed to undermine conventional ideologies that either deny women's sexuality or consider it monstruous, unnatural[7]; Lydia inverts the figure of the female siren, luring men to perdition. As Susan Gubar has observed, the monstrous woman of Augustan satire allowed "the satirist to exorcise his fear of mortality and physicality by projecting it onto the Other," while also functioning as a sign of his fascination with materiality.[8] In Swift's "Strephon and Chloe," for example, the woman, beautiful, slim, ethereal, passive, lures her lover into marriage by convincing him of her lack of corporality. Lydia, on the other hand, is an inverted picture of this façade, for she is not very attractive, and is stout, active, loud, indeed raucous. Her laughter is disruptive and her flirting outrageous; soldiers appeal to her especially, as they did to her mother in her youth (PP, 229) and still do in her old age (now vicariously, as husbands for her daughters (PP, 29)). Although both the protagonist and the narrator deplore these two women's conduct, the author lets them achieve all their ends. In spite of the severity of contemporary society's sanctions against feminine "misbehavior," even "sin" is dealt with lightly. Lydia's "disgrace," her decision to elope and live with Wickham even though he does not propose to marry her, for instance, could have produced very grave results: if Darcy had not intervened, she would probably have been eventually abandoned by her "seducer" and been forced either to prostitute herself or to go back to her family, who may have confined her, "secluded from the world, in some distant farm house" (PP, 309). In *Pride and Prejudice*, however, this "oversexed" female is allowed to marry and go on being her irresponsible self, "untamed, unabashed, wild, noisy, and fearless" (PP, 315), blissfully unaware of the danger she has been in.

Also, the behavior of Mrs Bennet, Lydia, and even Kitty as females grotesques serves the carnivalesque function of undermining the dignity of the two eldest Bennets, Jane and Elizabeth, as heroines, for, though they are not guilty of the same folly, they must suffer the humiliation of seeing their family publicly exposed to ridicule. Their recurrent confusion while their close relatives make a spectacle of themselves thus serves to subvert novelistic heroism itself. Furthermore, in keeping with the "universality" of carnival laughter, which was directed at the "carnival's participants" themselves (RHW, 11), in this novel we are made to regard the characters we identify with as readers as less than sacrosanct; growth, for both Elizabeth and Darcy, for example, is a result of their humiliation. Their love relationship is likewise neither idealized nor insulated from debasement. The ways in which the process of falling in love and seeking a husband in *Pride and Prejudice* is itself desecrated, seen in its ludicrous or mundane aspects, made many early readers dislike the novel. For these readers were used to fictions treating love as "an unassailed ideal." According to B. C. Southam, in the view of many of Austen's contemporaries, "The ungentlemanly and unladylike manners of the Bennet family were not the stuff for fiction." Such readers objected to the novel's aiming laughter at romance, for they

> wanted to preserve literature as a kind of higher, happier reality, and Jane Austen's novels were a particular threat to the greatly prized unreality of romantic and sentimental fiction. While few readers could deny that they enjoyed reading the novels--for the vitality of the characters, the wit, the accuracy and realism of her picture of society--praise comes grudgingly, fenced round with qualifications: that her characters are socially and morally vulgar, that the novels are simply entertaining, that the "instruction" (what we might term the adduceable "moral" of the story) is not inspiring or elevating, that the commonplace is perfectly rendered but the commonplace is not what we look for in literature.[9]

In this sense, parody is omnipresent in *Pride and Prejudice*, although it is not the type of parody aimed at individual works which can be found in *Northanger Abbey*; rather, the novel seems written against the background of a profound understanding of the prevalent literary attitudes and the "official" literature of Austen's times.

If, for example, we compare *Pride and Prejudice* with Burney's *Evelina,* a novel to which Austen's has some similarities and many points of contrast,[10] we observe that the treatment of grotesque relatives of the heroines is rather different. The gross misbehavior of *Evelina*'s grandmother, Mme. Duval, though carnivalesque in its treatment of parental authority, cannot really affect the way others see the angelic heroine. The old lady's grotesqueness momentarily threatens the peace of mind of the heroine, but the ridiculous predicaments in which she is often involved cannot taint the hallowed love relationship. In *Pride and Prejudice*, on the contrary, "the total want of propriety so frequently, so almost uniformly betrayed" by everyone in the Bennet household but Elizabeth and Jane (and by Lydia and Mrs Bennet especially) makes Darcy object to Jane's marriage to Bingley and hesitate to love Elizabeth himself (PP, 198).

Traditional feminist heroines are exceptional women whose extraordinary qualities exempt them from the common fate of females. This novel counters such a stance by submitting its most sympathetically presented characters to humiliating treatment. Lydia's elopement and marriage, furthermore, carnivalistically degrade both Elizabeth, whose chances of marrying Darcy appear diminished at a time she is beginning to love him, and Darcy himself. For Darcy must accept what Lady Catherine calls the "pollution" of Pemberley's "shades," by accepting to become brother-in-law to Wickham, a scoundrel and his father's steward, and brother to Lydia, a woman condemned by the contemporary double-standard on sexuality.

In the end, the novel's attitude to these disruptive females, Lydia and Mrs Bennet, is ambivalent, for they are both shown as distorted products of a mistaken education of women, and as such contrasted to Elizabeth and Jane in sense and moral attitudes, and made to act as subvertors of a social order inimical to women. As will be discussed below, the social situation of women, the lack of "honourable provision" for their fate (cf. PP, 122), other than marriage, helps to excuse their flouting some of society's rules for feminine conduct (either seriously, as Charlotte does in her mercenary marriage, or farcically, as Lydia does in her eloping while convulsed by laughter (PP. 291)).

Closely linked with the use of fools and disorderly women for purposes of profanation is the employment of carnivalistic mésalliances in *Pride and Prejudice*. By juxtaposing personal characteristics, ideas and discourses that in official ideology appear distant and well-differentiated, the novel "brings together, unifies, weds and combines the sacred with the profane, the lofty with the low, the great with the insignificant, the wise with the stupid" (PDP, 123).

The author of *Pride and Prejudice* seems to revel in creating mésalliances, which range from the juxtaposition of characters to the mingling of seemingly incompatible discourses, going through the blending of discordant characteristics in a single character. The list of instances of the first of these types of mésalliances is long: the most intelligent characters (Mr Bennet, Charlotte Lucas) appear married to the most foolish (Mrs Bennet, Mr Collins); the plainest ones (Mary King, Miss de Bourgh) may be temporarily or imaginarily linked to the handsomest (Wickham, Darcy); the most obtuse mother (Mrs Bennet) has the wittiest daughter (Elizabeth), while the strongest and most domineering (Lady Catherine) has borne the mousiest female (Miss de Bourgh). Many characters also exhibit seemingly paradoxical combinations of traits. Thus, the socially highest-ranking characters (Lady Catherine, Darcy) are also the most rude, while some of those with the greatest "elegance of mind" (the Gardiners) belong to the least fashionable social groups. Similarly, one of the most principled characters (Darcy) is temporarily judged to be the most blameworthy, while the most unprincipled of all (Wickham) has the best manners and for a time appears totally blameless. Some characters seem to be embodied oxymorons; Lady Catherine, for instance, is characterized by her "dignified impertinence," while Collins is a queer mixture of servility and self-importance.

Furthermore, the mingling of discourses, as well as the placing of discourses in the least appropriate circumstances, produces the most ironic passages in the novel, as both Mr Collins and Mary Bennet spout lofty inanities and absurd moralizing. On the occasion of Lydia's elopement, for instance, Mr Collins' letter to Mr Bennet is a mixture of selfish gloating (as Collins reflects that, had Elizabeth married him, "I might have been involved in all your sorrow and disgrace") and ruthless unconcern for the feelings of others (the Bennets' "present distress," writes Collins, "must be of the bitterest kind, because proceeding from a cause which no time can remove.") By way of palliation he goes on to say, "The death of your daughter would have been a blessing in comparison to this." He then blames the Bennets for their "faulty degree of indulgence" in bringing up Lydia, but offers the "consolation" that "her own disposition must be naturally bad, or she could not be guilty of such an enormity, at so early an age." All of these cruelly insensitive remarks are introduced by professions of pious condolence: "I feel myself called upon, by our relationship, and my situation in life, to condole with you on the grievous affliction you are now suffering under . . . No arguments shall be wanting on my part, that can alleviate so severe a misfortune" (PP, 296-7). His reference to his "situation in life," Collins' cliché for his profession as Christian minister, makes his cruel bluntness all the more ironic.

On the same occasion, Mary Bennet consoles "herself with . . . moral extractions from the evil before them." After telling Elizabeth "we must . . . pour into the wounded bosoms of each other, the balm of sisterly consolation," she coolly draws from the event "this useful lesson; that loss of virtue in a female is irretrievable" and "that her reputation is no less brittle than it is beautiful" (PP, 289). Such abstract reflections, showing detachment and indifference to Lydia's fate, make Elizabeth lift "up her eyes in amazement." This cold-hearted condemnation of a sister to "endless ruin" because of "one false step" can hardly stem from "sisterly love," any more than Collins' advice to Mr Bennet to cast off Lydia and not even allow her name "to be mentioned in your hearing" has anything to do with the "christian forgiveness" it purports to recommend (cf. PP, 363-4). Thus the novel unmasks the ruthless character of moralistic condemnations of feminine misconduct, even when accompanied by a false "loving" pathos.

Mary's philosophizing is all the more interesting because it proceeds from the most studious and well-read of all the women in this novel. This passage must be considered in relation with two other conversations dealing with feminine education: the one among Bingley, his sister, Darcy and Elizabeth at Netherfield, the other between Elizabeth and Lady Catherine at Rosings. In the first, Miss Bingley holds up the ideal of the "accomplished woman," which her brother satirizes as the abilities to "paint tables, cover screens and net purses." For Miss Bingley the list of "accomplishments" a woman must have included the usual performing abilities and social graces acquired at fashionable boarding-schools. Darcy adds to the requirements; an accomplished woman must possess "something more substantial, in the improvement of her mind by extensive reading." Elizabeth, on the other hand, exclaims that she has never met such a paragon: "I never saw such capacity, and taste, and application, and elegance, as you describe, united" (PP, 39-40). Her remarks can be read as a protest against the injustice of demanding perfection from women, against the confining stereotype one critic calls "a carbon-copy elegant female."[11] Similarly, in the conversation with Lady Catherine, Elizabeth defends the method by which her parents provided her and her sisters with masters *if* they wished to learn (PP, 165). With regard to her rejection of the "accomplished woman" stereotype, Elizabeth seems to be in perfect agreement with the positions of contemporary feminists like Wollstonecraft.[12] But the passage showing Mary Bennet's misogynist moralizing may be read as engaging in dialogue with the cry for feminine education. For Mary *has* been educated, and has read extensively, but what she has been taught by her studies reflects the accumulated anti-feminist "wisdom" of the ages. We must do more than expose women to the moralistic drivel about females men have produced and are also taught, Austen seems to be saying, before women's education can truly become a solution to the feminine predicament.

Through these and similar passages we see that the mingling and juxtaposition of discourses in *Pride and Prejudice* serves as basis for ideological reflection on both love and the situation of women. The prattle of fools and incongruous mésalliances are two of the most astute means used by Austen to expose conventional wisdom and "pathos-charged lies."

Nevertheless, these narrative devices (fools, disorderly women and mésalliances) do not merely function in a negative way, pointing up society's failings, the ludicrousness of certain social languages. The delight we derive from the eccentric discourse of the novel's fools serves to carnivalize life, to allow us to adopt an irreverence which holds few things sacred and defeats even the solemnity of death. This irreverence is not destructive and individualistic, like that of iconoclasts, but is based on a deep sense of community. Before we investigate the ways in which *Pride and Prejudice* propitiates a dialogic understanding of the meaning of society and community, however, we must briefly consider the novel's determination to treat "serious" themes such as sexual misconduct and death laughingly through the agency of the novel's clowns, acting as "heralds of the laughing truth," as the unveilers of the hypocrisy of official, sacred truth (RHW, 92-93).

In keeping with the character of folk humor, which "denies, but revives and renews at the same time," avoiding "bare negation" (RHW, 11), *Pride and Prejudice* both decries anti-feminist discourses and allows us to view the situation of women and their need to enter into "love" relationships in a light vein. In this sense, laughter in this novel is festive, rather than coldly satirical or condemnatory. It is not surprising, therefore, that what would have been seen by the novel's contemporaries as Lydia's damning sin carries no serious consequences. For evil in this novel, whether physical or spiritual, is laughable; such generally serious topics as illness and even death are the subject of many jokes. Thus, Mrs Bennet, whenever she cannot get her way, feels both indisposed and "cruelly used," and complains that "nobody feels for my poor nerves!" (PP, 113). Her suffering stems from her inability to withstand frustrations; as she says herself, "It makes me very nervous and poorly to be thwarted so in my own family" (PP, 140). Being "thwarted" because Lady Lucas will have a daughter married before she will throws her into a "most pitiable state," an "agony of ill humour" (PP, 129).

Both Mr and Mrs Bennet, as well as Collins, refer to death repeatedly, in a carnivalesque attitude by which fear of death is defeated. Thus, Mr Bennet ironically tells his wife that if Jane dies of an illness contracted when, as Mrs Bennet had hoped, it rains after Jane leaves to visit the Bingleys on horseback, it will be a comfort to know "that it was all in pursuit of Mr Bingley, and under your orders" (PP, 31). Collins, for his part, seems to gloat as he refers to "the melancholy event" (Mr Bennet's death) that will make Collins the happy owner of Longbourn (PP, 106). As soon as the Lucases find out that Collins has proposed to their daughter Charlotte, Lady Lucas begins to calculate "how many years longer Mr Bennet [the present owner of Longbourn] was likely to live" (PP, 122). Mrs Bennet takes "comfort" in the face of Bingley's desertion of Jane, in the supposition that "Jane will die of a broken heart, and then he will be sorry for what he has done" (PP, 228). The lady also entertains "terrrific fears" when Lydia elopes, not about what is very likely to happen to her, but about melodramatic, improbable events: "I know [Mr Bennet] will fight Wickham [Lydia's "seducer"] . . . and then he will be killed, and what is to become of us all? The Collinses [who will benefit from the entail on Mr Bennet's property] will turn us out, before he is cold in his grave" (PP, 288). Mrs Bennet also talks to her husband about his own death, provoking his "consoling" reply, "Let us flatter ourselves that *I* may be the survivor" (PP, 130). These absurd or joking references to death change it into a ludicrous mask, and so make it lose its threatening meaning. Such a victory over the fear of death is one aspect of the attitude of carnival laughter, which "builds its own world versus the official world," creating "a whole comic world" (RHW, 88). In a similar vein, for example, the reiteration of merry cries by revellers during the Roman carnival, calling for death to those who did not obey the festival's requirements, suspended the grim associations of death sentences.[13]

The degradation of official attitudes towards human reality is also achieved through Austen's use of clowning. Through the presence of clowns in *Pride and Prejudice* Austen enhances her readers' enjoyment of the stupidity of the novel's fools without dwelling on the deleterious effects of their behavior. Clowning also allows us to relish the ludicrous aspect of the uncrowning of sympathetic characters, in spite of their pain or embarrassment.

The two characters who repeatedly play the clowning role in the novel are Elizabeth and her father, Mr Bennet. The very first time we see Elizabeth she is engaged in laughing at herself and Darcy, after he scorns her as a dancing partner; she tells the story among her friends "with great spirit . . . for she had a lively, playful disposition, which delighted in any thing ridiculous" (PP, 12). Through laughter, then, Elizabeth overcomes the humiliation of being physically appraised as a female by men at a ball and then judged as "only just tolerable" by Darcy (PP, 19). Further, unlike the censorious satirist, whose negative laughter places him "above the object of his mockery" (RHW, 12), Elizabeth counters exclusionary criticism with mockery of both Darcy and herself; in her own story she appears as the laughable wallflower, slighted by an arrogant, ridiculously self-important man.

In her social encounters with Darcy Elizabeth repeatedly answers his male arrogance.[14] As he listens to her "teazing Colonel Foster to give us a ball at Meryton," for instance, Elizabeth senses his superior attitude: dances are "a topic which always makes a lady energetic," he says condescendingly. In consequence, Elizabeth decides to be impertinent herself to avoid "growing afraid of him," as she tells Charlotte (PP, 24). In a later gathering she half-mockingly warns him that she will not be intimidated by him, for she has interpreted his question ("Do you not feel a great inclination . . . to seize such an opportunity of dancing a reel?") as motivated by an intention of despising her taste for dancing.[15] Thus she informs him that "I always delight in overthrowing those kind of schemes, and cheating a person of their premeditated contempt. I have therefore made up my mind to tell you, that I do not want to dance a reel at all--and now despise me if you dare" (PP, 52).

Her attitude, therefore, is one of "archness" aimed at using laughter to triumph over fear; Darcy's social superiority, his patriarchal haughtiness, cannot cow her while she laughs. This is precisely the function of the medieval clown, using "festive folk laughter," says Bakhtin, to triumph over "power, . . . earthly kings, . . . the earthly upper classes, [over] all that oppresses and restricts" (RHW, 92), including (although Bakhtin does not say so) masculine supremacy. It is significant that all the exchanges between Darcy and Elizabeth referred to in the preceding paragraph are related to the subject of dancing, a subject, as Darcy hints, dear to a lady's heart (PP, 24.) This gentleman avoids and despises dancing, while a foolish female such as Lydia delights in this exercise as in nothing else. Elizabeth herself loves to dance, as do most of Austen's heroines. Dancing, it would seem, allowed women both a form of licit sexual contact and strong rhythmic exercise, two pleasures severely restricted for women during Austen's times. It could be seen, therefore, as a symbol of non-threatening feminine enjoyment; Darcy's contempt for it intensifies his negative masculine power, his siding with feminine oppression and patriarchy. In this and other passages, Elizabeth, like her father, acts as a clown when she speaks with unique freedom "in otherwise unacceptable languages" (cf. DN, 405); or, as her mother says, when she makes free to "run on in the wild manner you are suffered to do at home" (PP, 42). The ways in which her speech motivates "distortions and shufflings of languages and labels"[16] makes Darcy tell her "you find great enjoyment in occasionally professing opinions which in fact are not your own" (PP, 174).

Indeed, Elizabeth enjoys not only ironically distorting languages, but also observing absurdity in others. As she puts it, "Follies and nonsense, whims and inconsistencies *do* divert me, I own, and I laugh at them whenever I can" (PP, 57). Often her delight is made explicit by the text and steers our attention to the laughable aspects of an episode. Thus, for instance, we see Collins' proposal through her eyes, and share her reaction when "Mr Collins, with all his solemn composure" talks of "being run away with by his feelings," making Elizabeth "so near laughing" that she could not trust herself to speak in order to interrupt him (PP, 105). Even when she is not laughing, her mere presence in a scene where foolish behavior occurs is enough to make us sensitive to it, as it often happens when the Bennets chat at home, in a family party or with their close friends, the Lucases. Thus, her satirical bent affects us as readers; because we know she must be enjoying many displays of folly, our attitudes are directed to laughter.

However, even when Elizabeth is pained by her family's public displays, we are still made to enjoy the scene thanks to Mr Bennet's peculiar attitude. His wit and intelligence are obvious from the beginning; his judgment of Mr Collins' first letter, for instance, as evidencing "a mixture of servility and self-importance" (PP, 64), is later shown by Collins' behavior to be an astute portrait of the man. As we become aware of his intellectual acuity, as well as of his love of and closeness to the protagonist, we come to be partially led by his attitudes to the action as it unfolds. Although Mr Bennet, "except in an occasional glance at Elizabeth," requires "no partner in his pleasure" in witnessing absurdity, the narrator's reports of his inner reactions allow us to share in his "keenest enjoyment" (PP, 68). Once Mr Bennet's attitude has been established, our reading of his family's embarrassing behavior will often be directed by his stance, as we see him, for instance, look as amused as any stranger could whenever the Bennets choose to expose themselves during social occasions (cf. PP, 101).

Inasmuch as Mr Bennet and Elizabeth function as clowns, their interactions with other characters often lead us to reflect on social codes and languages. Although there are strong individualistic tendencies in Mr Bennet, tendencies which, in the view of both the narrator and Elizabeth, often lead him to irresponsibility, his verbal interactions with Mrs Bennet or with Collins often serve a double function. For they may act both as evidence of his psychological quirks, such as his penchant for defending his seclusion, and as indices pointing to a possible unmasking of social conventions. Thus, for instance, Mr Bennet's ironic admonition to Collins to "stay quietly at home" for fear Lady Catherine may be displeased, rather than return to visit the Bennets, can be seen from two different viewpoints. With regard to Mr Bennet's desire as an individual, the advice is actually aimed at keeping away the boring Collins, who tends to invade Mr Bennet's library; from this viewpoint the humor lies in the speaker's thinly disguised breach of hospitality. With regard to the relationship between Collins and Lady Catherine, however, the exchange serves to underscore Collins' utter servility toward his patroness, which may lead him to place her interests before those of his own family. To Mr Bennet's injunction, "You had better neglect your relations, than run the risk of offending your patroness," Mr Collins responds, "I am particularly obliged to you for this friendly caution, and you may depend upon my not taking so material a step without her ladyship's concurrence" (PP, 123). In this way the requirement of near-feudal humility and obsequiousness before the great is ridiculed.

Elizabeth's "clowning," on the other hand, often follows a more communital bent. Once, for instance, while dancing with Darcy, who remains unsociably silent, she decides to "punish" her partner by obliging him to talk, and thus makes some slight observation, and then addresses him again:

> "It is *your* turn to say something now, Mr Darcy. -*I* talked about the dance, and
> you ought to make some kind of remark on the size of the room, or the number
> of couples."

After a few additional remarks in this vein, exposing the social norm that requires such small talk between dancing partners, as well as the conventional character of what is usually said ("Perhaps by and bye I may observe that private balls are much pleasanter than public ones") Elizabeth suggests that, inane as such conversations may be, the need for social bonding may make them desirable:[17]

> "One must speak a little, you know. It would look odd to be entirely silent for half an hour together, and yet for the advantage of *some*, conversation ought to be so arranged as that they may have the trouble of saying as little as possible."

To Darcy's question about whether she refers to her own wish to be silent or to what she thinks to be his, Elizabeth archly replies that they are both "of an unsocial, taciturn disposition, unwilling to speak, unless we expect to say something that will amaze the whole room, and be handed down to posterity with all the éclat of a proverb" (PP, 91). Elizabeth's satire on the individualistic arrogance of those who scorn small talk is a thinly veiled reproach against Darcy, who recognizes it as such, replying, "This is no very striking resemblance of your own character, I am sure. . . . How near it may be to *mine*, I cannot pretend to say."

We will later consider the question of whether this "portrait" of Darcy is indeed "faithful" or unjust. For now, I will merely point out that Elizabeth's clowning is, like folk humor, ambivalent, simultaneously laughing at convention and recognizing the need for social customs as bonds among people. This issue is related to the complex question of the proper role of the community and its formal and informal discourses in a person's life, a question which is central in this novel,[18] and which must be discussed as socio-philosophical background for the understanding of the heroine's development.

One avenue into the consideration of the novel's conception of community is the question of the proper attitude to the formalities of social intercourse. The first time social formalities are alluded to in *Pride and Prejudice* comes, as we have seen, when Mrs Bennet, arguing with her husband, says that the Bennet ladies will not be able to visit Bingley, a newcomer, until Mr Bennet goes. In the following chapter it is Mr Bennet who refers to the next ball his daughters will be attending, and declares his intention to introduce Mr Bingley to a friend of the Bennets, Mrs Long. Since Mrs Bennet does not know her husband has already paid the required courtesy call to Bingley, her response is, "Nonsense, nonsense." Mr Bennet then pretends to misunderstand her, asking her, "Do you consider the forms of introduction, and the stress that is laid on them, as nonsense? I cannot quite agree with you there" (PP, 7).

Is the observance of social formalities and customs nonsense? Any revision of the critical literature dealing with this issue in *Pride and Prejudice* will lead to a variety of complex questions. For instance, is the importance of such observances recognized in this novel as further evidence of the tyranny of society over the individual, who would be in danger of becoming "indistinguishable from his social role"?[19] Or are social norms conceived in the novel as an external sign of a deeper "social totality," which provides the proper framework for the self?[20] Is the question of social manners in this novel to be framed within the broader perspective of a fictional conflict between tradition and "class pride," represented by Darcy, and "aggressive individualism," represented by Elizabeth?[21] Is the etiquette of introductions one more aspect of that Austenian stress on social rituals that seems unintelligible to modern readers unless we place ourselves within the context of contemporary culture, in order to understand the "moral rationale" of her age? Furthermore, does Austen's picture of this age contain "civilized forms," such as the social norms for introductions, and "chaotic energies," such as Mrs Bennet's irrationality, both productive of meaning?[22]

All the different conceptualizations of the social framework and its demands on characters seem to be related to an underlying question: Is Austen's stance in *Pride and Prejudice* more sympathetic to the claims of society (or of form, established structures, etc.) or does the novel lean more to favoring the needs of the individual (or the self, or the pleasure principle)? Part of the difficulty in resolving this question may be due to the fact that, as Claudia Johnson has said, "Austen has contrived *Pride and Prejudice* in such a way that virtually every argument about it can be undercut with a built-in countervailing argument, a qualifying 'on the other hand' which forestalls conclusiveness."[23] Thus, an analysis of Austen's method should start out from an awareness of her structuring her fiction in what, in Bakhtinian terms, can be called a "zone of direct contact with inconclusive . . . reality," a reality seen as contemporary and fluid.[24] In such an approach, this novel will appear as "a system of languages that mutually and ideologically interanimate each other."[25] Therefore, Austen's representation of community may be analyzed from the viewpoint of the interaction between a central narratorial voice, the voices of individual characters, and the voice of the community, or neighborhood. Through such an analysis, the present study will ask in what sense the bonds among members of certain communities appear to be viewed sympathetically by Austen, and in what sense, or from what perspective, they seem to be painted in very negative terms.

I am using the term "community" rather than "society" in order to distance this discussion from the commonplace, in critiques of this novel, of equating collectivity with social order, with the "powers that be" in a patriarchal, class society. It is due to this equation that Elizabeth Bennet so often appears as "the champion of the prerogatives of individual desire," jeopardizing "both the social order, which demands self-denial, and the moral order, which is based on absolute Christian principles."[26] A radical change in perspective is needed in order to break off from the cycle of critical action-reaction in which Elizabeth (or her creator, or both) is alternately praised or blamed for her individualism, or, lately, blamed for not being individualistic enough. I will therefore view collectivity in this novel, not as status quo, as established powers, but from the popular standpoint of a utopian carnivalesque spirit. By this change in perspective we may recognize the gay assertion of community in *Pride and Prejudice*, an assertion which often leads both to self-mockery and to the grotesque exaggeration of collective failings.

In the novel's initial statement, the narrator already assumes an ironic tone resulting from the overlaying of the voice of a "neighbourhood's families" and the voice of the educated, enlightened individual. An analysis of the first paragraph in Chapter III, where the voices of individual characters mix and merge with the narrator's report of their verbal exchanges, may serve an introduction to the discussion of the concept of community. This chapter opens soon after Mr Bennet's admission that he has already visited Mr Bingley:

> Not all that Mrs Bennet, however, with the assistance of her five daughters, could ask on the subject was sufficient to draw from her husband any satisfactory description of Mr Bingley. They attacked him in various ways; with barefaced questions, ingenious suppositions, and distant surmises; but he eluded the skill of them all; and they were at last obliged to accept the second-hand intelligence of their neighbour Lady Lucas. Her report was highly favorable. Sir William had been delighted with him. He was quite young, wonderfully handsome, extremely agreeable, and to crown the whole, he meant to be at the next assembly with a large party. Nothing could be more delightful! To be fond of dancing was a certain step towards falling in love; and very lively hopes of Mr Bingley's heart were entertained. (PP, 9)

In the narrator's opening report of several exchanges between the Bennet ladies and Mr Bennet, the former seek in vain to obtain information from the latter. (As in the first chapter, we observe here a war over information, only now its holder refuses to relinquish it; power for Mr Bennet lies not in communication but in reserve.) The second sentence refers, in Johnsonian parallel construction, to three types of speech acts (questions, suppositions, distant surmises) resorted to by the ladies. This use of three parallel noun phrases is later mirrored in the description of Bingley, which is the narrator's report of Lady Lucas' report of her husband's report. Thus, structural linguistic similarity is used to link a collective communicative effort (by Mrs Bennet and her five daughters) and a first overlaying of voices (a report of a report of a report). Immediately, the narrator relates, in free indirect speech, the reaction of Mrs Bennet and her daughters. Their collective exclamation of delight provides the first truly *hybrid* construction,[27] in which the narrator's ironic, skeptic voice momentarily adopts the ecstatic tone of the ladies' anticipation. The mention of the assembly in the preceding sentence makes this exclamation seem like a rumor spreading through all the households where there are ladies who attend balls. The narrator mocks fortune- and bachelor-hunting families, with their collective "lively hopes," but the mockery is tempered by references to ladies' love of dancing, a love, after all, which Austen's heroines usually share. The passive voice at the end generalizes, making the passage more inclusive, the sense of collectivity stronger. Thus the narrator's attitude toward these collective reactions acquires a gay, mocking ambivalence.

The narrator's voice becomes increasingly more collective as the chapter progresses, as we are told of neighbors' speculations about Bingley's trip to London. A crescendo of gossipy voices both mirrors and produces a report about the large number of ladies Bingley will purportedly bring to the ball. When Bingley at last appears at the ball, however, it turns out he has only brought "his two sisters, the husband of the eldest, and another young man." The appearance of the latter is followed by "the report which was in general circulation within five minutes after his entrance, of his having ten thousand a year." Each of the groups present, "the gentlemen" and "the ladies," then speaks in one voice: "The gentlemen pronounced him to be a fine figure of a man, the ladies declared he was much handsomer than Mr Bingley, and he was looked at with great admiration for half the evening" (PP, 10). When Darcy fails to dance with any lady, or to speak to anyone, outside his own party, "His character was decided. He was the proudest, most disagreeable man in the whole world, and everybody hoped he would never come again" (PP, 11). Thus we see how the progressive inclusion of more voices in reported utterances leads the narrator to ironically blend her voice into the collective voice ("everybody")[28] passing judgment on Darcy. This narratorial irony is evident in the change in collective appraisals of Darcy's appearance, from approval influenced by the report of his income, to condemnation (his "having a most forbidding, disagreeable countenance") reached as soon as he is "discovered to be proud, to be above his company, and above being pleased" (PP, 10). But the narrator, though here inviting the reader to laugh at this inconsistency, will later on endorse the reproach to Darcy for his excessive pride, so that the community's collective voice, demanding from newcomers a willingness to accept efforts to please them, will be partially vindicated.

An examination of Darcy's relations to others can shed light on the narrator's attitudes toward the community. There are three issues involved in the antipathy between Darcy and the Meryton neighborhood, and they are related to three areas of social contradictions: social class, gender, and the conflict between London and provincial, rural communities. Darcy's entrance into the assembly hall creates a commotion because he is both sexually attractive and socially desirable. His manners and income make him highly likely to have that ultimate status symbol for the rural gentry, a house in London. However, his behavior soon causes him to be generally detested because he is seen to be unreachable, which in turn is due to his hauteur, his contempt for the gathering. "At such an assembly as this," he tells Bingley, dancing "would be insupportable" (PP, 11).

Darcy's failings are, for the first half of the novel, exaggerated. Mrs Bennet is sure he thinks "the country is nothing at all" (PP, 43). Elizabeth considers him a snob who, if forced to enter such a middle class sector of London as Gracechurch Street, where the Gardiners live, "would hardly think a month's ablutions enough to cleanse him from its impurities" (PP, 141). Darcy will later show himself to be above such snobbery, or else will have overcome such leanings, after Elizabeth's rejection changes him, for he will be very civil to the Gardiners. But he is indeed guilty of considering himself above Elizabeth, both as male and as her social superior, as will be evident in his mode of proposing to her. As he admits, he has struggled to repress his love for her because the "condition in life" of her relations is "decidely beneath my own" (PP, 192); as he proposes to her, "his countenance" expresses "real security" that she will accept him (PP, 189), for his vanity has convinced him that she can only feel flattered by his love (cf. PP, 369).

These flaws in Darcy's character become evident not only in his relationship with Elizabeth. Although her accusations of concrete wrongdoing toward Wickham and Jane and Bingley will prove to be largely unfounded, she is right when she accuses him of arrogance and conceit, of "selfish disdain of the feelings of others" (PP, 193). Darcy's real failing, then, lies in his failure to enter into community with others, in his individualistic family pride. He will later confess to Elizabeth that his parents had spoilt him, that they "allowed, encouraged, almost taught me to be selfish and overbearing, to care for none beyond my own family circle, to think meanly of all the rest of the world" (PP, 369). Although his pride is partly based on his social class and family tradition,[29] the fault for which he is consistently reproached throughout the novel is his failure to "trouble himself" to relate to others (PP, 175). The stance he adopts during a musical party is emblematic of his attitude vis-a-vis his fellow beings; he stands off alone, not, like Mr Bennet,[30] in order to laugh at others, but in order to pass judgment on them "in silent indignation" (PP, 25). By stressing Darcy's failure to commune with others, then, the novel emphasizes the importance of community as the proper context for personal behavior. But the collective or social reality which the novel upholds is not the force of traditions or the strength of class or established moral structures, which discriminate and exclude. In my view, what is at play here is an approach to human relations in which elements of utopian community are important, for they make up a mask-like bond of the self with others (at least with all others one may meet socially).

In contrast to Darcy, Elizabeth repeatedly shows her awareness of the

importance of establishing a sense of community with her peers. She exhibits
a sense of the importance of collectivity whenever she thinks in terms of what
"would be better for the neighbourhood" (PP, 178).[31] At one point it is Mrs
Gardiner who shows regional allegiance ("I should be sorry," she says to
Elizabeth, "to think ill of a young man who has lived so long in Derbyshire"),
while Elizabeth, angry at Darcy for his supposed mistreatment of Wickham,
and at Bingley for his apparent neglect of her sister, Jane, proclaims herself
"sick" of "young men who live in Derbyshire" and of "their intimate friends
who live in Hertfordshire." For this speech she is rebuked by Mrs Gardiner
(PP, 153-4), a sensible woman whose words carry some weight in the novel.
As we shall discuss below, it is precisely her tendency to trust her own
perceptions of others too rapidly, blocking herself against understanding
other people's motives, that leads her into error. Her sins, therefore, are, like
Darcy's, sins against community.

Finally, Elizabeth, in spite of her occasional (but serious) lapses from
a more communital attitude, boldly shows her identification with her
neighborhood by her use of unpretentious, homespun speech, especially when
confronted with the high and mighty. Thus, she employs a colloquiallism in
response to the news of the arrival of Miss de Bourgh: "I expected at least that
the pigs were got into the garden, and here is nothing but Lady Catherine and
her daughter!" (PP, 158). Again, she quotes a homely proverb to Darcy's face,
soon after she notices his listening to her conversation with others at a party.
Elizabeth defies what she takes to be his contempt by repeating to him "a fine
old saying which every body here is of course familiar with--'Keep your breath
to cool your porridge'" (PP, 24).[32] Elizabeth feels the loyalty to her community
that is characteristic of people used to life in a country village. Her "attachment
to Hertfordshire" is recognized by Darcy; it is a mark of his London
presumptuousness that he considers it a compliment to suggest that Elizabeth
has no right "to such a very strong local attachment," condescendingly
hinting she is too superior to "have been always at Longbourn" (PP, 178-9).

For Elizabeth, it is not really a question whether strong bonds to a
community are good or bad; it is, rather, that they are unavoidable. In this
sense, the novel seems imbued with a sense of the interpenetration of the
individual and the social aspects of human experience, of the fact that it is
impossible to establish the frontier between the two. For we may say,
following Volosinov, that the individual is constituted precisely by his/her
interaction with others in a social framework. *Pride and Prejudice*, like *Emma*,
conceives the relations between its central characters and the community in
which they live in very similar terms to what Volosinov describes as the
dialectical relations between psychology and ideology: "the content of the
individual psyche is by its very nature just as social as is ideology," since "the
very . . .consciousness of one's individuality . . . is ideological, historical, and
wholly conditioned by sociological factors," while "ideological phenomena

are just as individual as psychological phenomena."[33]

Of course, the novel is far from always showing sympathy towards the collective voice, towards "every body"; nothing could be farther from Austen than a romantic idealization of any group of people. The entire series of episodes involving Wickham seems especially designed to discredit that *vox populi* which is so unanimous in abhoring Darcy that Elizabeth can truthfully say, "Every body [in Hertfordshire] is disgusted with his pride" (PP, 78). When Wickham circulates his story of the evil Darcy has done him, "every body was pleased to think how much they had disliked Mr Darcy before they had known any thing of the matter" (PP, 138). For some time, these people are enamored of Wickham, who, as Mr Bennet later will say, "makes love to us all" (PP, 330). But when Darcy's letter reveals Wickham's evil deeds, Elizabeth is forced to recollect that she can adduce in his defense "no more substantial good than the general approbation of the neighbourhood, and the regard which his social powers had gained in the mess" (PP, 206). After Wickham and Lydia elope, the fickle public will turn totally against him, as his many creditors begin to suspect he will not pay his debts: "All Meryton seemed striving to blacken the man, who, but three months before, had been almost an angel of light." We again encounter that character that so often appears in this novel, "every body": "Every body declared that he was the wickedest young man in the world; and every body began to find out, that they had always distrusted the appearance of his goodness" (PP, 294-5). This collective character, then, is blind to the faults of those who flatter it, implacable against those who provoke its resentment, and quite ready to distort facts in order not to face up to its own mistakes.

"Every body" is simply another name for that omnipresent "they," the "neighbours," the "country," an entity whose opinion is powerful enough, on one occasion, to move Elizabeth to oppose Lydia's plan of walking to Meryton the same afternoon the sisters arrive from a trip: "It should not be said, that the Miss Bennets could not be at home half a day before they were in pursuit of the officers" (PP, 223). Elizabeth's fear of the generalized surveillance by members of the community shows its effective social control. The same group of people whose gossip is feared will rejoice when evil befalls the Bennet family in the form of Lydia's elopement, Elizabeth suggests; therefore they should offer no condolences: "Let them triumph over us at a distance, and be satisfied" (PP, 293). Thus she ironically deflates the seriousness of the tragic moment, defeating the fear of, in Jane's words, "the horror of what might happen" to Lydia (PP, 292); she also exaggerates the satisfaction many people feel when others suffer mishaps. In a verbal thrashing the narrator likewise describes the "spiteful old ladies in Meryton" reacting with glee to the news of Lydia's marriage to Wickham, "because with such a husband, her misery was considered certain" (PP, 309). By turning the gossiping old ladies into grotesque monsters, Austen achieves the typical carnivalesque triumph: "All that was frightening in ordinary life is turned into amusing or ludicrous monstrosities" (RHW, 47).

This transformation of fear into laughter, it is true, does not obliterate the "monsters." The neighbors' surveillance and intrusions can be seen as an indication of the applicability of the Foucauldian concept of the panopticon to Austen's narratives. However, it would be a mistake to attempt to explain Austen's complex view of human collectivity solely by applying Foucault's discussion of the ways in which social relations serve as a form of surveillance leading to self-discipline (cf. *Discipline and Punish*). For community in Austen does not only mean the micro-distribution of power through vigilant social control Foucault describes; it is, rather, carnivalistically ambivalent, *both* the site of generalized struggle *and* the occasion for self-revelation, growth and intimacy. As said above, both Darcy's and Elizabeth's flaws relate to sins against the community, showing the novel's approval of an attitude of openness to others. Furthermore, *Pride and Prejudice* can be shown to endorse an attitude of christian humility: Most of us are quite ready to see faults in others, but very reluctant to admit them in ourselves. Thus, to feel above one's neighbors is a temptation that must be avoided. Elizabeth's *Bildung* will be a lesson in the idea that, vulgar and malevolently inexcusable as the many-headed monster, the Other, often seems, one may occasionally have to admit that one is not fully exempt from its shortcomings. In conclusion, the story of Elizabeth Bennet upholds the need to observe conventions, even while laughing at them, in as much as they serve a bonding function; in this sense it shares carnival's "universal spirit," which is "a special condition of the entire world, of the world's revival and renewal, in which all take part" (RHW, 7). It is true that the "entire world" of this text extends to both genders but does not include workers, servants, or the poor on an equal footing; on the other hand, the "entire world" of popular festivities during the middle ages and the Renaissance did not include women as men's equals either. In other words, this novel's sense of the importance of an orientation towards the community is carnivalesque in the sense that (and inasmuch as) it implies a dissolution of gender hierarchies, while medieval carnival meant the suspension of class hierarchies.

Community bonds, nevertheless, tend to be bonds of war. Beyond the fierce competition among families with marriageable daughters, conflict constitutes much of the fabric of social intercourse. And, of course, this strife is conducted mainly in two arenas: gender and social class. The novel reveals, in addition to conflicting views on women, the struggle that underlies much of the process of social interaction. One of the most intense and most central social conflicts in the novel is that between characters with connections to "trade," meaning those who work for their money (or whose male relatives do so), and characters belonging to families who for generations have held large estates. Elizabeth Bennet's status is ambiguous, for her father belongs to the second group, while her mother originally belonged to the first, as is evident in the fact that in Mrs Bennet's family there are two attorneys (much to Miss Bingley's malevolent satisfaction (see PP, 36-7)). Darcy and his aunt, Lady Catherine, on the other hand, belong to the second group. The conflicts among these three characters represent central points in the evolution of the plot; our sympathies as readers seem to be directed by the narrator toward the values of the working middle class, and against the aristocratic emphasis on nobility of birth.

Among the most interesting manifestations of social conflicts in the novel we find the arriviste efforts of people whose fortune originated in trade in the past, but who have now enlarged the ranks of the idle. Thus, for instance, Sir William Lucas' knighting convinces him that he cannot remain in trade, and moves him to feel "disgust" toward "his business and his residence in a small market town," both of which he soon gives up to settle in Lucas Lodge, "where he could think with pleasure of his own importance" (PP, 18). Similarly, Miss Bingley and Mrs Hurst wished to forget that "their brother's fortune and their own had been acquired by trade" (PP, 15). These two elegant ladies are consummate snobs, who "would have had difficulty in believing that a man who lived by trade, and within view of his own warehouses, could have been so well bred and agreeable" (PP, 139). The man in question is Mr Gardiner, Mrs Bennet's brother; he and his wife constitute living proof of that "elegance of mind" which the novel presents in opposition to the social distinction of "people of fashion." Mr Gardiner, aside from working for a living, has a lifestyle in many ways indistinguishable from that of those who look down upon him. This fact is hard to believe for someone like Lady Catherine, who exclaims in surprise when Elizabeth Bennet informs her that Mr Gardiner "keeps a man-servant" (PP, 212).

One interesting aspect in this novel's treatment of social relationships as bonded war lies in the ways in which conflict is inscribed in the language of everyday interaction. That war is a generalized reality in social interaction is recognized by the principal characters and by the narrator herself, for they all consistently use the language of war to refer to linguistic exchanges. Thus, for instance, one of the most common words used to refer to a character's effort to sway another character's opinion, or to obtain information or a commissive[34] from another character, is "attack." As we have seen, the Bennet ladies "attacked [Mr Bennet] in various ways," when trying to get him to describe Mr Bingley. On a visit to Netherfield, Lydia addresses Bingley in a "sudden attack" reminding him of his promise to give a ball (cf. PP, 45). Miss Bingley's account of Wickham's relations to and dealings with the Darcy family is called by Elizabeth "a paltry attack" that cannot influence her opinion. And when Miss Bingley, jealous of Darcy's attentions to Elizabeth, wishes to offend her, she makes thinly veiled comments about Elizabeth's officer-crazy sisters and the removal of the militia from Meryton; Elizabeth must exert "herself vigorously to repel the ill-natured attack" (PP, 269).[35] Mrs Bennet often "attacks" her daughters, as she does Elizabeth to get her to accept Collins' marriage proposal (PP, 112). More incongruously and unfeelingly, she vents her disappointment in Bingley's failure to return with "attacks" on Jane demanding her confession that "if he did not come back, she should think herself very ill used" (PP, 129). In addition to "attack," a partial list of words related to martial arts often used in the novel to describe verbal and other forms of social interaction would include "defy," (cf. PP, 24, 80), "victory" (PP, 43), "provoke" (PP, 52), "dispute" (PP, 51), "manoeuvre," "repulsed" (PP, 102), "combated" (PP, 142), "triumph" (PP, 43, 148, 160, 310, 311, 312), "challenge," "courage," "intimidate" (PP, 174, 357), "fight" (PP, 287), "submit," "recede" (PP, 356).

Nor is martial language confined to hostile relationships. Making comic use of a long courtly-romantic tradition, the narrator refers to sexual and romantic interactions with a profusion of military terms, that tend to trivialize war as they stress the omnipresence of conflict. Thus, for instance, Elizabeth's intentions as she dresses herself for the Netherfield ball are described, in ironic "love-is-war" clichés, as preparation "for the *conquest* of all that remained *unsubdued* of [Wickham's] heart, trusting it was no more than could be *won* in the course of the evening" (PP, 89; emphasis added). Friendship and love are sometimes at war with each other; thus, Elizabeth trusts that "the influence of [Bingley's] friends," who have tried to keep him away from Jane, might be "successfully combated by the more natural influence of Jane's attractions" (PP, 142). Again, Mr Bennet jokingly congratulates Elizabeth "on a very important conquest" when Collins' letter relates gossip about Darcy's interest in Elizabeth (PP, 362).

Merry hostilities in *Pride and Prejudice*, rather than being limited to adversaries, become even more prevalent between intimates, for intimacy provides information that can be used against one's friends. Thus, Elizabeth tells Miss Bingley that she has the means of retaliating against Darcy after he has made an "abominable" speech about certain common feminine motivations: "We can all plague and punish one another. Teaze him--laugh at him.-- Intimate as you are, you must know how it is to be done" (PP, 57). The novel also insists on the generalized war based on everyone's desire to be proven right in his/her appraisal of everyday situations. Only someone as candidly benevolent as Jane can think that her sister's love for her will prevent her "triumphing in her better judgment at my expence," when Elizabeth proves right about Miss Bingley (PP, 148). Elizabeth, on the contrary, recognizes that Darcy would

> triumph . . . could he know that the proposals which she had proudly spurned only four months ago, would now have been gladly and gratefully received! He was as generous, she doubted not, as the most generous of his sex. But while he

was mortal, there must be triumph. (PP, 311-2)

Although it is generalized, war is most intense when sexual and social forces collide. The two most violent battles in the novel occur when Darcy first proposes to Elizabeth, and when Lady Catherine visits Elizabeth to dissuade her from marrying Darcy. From a linguistic viewpoint, however, the most interesting of these two verbal confrontations is the second one, the one between Elizabeth and Lady Catherine.[36]

This lady uses discourse weapons that are commensurate to what she represents: all the most negative aspects of worldly power. She adds an overbearing personality, built upon the habit of commanding, patronizing and intimidating her inferiors, to her excessive reliance on the weight of a noble family, status, money, and a large estate as basis for her claims to the regards of others. This lady's language, her rage, are symptomatic of the gulf that still remained between the aristocracy and some segments of the middle classes. As a person "connected to trade," Elizabeth is considered by Lady Catherine unworthy of her newphew, Darcy, whom she wants to marry her daughter; she cannot abide to see these two "divided" by "the upstart pretensions of a young woman without family, connections, or fortune." Stressing the superiority of her ancient family (and Darcy's), Lady Catherine tries to convince Elizabeth that her marriage to Darcy would be a monstruous mismatch (PP, 356-8). In this confrontation with Elizabeth at the latter's home, Longbourn, Lady Catherine's behavior merely underscores the patronizing, overbearing impertinence she has already shown towards the Collinses and their guests and towards the villagers she presides over at her estate, Rosings (cf. PP, 160-76, 210-4).

The confrontation reaches its climax when, after Lady Catherine's many insults, threats and accusations, she changes her command to reject Darcy to a demand that Elizabeth confess that she is "resolved to have him." This Elizabeth will not admit, affirming only her right to pursue her own happiness[37] "without reference to *you*, or to any person so wholly unconnected with me." Thus she rejects the lady's claims of the supremacy of family and superior birth. And yet Elizabeth's position, though imbued with the revolutionary spirit of rationalism, is not fully individualistic: to the charge that the marriage will make Darcy "the contempt of the world," the young lady's reply is not an expression of readiness to brave such contempt in romantic assurance of the sufficiency of love. Rather, she insists that "the world in general will have too much sense to join in the scorn [shown by Darcy's family]."

In summary, Elizabeth uses irony and reason as her argumentative weapons in defense of her personal dignity, while Lady Catherine appeals to the power of rank and the established claims of family and age, attempting to force her interlocutor to comply to her demands by means of intimidation.

Thus we may say that the discourse tools employed by each represent the positive qualities of the first and the faults of the latter, who embodies what is most unpleasant and reprehensible about the exercise of social power.

Pride and Prejudice presents a complex view of society, in which strong bonds among people in a community appear as the unavoidable context for interpersonal relationships. These bonds seem to be conceived more as an attitude of openness to the possibility of utopian fellowship than as an idealization of the actual virtues of country life or English culture. Paradoxically, one of the strongest bonds among people is their common store of language, manners and customs, which sustain a form of social interaction that can be described as institutionalized, merry warfare. Thus war is inscribed in language and in the rules for social intercourse. Furthermore, the narrator's irreverent tone and the ironic views of the protagonist show a festive awareness of the human failings that country communities often exhibit. In fact, such failings are sometimes comically, grotesquely exaggerated and mocked.

Similarly, the "villainess" in the novel, Lady Catherine, turns out to be more ridiculous than intimidating, in spite of all her near-feudal social and economic power. This lady uses power to dominate others while pretending to protect them. The fictional universe in *Pride and Prejudice*, however, contains a realm of beneficent use of power, a small utopian community in which the old oppressive order has died and the world has been reborn. This realm is a very complex fictional reality, being both limited to a chosen few and forced to coexist with perpetual, unavoidable conflict. Nevertheless, even with these qualifications it still qualifies as a utopian realm, for it is a domain of abundance and munificence, seen from the perspective of the socially despised, which in this novel generally means women and occasionally servants. It is a world where masters are judged by their dependents, where snobbery is forbidden, where wives laugh at their husbands as freely and fearlessly as they could laugh at themselves, where cynics become sociable, and where community bonds thrive. The story of this world's victory is also the story of Elizabeth's growth to maturity.

The seeds of this complex utopian world are present from the start, though they begin to germinate only in the third volume, and fructify in the conclusion. This utopia is achieved, largely, but not exclusively, through the heroine's development. While *Northanger Abbey* describes social worlds full of imperfections that are largely overcome in its utopian ending, in *Pride and Prejudice* we find utopian elements from the beginning. As Claudia Johnson observes, "*Pride and Prejudice* is a categorically happy novel, and its felicity is not merely incidental, something that happens at the end of the novel, but is rather at once its premise and its prize."[38] From the start, the very climate of the Bennet household shows some utopian elements due to its patriarch's *de facto* abdication of many of his prerogatives and to the Bennet parents' lack of authoritarianism, the "benevolent neglect" they show toward their daughters. Their parental "laissez-faire" attitude, although excessive in the case of Kitty and Lydia,[39] has contributed to make the protagonist's character bold and independent, and must have had some influence in the formation of her carnivalesque wit. The fact that she has been allowed to "run on in [a] wild manner . . . at home," as her mother puts it, has made her unconventional and original. Thus she is, in Bingley's words, a "studier of character" (PP, 42) who appears to be no respecter of persons.

Elizabeth's habits of festive, mocking observation and analysis of the behavior of others place her in a sense outside of established social categories. She is not cowed by "the mere stateliness of money and rank"; it would take "extraordinary talents or miraculous virtue" to make her feel "trepidation" (PP, 161). Nor is she properly submissive before male greatness. While Miss Bingley fawns upon Darcy, hoping to marry him, Elizabeth challenges and laughs at him whenever she can. As she will later tell Darcy, "my behavior to *you* was at least always bordering on the uncivil" (PP, 380). Furthermore, she does not show respectful acquiescence before her elders; as Lady Catherine observes, "you give your opinion very decidedly for so young a person." When she laughs at Lady Catherine's inquisitiveness, refusing to answer her questions, this lady is astonished; "Elizabeth suspected herself to be the first creature who had ever dared to trifle with so much dignified impertinence" (PP, 165-6). Elizabeth's determination *not* to fawn upon men and to think for herself, her penchant for laughter, her disregard for "feminine" decorum (shown, for instance, in the cross-country trek that muddies her petticoats), all make her a rationalistic version of the "disorderly woman" who nevertheless preserves high standards of dignity. This character does not even respect the clergy, for she, like her father and the novel's narrator, repeatedly laughs at Collins' absurd and contradictory mixture of humility and pretentiousness, nowhere as evident as in his views of the clerical profession ("I consider the clerical office," Collins tells her, "as equal in point of dignity with the highest rank in the kingdom--provided a proper humility of behaviour is at the same time maintained"--PP, 97). Indeed, Bakhtin's words describing medieval laughter can be applied to Elizabeth, for she also distrusts "the serious tone" and feels "confidence in the truth of laughter," which "eliminates fear and opposes dogmatic, official truth" (RHW, 95). It is her propensity to laugh at every absurdity, even when shown by those who appear to be above her, that places her in the utopian realm of carnival laughter, which "offered a completely different, nonofficial, extraecclesiastical and extrapolitical aspect of the world, of man, and of human relations," building "a second world and a second life outside officialdom" (RHW, 6).

Nevertheless, sometimes Elizabeth's attitude falls short of carnivalesque utopian equality and universal profanation, for she judges others too hastily and trusts her own impressions too blindly, clinging to her misperceptions.

The utopian spirit of festive laughter, according to Bakhtin, "created no dogmas and could not become authoritarian" (RHW, 95); Elizabeth, on the other hand, sometimes seems in danger of trusting the authority of her own impressions too much. Of course, her independence of mind and joyful wit are admirable; our sympathies as readers are directed in favor of her intelligence and strength of personality. As Susan Morgan puts it, "Elizabeth's freedom is basically the freedom to think for herself."[40] But precisely because she knows the power of her intelligence, she is susceptible to making mistakes. In the words of Andrew H. Wright, "Elizabeth's prejudice stems from a pride in her own perceptions." She shares with Darcy both this power and this liability. Wright argues that it is, ironically, because of their "deep percipience" that both are "subject to failures of perception."[41] In this novel it becomes clear that everyone is occasionally subject to such failures, whether or not their intelligence is superior like Elizabeth's or Darcy's.

The significance of this novel's uncrownings is not limited to the humbling of two individuals, but refer us to the inversion of the heroic dignity of novelistic lovers. Nevertheless, on a psychological level, *Pride and Prejudice* is the story of their personal uncrowning, their humbling as they realize that they are liable to make the same mistakes other, more vulgar souls make, and for very similar reasons. Thus we see once more how ideology, seen as the "mind" of social groups, interpenetrates psychology, or the study of the mind of individuals. Paradoxically, Elizabeth and Darcy's moral and intellectual advantage over the group ("the neighborhood") consists precisely in the ability to face this humiliation and ultimately accept it.

Although both characters will undergo similar humblings, during the first half of the novel it is Darcy's failings that we focus on. For we not only follow most of the action through the eyes of Elizabeth Bennet; the narrator also tends to appraise people and events from a perspective very close to the protagonist's. A look into the relation between Elizabeth's voice, her consciousness, and the narrator's utterances will allow us to reflect on the novel's attitude to such epistemological questions as the possibility of certitude and the conditions affecting perception, questions that are basic to an understanding of Elizabeth's personal development. For Elizabeth's style of discourse is in many ways similar to the narrator's, and yet the difference between them, especially in the first volume, is that between a slightly sardonic, somewhat monologic irony and an irony more deeply imbued with the carnivalesque spirit. As Bakhtin points out, when irony is festive rather than negative or bitterly satirical, it is speech "with reservations," aimed at transcending dogmatic, authoritarian culture; ironic laughter strives to transcend the tendency to speak in proclamations.[42]

Nevertheless, although Elizabeth's viewpoint is partly flawed, even before she appears in the novel we are placed in a perspective very close to hers. Mr Bennet, for example, is presented in a more favorable light in Volume I,

Chapter I (p. 5), than he is at the end of the second volume, when Elizabeth's experience allows her to reflect on his failings. In the earlier passage, he is only said to be "odd" and "sarcastic," and the contrast to his wife's "mean understanding, little information and uncertain temper" makes him appear to advantage. In the later passage, we are made to reflect on the consequences of his shortcomings at a time when Elizabeth is forced by events to overcome her partiality as her father's favorite. She then dwells on the thought that, in laughing at his wife before their daughters and exposing her "to the contempt of her own children" he has neglected his conjugal and parental duties: Elizabeth "had never felt so strongly as now, the disadvantages which must attend the children of so unsuitable a marriage, nor ever been so fully aware of the evils arising from so ill-judged a direction of talents" (PP, 236-7). If Elizabeth feels these disadvantages more strongly "*now*," it is not only because Lydia has been behaving even more wildly, or Kitty more peevishly; it is also because she has herself undergone a transformation. At Hunsford Parsonage, after discovering she has been unfair to Darcy, she has changed, and is now more likely to be aware of how her own gratitude may have influenced her desire to "banish from her thoughts" her father's faults.

Mr Bennet's occasional individualistic stance places him, at times, beyond carnivalesque eccentricity and outside the clown's dialogism. Individualism is foreign to the clown's ambivalent stance, his firm rooting in social languages. As Bakhtin says, the "clown's speech [is] determined by his specific social orientation (by his privileges as a clown)" (DN, 405). The clown's unique "right to speak in otherwise unacceptable languages" is itself grounded in the clown's *social* role. This role was to act as the herald of "laughing truth," not in "a subjective, individual . . . consciousness" but as "the social consciousness of all the people" (RHW, 92-95). Mr Bennet, then, is a complex character whose eccentricity allows him to play a clowning role, while at the same time that very trait leads him to an individualistic stance that places him beyond the clown's firm anchoring in "the social consciousness of all the people". This ambivalent character is at the root of Elizabeth's painful realization of his father's faults; if he always played the clown, his eccentric utterances would not be judged at the level of individual morality. It is only when Elizabeth overcomes some of her own tendencies to individualism that she is able to face her father's faults. Since the narration follows Elizabeth's mental processes, we as readers also see those faults more clearly after this point than we had before.

The reader's closeness to Elizabeth is also based on the considerable similarity between the narrator's voice and Elizabeth's style of speech and thought. As Lloyd W. Brown observes, "it is Elizabeth herself whose personality and style pervade the tone of *Pride and Prejudice*." Indeed, the novel's protagonist is given to pronouncements that seem very similar to the narrator's "epigrammatic summaries of character and situation." For example, in terms that remind one of the narratorial description of Mrs Bennet in the first chapter, Elizabeth will say of Collins that he "is a conceited, pompous, narrow-minded, silly man" (PP, 135). In addition to such judgments, Elizabeth's style and the narrator's also share a carnivalesque bent, what Lloyd Brown calls their "mocking inversion of traditional values."[43] Elizabeth not only clownishly mocks Darcy's pompous self-importance; she is also "impatient" with conventions and sentimentality, as she shows, for example, when she counters her mother's novel-like portrayal of Jane being wooed with sonnets at age fifteen, observing that poetry is most efficacious "in driving away love" (PP, 44).

In spite of the nearness of her general stance to the narrator's irony, Elizabeth at times seems in danger of falling into her father's too-individualistic, negatively satiric stance. Thus, for instance, she protests that to find Darcy agreeable would be even greater misfortune than to continue to find reason to hate him: "To find a man agreeable whom one is determined to hate! Do not wish me such an evil" (PP, 44, 90). She exhibits her proud penchant for paradox again, when her disappointment in Wickham and Jane's in Bingley leads her to rejoice over the fact that she will soon be in the company of Collins: "Stupid men are the only ones worth knowing after all" (PP, 154).

Elizabeth's tone is generally assertive, but her confidence in her own judgment will come to seem excessive. Faced with contradictory reports about the dealings between Wickham and Darcy, for example, Elizabeth retorts to her sister's expression of distress, "One does not know what to think," with a confident, "I beg your pardon; —— one knows exactly what to think" (PP, 86). Similarly, Elizabeth will treat "The idea of [Bingley's] returning no more . . . with the utmost contempt" (PP, 120). And yet "the idea" will prove correct, and what she knew "exactly" will turn out to be false. For Elizabeth fails to take into consideration what the narrator of *Pride and Prejudice*, for all her self-confident wit and perceptiveness, never forgets: that our views of people and events are too often colored by our sympathies or antipathies, our gratitude or resentment, our wants and needs.[44] The narrator often seems to endorse Elizabeth's judgment of people, as it happens when Jane has a more favorable impression of Bingley's sisters than Elizabeth's:

> . . . with more quickness of observation and less pliancy of temper than her sister, and with a judgment too unassailed by any attention to herself, [Elizabeth] was very little disposed to approve them. They were in fact very fine ladies; not deficient in good humour when they were pleased, nor in the power of being agreeable when they chose it; but proud and conceited. (PP, 15)

We observe here almost the same "finality of utterance" that one critic attributes to Elizabeth's interventions in dialogue.[45] And yet the narrating voice suggests that Elizabeth's stringent judgment was not only based on her greater "quickness of perception," but also on her having been "too unassailed by any attention to herself" to like Miss Bingley.[46] (This statement will in hindsight seem an instance of litotes, because of the intense jealousy and rivalry Miss Bingley will develop towards Elizabeth.)

As the novel progresses, such narratorial statements ironically relating a character's views to his/her interests or affections, and thus relativizing such views, become more prevalent, while direct addresses to the reader in a seemingly authoritative tone become less frequent and less definitive. The narrative voice is often charged with an irony that gives its statements, in the words of Julia Prewitt Brown, "a flashing ambiguity": "The narrative voice, then, provides some limit, some barrier, which the action strives ceaselessly (and successfully) to overcome. The narrator's provision of certitude, despite its accuracy, is temporary."[47]

It is typical of this narrator that she will qualify what would otherwise seem to be decisive declarations by adding words such as "perhaps" that turn assertions into statements of probability. For instance, when Wickham begins to court Maria King immediately after she inherits a fortune, the narrator attributes Elizabeth's reaction to her regard for him, but turns her own appraisal into a probabilistic judgment. When Mrs Gardiner seems dubious about Wickham's attitude, Elizabeth defends him, "Pray, my dear aunt, what is the difference in matrimonial affairs between the prudent and the mercenary motive?" Elizabeth has formerly condemned Charlotte for her mercenary marriage, has even reproached Jane for blinding herself, out of friendship, to Charlotte's unprincipled decision: "You shall not defend her, though it is Charlotte Lucas" (PP, 135-6). And yet Elizabeth likes Wickham too well to apply the same principle to him. As the narrator observes, "Elizabeth, less clear-sighted *perhaps* in his case than in Charlotte's, did not quarrel with him for his wish of independence" (PP, 149-50 —— emphasis added).[48] Moral principle, the text seems to say, may be unitary, but when individuals apply it they can never be absolutely certain of their own motivations and perceptions. Skepticism about judgments about someone else would logically extend to the narrator's own statements. In the end, the reader may feel that, in spite of initial appearances, in spite of the narrator's seeming endorsement of the view that to condemn Charlotte's decision is to be "clear-sighted," there was considerable more justification for Charlotte's marriage than for Wickham's courting the new heiress, for the former has no other "provision" to choose from, while the latter has wasted several opportunities to make a livelihood. Elizabeth's monologic tendencies, then, manifest themselves in her readiness to condemn others and in a somewhat complacent reliance on her own judgment. Correction will come in the form of uncrownings; before analyzing the process of her humiliation, however, we must understand more deeply the carnivalesque creativity that serves as backdrop for Elizabeth's *Bildung*.

Elizabeth is not alone in her tendency to let her judgment be influenced by her affections. Ironical ambiguity and a consciousness of the inevitability of prejudice become more and more evident the farther we get into the novel, not only in the mercenary judgments made by "every body," on the basis of Darcy's income or Wickham's debts. In *Pride and Prejudice* it is recognized that, as Mr Bennet tells Elizabeth, "human nature is too prone" to forget its own guilt, its own humbling (PP, 299). Often, partial, prejudiced mental processes are not just sceptically recorded, but amusedly, almost fondly, narrated, and not described as culpable. Charlotte, for instance, moved by sincere love for her friend Elizabeth, hopes she might marry Darcy's cousin, Colonel Fitzwilliam. Immediately, however, the narrator hints that Charlotte's self-interest leads her to reflect that, in spite of the colonel's personal "advantages," it would be better if it were Darcy who would propose to Elizabeth, for "Mr Darcy had considerable patronage in the church, and his cousin could have none at all" (PP, 181). If Elizabeth marries him, it is implied, Darcy may help Collins, Charlotte's husband's, by granting him another living; his cousin cannot. Even in such idle musings about the future of one's friends, therefore, self *will* intrude.

The most intelligent and trustworthy characters, from Darcy to Elizabeth to the Gardiners, at some point or another base their opinions, perceptions, even memories, on what they would like to believe. We find, for instance, that Darcy did not maneuver to separate Bingley and Jane solely because he had his friend's best interest at heart. Darcy believes he has not been biased, and he proudly asserts in his letter to Elizabeth that he had observed Jane and concluded she was not in love with Bingley: "That I was desirous of believing her indifferent is certain--but I will venture to say that my investigations and decisions are not usually influenced by my hopes or fears" (PP, 197). In spite of Darcy's confidence in his own dispassionate conclusions, it will become clear that he "had formed [the] plan" of seeing his friend Bingley married to his sister; the narrator ironically suggests that "It is probable that [the plan] might add something to his lively concern for the welfare of his friend" (PP, 265).[49]

Even Mrs Gardiner, so often the voice of reason, at times "remembers" very conveniently. After meeting the charming Wickham, she

> tried to remember something of [Darcy's] reputed disposition when quite a lad, which might agree with [Wickham's accusations], and was confident at last that she recollected having heard Mr Fitzwilliam Darcy formerly spoken of as a very proud, ill-natured boy. (PP, 143)

And yet we will later hear Darcy commended by Mrs Reynolds, the housekeeper at Pemberley, for the sweetness of his temper as a boy. When Mr and Mrs Gardiner, arguably the most sensible characters in the book, suspect Darcy and Elizabeth are in love, it will become "a matter of anxiety to think well" of Darcy. At Lambton, moreover, they "could not be untouched by his politeness": "There was now an interest in believing" the housekeeper's praise of Darcy; their conclusion "that the authority of a servant who had known him since he was four years old . . . was not to be easily rejected" could not be an impartial one (PP, 264)[50]

Furthermore, such relativity is gradually reinforced after both Elizabeth and Darcy have been humbled by their interaction at Rosings. Initially, the narratorial voice has fluctuated between irony and seeming conclusiveness, a partial tendency to monologic pronouncements that appears to be linked to Elizabeth's own dogmatic tendencies.[51] As we have seen, blinded by her attraction to Wickham, and too quick to apply moral precepts in the case of Charlotte's marriage, as though, under patriarchy, the social consequences of gender had no relevance in choosing a course of action, Elizabeth has been misjudging the people around her. She will have to learn, however, that her greatest injustice has been her marked condemnation of Darcy.

Elizabeth's personal development must be placed within this context of relativization of the main characters' aspirations to certitude and impartiality in the process of acquiring knowledge and applying moral principle. An outline of Elizabeth's general process should be helpful as introduction to an analysis of what we shall call her two major uncrownings. Her process can be seen to fall into four parts: In the first volume, Elizabeth makes a series of judgments; in the second, she realizes her mistakes and is therefore humbled at Rosings; in the third she is humbled again by Lydia's elopement; later, her strength carries her through Lady Catherine's attack, her behavior giving hope to Darcy, which leads to a happy resolution. Superimposed on her learning process we find the evolution of her laughter: Her first stage is characterized by ebullient self-assurance. By the end of the first volume, and for part of the second one, it seems that she does not need as much to grow as to overcome the adversities of a very unfair situation. As she grapples with adversity, her problem does not appear to be epistemological but simply moral. Then, at Rosings, Elizabeth will abruptly have to face her mistakes and to revise her approach to knowledge; this phase increases her moroseness. Her trip back home will be equivalent to her crossing a threshold; later, her nearness to Jane will reanimate her. By the end of the second volume, "everything wore a happier aspect" (PP, 238). The prospect of a sightseeing tour appears as a partial release from the limitations of her home and society. Her reunion with Darcy at Pemberley is interrupted by news of Lydia's elopement; her despairing of a renewed relationship with Darcy will not dampen her ability for spirited self-defense when facing Lady Catherine, and she is rewarded by love. In consequence, she not "only smiles"; she laughs (cf. PP, 283).

When seen as an overlay on her learning process, the evolution of her laughter shows Elizabeth as clown/queen. As heroine, she has been crowned and invested in a narrative dignity that is based on her high intelligence and moral character and celebrated by the proximity between her consciousness and the narratorial report, but which is simultaneously undermined by Darcy's snub and her family's folly. Such humblings act as foreshadowing for the episode when Elizabeth comes to realize how deeply she has been mistaken when she has let her attraction toward Wickham and her indignation toward Darcy make her narrow and dogmatic. While she laughed at Darcy's self-importance, she was impervious to his pompous disdain and to the malevolence of the Bingley sisters. At that point, it was Darcy who assumed the position of the Rabelaisian "gloomily serious agelasts," who, strutting majestically, were both unable and unwilling to laugh (RHW, 212). However, as Elizabeth assumes the absolutist attitude of flatly condemning Charlotte, Darcy, even Bingley, thus refusing to admit the limitations of her own judgment, she becomes indignant and dissatisfied. Then, like the carnival king, she has her disguise and mask torn off. The abuse she heaps on herself when her own reflections on Darcy's letter make her realize her mistake becomes her uncrowning, "equivalent to a change of costume, to a metamorphosis" (RHW, 197).

Although the first volume is so mirthful, so replete with the absurdities of Mrs Bennet, Collins, and Sir William Lucas, as it closes Elizabeth's situation seems to be characterized by increasing hardships. Because she has no fortune to inherit, she must be on her guard against falling in love with a very poor man, Wickham, apparently the victim of Darcy's cruelty (although she recognizes that, if she does fall in love, it would probably not "be wisdom to resist" (PP, 145)). Throughout most of the volume Elizabeth's festive spirit has been sustained even in humiliation by the confidence that everything will turn out as it should in the end. By the last chapter in the volume, however, "Even Elizabeth began to fear" (PP, 129); by the first chapter of Volume II, "Hope was over, entirely over" (PP, 133), in the matter of Jane and Bingley at least. With Charlotte married to Collins, Jane unhappy, Wickham unattainable, it begins to seem to Elizabeth that there is little chance of happiness for women in this world. As Jane tells her, Elizabeth is in danger of becoming embittered (PP, 135). Her ability to laugh seems momentarily in peril; for all her love of absurdities, "she had known Sir William's [and, I might add, those of all her neighbors] too long" (PP, 152).

Ironically, Elizabeth will regain her ability to laugh when she learns to recognize her own "follies and inconsistencies," although the lesson is painful. As Bakhtin says, "indignation, anger and dissatisfaction . . . divide, while laughter [what Bakhtin calls "joyful, open, festive laugh," rather than the "closed, purely negative, satirical laugh"] only unites." This "laughing laugh," furthermore, "can be combined with profoundly intimate emotionality (Sterne, Jean Paul and others)."[52] While Elizabeth continues to dwell exclusively on the defects of others, however, she will be unable to laugh. For a while, the only alternative to Elizabeth's dissatisfaction seems to be Jane's forbearance and resignation. We begin by agreeing with Elizabeth against Jane; we will later come to see the flaws in the former's attitude as well. (I might add that the contrast between Elizabeth and Jane helps to make us, as readers, more prone to fall into Elizabeth's errors. Because we have been seeing Elizabeth's judgment as superior, we tend to identify with her and her views. Therefore her uncrowning becomes ours also.)

Of no earthly matter does Elizabeth seem as sure as she is of Darcy's guilt in having made Jane unhappy by separating her and Bingley and in having ruined Wickham's future. When, incensed by Darcy's arrogant manner of proposing to her, Elizabeth throws these accusations in his face, she talks in terms of absolute conviction, saying, "You dare not, you cannot deny . . ." and, "Can you deny that you have done it?" It is not the evidence she possesses (chiefly Colonel Fitzwilliam's revelations) that provides the certainty, however; the source of her assurance seems to be the indignation she feels. Her anger increases when she notices "his smile of affected incredulity" (PP, 191). When he suggests she is only resentful because of his lack of "policy," his sincerity and "abhorrence" of "disguise" in the manner of his proposal, her reply is categorical: it was not "the mode of your declaration," ungentlemanly as it was, that led her to reject him, but the fact that "I had not known you a month before I felt that you were the last man in the world whom I could ever be prevailed on to marry" (PP, 193). It is both ironic and chracteristic of Darcy that he is stung by the insult of not being "gentlemanly" in the style of his proposal more than by her more serious accusation about his "selfish disregard for the feelings of others."

As a result of this confrontation, both Darcy and Elizabeth will change radically. Before this incident, Darcy had admitted only to faults of "temper":

> "I have faults enough, but they are not, I hope, of understanding. My temper I dare not vouch for.--It is I believe too little yielding--certainly too little for the convenience of the world. I cannot forget the follies and vices of others so soon as I ought, nor their offences against myself." (PP, 57)

Before Elizabeth rejects him, Darcy's pride does not allow him to see that his "understanding" of his own worth relative to others' leads him to offend other people himself. This disdain toward his fellow beings is related to his belief that he can know himself and others with such finality as his preceding statements show. Therefore he cannot understand, at the time, how damning is Elizabeth's reply, "you have chosen your fault well.--I really cannot laugh at it" (PP, 58). Luckily for Darcy, however, Elizabeth's angry rejection will shake him; later, her teaching him to be laughed at will in time instruct him in what, according to Bakhtin, clowns teach: "the inadequacy of all available life-slots to fit an authentic human being" (FTCN, 161).

Elizabeth, for her part, will eventually discover that the discernment she prided herself on was influenced by prejudice. Her vanity was wounded by Darcy's slight, and flattered by Wickham's attentions; therefore she has believed what was most in accordance with these feelings. As Elizabeth herself will conclude, "Had I been in love, I could not have been more wretchedly blind. But vanity, not love, has been my folly" (PP, 208). Reason, undoubtedly, greatly helps Elizabeth to accept this humiliating but just discovery (her own words). But what makes her take the first step in accepting Darcy's version of his dealings with Wickham is the realization that what seemed objectively unanswerable can be plausibly argued from a very different viewpoint:

> . . . every line proved more clearly that the affair, which she had believed it impossible that any contrivance could so represent, as to render Mr Darcy's conduct in it less than infamous, was capable of a turn which must make him entirely blameless throughout the whole. (PP, 205)

Once she accepts that a different "turn" in the representation of events is possible, she can contrast the two contradictory accounts, Darcy's and Wickham's, both seemingly coherent. It then becomes necessary to seek external evidence. In Wickham's aid, she can only invoke "the general approbation of the neighbourhood," mostly based on his graceful social manners. In support of Darcy's version, however, she can bring confirmation in the form of what Colonel Fitzwilliam told her only the previous morning. Most importantly, Darcy tells Elizabeth his own family secrets, his sister's aborted decision to elope with Wickham. It is Darcy's trusting her with such potentially humiliating information that clinches the matter for Elizabeth. Indeed, the very fact that he has written to her constitutes evidence that he has changed, that he is no longer inflexible, no longer disdainful of the opinions of others.[53] Undoubtedly, his logical discourse, the force of his arguments and his moral tone, make his story more plausible. But what is most convincing is Darcy's first gesture of recognition of his need of her favorable opinion, his first effort to exert himself to obtain it. Influenced by Darcy's incipient move to reject his own proud self-sufficiency, Elizabeth comes to conclude "she had been blind, partial, prejudiced, absurd" (PP, 208).

This moment, then, represents Elizabeth's most important uncrowning, the disrobing and unmasking that will transform her ("Till this moment," she says, "I never knew myself"-- PP, 208). In consequence of it, we may discern two parallel processes occurring internally in her. First, she will learn to be less authoritative, less monologic in her judgments. Accordingly, she will soon be reading and rereading Darcy's letter, experiencing profoundly how her feelings are relative to the viewpoint she assumes:

She studied every sentence; and her feelings towards its writer were at times widely different. When she remembered the style of his address, she was still full of indignation; but when she considered how unjustly she had condemned and upbraided him, her anger was turned against herself; and his disappointed feelings became the object of compassion. (PP, 212)

Second, she will realize she is liable occasionally to the same failings as "every body." For everyone's views tend to be influenced by his/her needs, wants, wishes; it is this very human limitation that makes people absurd and ludicrous, but it is also inescapable even for those who laugh.

Almost immediately after Elizabeth's crisis of self-revelation, we begin to see its consequences during one of the most carnivalesque chapters in the novel. Jane and Elizabeth, returning home, are joined by Kitty and Lydia "at the appointed inn where Mr Bennet's carriage was to meet them" (PP, 219). This meeting at the inn becomes a "threshold" moment, an encounter that will mark Elizabeth's passage from a position where she tottered on the edge of becoming a "negative satirist," placing herself "above the object of her mockery," to an attitude more expressive of "the point of view of the whole world": she who laughs also "belongs to it" (RHW, 12). Marking the occasion as one of feasting and over-abundance, the younger sisters "triumphantly displayed" a table laden with cold meat and showed their older sisters their many purchases, including a very ugly hat. Lydia's grotesque but "triumphal banquet" is also the occasion for her "free and jocular speech." Indeed, we may apply to her chatter Bakhtin's description of "prandial speech": "The popular-festive right of laughter and clowneries, the right to be frank, was extended to the table" (RHW, 279). Thus, she talks freely about Wickham as "a certain person we all like" in presence of the waiter, and then laughs at Jane and Elizabeth for their "formality and discretion" when they send the waiter away (PP, 220). Lydia's chatter is sprinkled with references to the business of "getting a husband," a process she appears to consider similar to acquiring ribbons, hats or any other commodity. She also narrates a recent prank when she and Mrs Forster dress a servant as a lady for a dance at Colonel Forster's, an episode in which we find such carnivalesque elements as travesty (male as female), mésalliance (the unknowing gentlemen's polite treatment of the disguised servant), and free and familiar contact (servant mingling with the gentlefolk, the ladies' mocking laughter (cf. PDP, 125)). This moment of folly, during which Lydia repeatedly says she could have died of laughter,[54] becomes the framework for Elizabeth's realization that she had once "harboured" views of Wickham's involvement with Mary King that were similar to what Lydia now expresses, though in much coarser fashion. The entire chapter underscores the differences and yet the humbling similarities between Lydia and Elizabeth. Our protagonist must accept that she, like Lydia, like "every body," may be partial and blind in her opinions.

This feast at the inn marks the beginning of Elizabeth's recovery of her laughter, while it celebrates the end of her excessive reliance on the trustworthiness of her own impressions, like a carnivalesque banquet in which "The end must contain a new beginning, just as death leads to a new birth" (RHW, 283). At Hunsford Parsonage, where she had been staying when Darcy proposed to her, and where she read and reread his letter, "the happy spirits which had seldom been depressed before, were now so much affected as to make it almost impossible for her to appear tolerably cheerful" (PP, 213). Once home, Elizabeth can once again confide in Jane, be comforted by her love and laugh good-naturedly at her reaction to the story of Wickham's wrongdoing:

> What a stroke was this for poor Jane! who would willingly have gone through the world without believing that so much wickedness existed in the whole race of mankind, as was here collected in one individual. (PP, 224-5)

Elizabeth can now try to "extort" a smile from Jane, pressing her in jest to "take your choice" of either Darcy or Wickham:

> "There is but such a quantity of merit between them; just enough to make one good sort of man; and of late it has been shifting about pretty much. For my part, I am inclined to believe it all Mr Darcy's, but you shall do as you chuse." (PP, 225)

It is now possible for Elizabeth to mock herself, saying Jane's excess of "regret and compassion" saves her the need to feel either: "if you lament over him much longer, my heart will be light as a feather." She can also allow that she has been vain in her dislike of Darcy, using it as a spur to her genius, "an opening for wit" (PP, 226). The phrase she uses to describe her own vanity, "I meant to be uncommonly clever in taking so decided a dislike to him, without any reason," is significantly similar to the narrator's ironic description, early in the second volume, of the conceit of the Meryton neighbors: "every body was pleased to think how much they had always disliked Mr Darcy before they had known any thing [against him]" (PP, 138). Elizabeth now has a more complex, more dialogical image of herself, for she knows she is, for all her acuity, liable to make the same mistakes in judgment as "every body." Paradoxically, just as she admits her misuse of her wit, her festive humor is restored. This paradox is related to the process of inner debate, Elizabeth's "dialogic relationship to [her] own self," as she has deliberated inwardly about Darcy's letter and her own reaction to it. Her engaging in active dialogue with herself has allowed the destruction of any remaining "naive wholeness" of her self image she may have had (cf. Bakhtin on the dialogism of soliloquies, in PDP, p. 120.)

As Volume II closes, Elizabeth is traveling with the Gardiners, happy even in having "one ceaseless source of regret in my sister's absence," for, she reflects, "A scheme of which every part promises delight, can never be successful; and general disappointment is only warded off by the defence of some little peculiar vexation" (PP, 238).[55] Through a series of incidents, their pleasure trip takes them to Pemberley, Darcy's home and a great and ancient house. There, Elizabeth will encounter a new Darcy, new both because he has changed and because her own transformation allows her to see his positive qualities.

Although Elizabeth has been censuring Darcy for his failure to enter into a spirit of community with others almost from the moment she saw him, she has consistently closed herself to any possibility of communicating with him even when he had tried to approach her. True, his manner was often condescending, but her prejudice blinded her even to his occasional flashes of humility. One evening at Netherfield, for instance, Darcy asks her whether she does not feel like "dancing a reel"; Elizabeth at first remains silent, and, when pressed, tells him she supposes he wants to despise her bad taste if she answers affirmatively: "I have therefore made up my mind to tell you, that I do not want to dance a reel at all--and now despise me if you dare." Darcy's reply, "Indeed I do not dare," astonishes Elizabeth, but does not move her to see him more favorably, partly because Miss Bingley's jealousy and rudeness towards Elizabeth create a further barrier between her and Darcy (PP, 52-3). But now it will become evident that both have benefitted from their painful combat, for they are both now more capable of entering into "new, purely human relations," into a transformed Pemberley. For, as will be shown below, this ancestral home will become a symbol for a special type of partial, utopian community capable of coexisting with conflict.

In spite of the changes both Darcy and Elizabeth have undergone, their mutual and then private, self-inflicted thrashings are not sufficient. Carnivalesque uncrownings are defined as "symbolic actions directed at something on a higher level, at the king" (RHW, 197); "the old world (the old authority and truth)" must die and give birth to the new (RHW, 207). In *Pride and Prejudice*, it is the traditional concept of novelistic love and the ideology of women as passive objects of male desire that must die. When at Pemberley Darcy and Elizabeth meet again, having chastised and thus uncrowned each other, they appear ready to begin a serious courtship, with all the traditional elements. Darcy courteously introduces his sister to Elizabeth; she is impressed by his kind treatment of her relatives, the Gardiners; they are surrounded by the setting of his money and his power. And then Lydia elopes.

This elopement will disrupt the progress of what might have been a conventional courtship, leading to a marriage incribed in the canons of patriarchal decorum. Instead of being feted at Pemberley and flatteringly wooed by a knight who will put his manor at her feet, Elizabeth will leave Pemberley in frightful anxiety after getting news of her sister's "shameful" act. It is this situation that will make Elizabeth aware of her feelings, as she, momentarily romanticizing her own situation, "sighed at the perverseness" of realizing she loves Darcy when apparently the family disgrace will make that love no longer possible (PP, 279). For Darcy's part, instead of showing off his ancestral home and discoursing on its traditions to his lady's relatives, he will leave to seek Wickham, a man he has reason to detest, and to persuade him to marry Lydia —— indeed to buy him for her. In order to marry Elizabeth, therefore, Darcy will have to deal with a rake and use his own money and power to "save" the reputation of her sister, a woman who has shown that her sexual drive is stronger than her "virtue" (cf. PP, 312). Elizabeth will then have to bear his aunt's insults with dignity.

Throughout this string of events, Elizabeth will recurrently appear tempted by novelesque notions of an impossible love for Darcy. Similarly, the whole family indulges in a novelization of Lydia's fate and its familial consequences. Thus, Jane characteristically sacrifices herself for everyone, while Mrs Bennet talks of duels and death, and stays secluded in her room as though she were an invalid, waiting for her meals to be brought to her on a tray. As Mr Bennet remarks, this "parade" gives "elegance to misfortune"; therefore, he ironically promises to "sit in my library, in my night cap and powdering gown, and give as much trouble as I can —— or, perhaps, I may defer it until Kitty runs away" (PP, 299-300). After Lydia comes back as Mrs Wickham, still wild and unrepentant, Elizabeth continues to cast herself as the heroine of a sentimental novel, lamenting that Lydia's marriage must ruin her own chances of happiness, for "it was not to be supposed that Mr Darcy would connect himself with a family, where to every other objection would now be added, an alliance and relationship of the nearest kind with the man whom he so justly scorned" (PP, 311). Finally, when Darcy and Bingley at last appear, ready to carry the two Cinderellas, Elizabeth and Jane, to a life of love and plenty, Elizabeth experiences, rather than the tender flutterings of sentimental fiction, both a very natural suspense and acute embarrassment over Mrs Bennet's vulgarity, her rudeness to Darcy, and her officious attentions to Bingley. The text nevertheless laughs at her "painful confusion," for which "years of happiness could not make Jane or herself amends":

> Yet the misery for which years of happiness were to offer no compensation, received soon afterwards material relief, from observing how much the beauty of her sister re-kindled the admiration of her former lover. (PP, 337)

Darcy, on the other hand, is, as he will later admit, similarly overcome by emotion and embarrassment during this reunion (cf. PP, 381). After both Elizabeth and Jane become engaged to their respective lovers, Elizabeth must still suffer from her entire family's ill-breeding and even Sir William Lucas's romantic absurdities. These ordeals undercut Elizabeth's and Darcy's heroic stature while at the same time debasing novelesque, romantic love and mocking the traditional presentation of the heroine as virginal, frail, all-spirit and only trembling body, and of the hero as a rock of self-sufficient strength.

Lydia's conduct, while becoming the occasion for the protagonists' debasing, will also lead indirectly to Elizabeth's gratitude for Darcy's role in securing her marriage; her thanking him will provide the occasion for Darcy's second proposal. This episode marks the beginning of the novel's happy ending, which confirms the full transformation of both Elizabeth and Darcy. Such a conclusion must be understood within the framework of their future home, Pemberley, where tendencies to utopian equality and fellowship will triumph, and festive, nonofficial truth will win over any narrow, dogmatic, or prejudiced views.

Although critics disagree on the meaning of Pemberley (as indeed they do about almost everything related to *Pride and Prejudice*) there seems to be a consensus among many that Darcy's ancestral home rises above any ordinary mode of existence.[56] Some see its elevation as positive; thus, for Frank Bradbrook, Darcy's home conforms a Gilpinesque "background of romance, sublimity, beauty and delight."[57] For Alistair Duckworth, it represents tradition and the wisdom of ancestors.[58] As Tony Tanner puts it, "Pemberley is an all but impossible dream of a space —— both social and psychic —— large enough to permit a maximum of reflecting speech and personal control."[59] Other critics, however, regard its uncommon qualities in a negative light. For Nina Auerbach, Pemberley seems to be the embodiment of "awesomely institutionalized" male power.[60] Katrin R. Burlin agrees, but she regards Austen's attitudes toward this masculine bastion as ironic. While Pemberley, according to Burlin, bombards Elizabeth "with a series of stunning images, all expansive, lofty, elevating," these "pictures of perfection" are ridiculed by the author: "*Pride and Prejudice* laughs at perfection."[61]

I believe we may make sense of Pemberley as a world "larger than life," accounting for both its beneficent possibilities and the novelist's ironic bent, if we regard it as a triumph of festive, relativistic laughter over negatively satirical skepticism, as well as a victory of irony over romance, if we consider it as carnivalesque utopia. From the moment we first see Pemberley described, the narrator seems to be playing with the image of an "alien miraculous world" that, in Bakhtin's description, characterizes romance (cf. FTCN, 84). Elizabeth comes to Pemberley full of fear of being treated as an interloper, a trespasser; even before any plans of visiting the ancient house are made, the mention of visiting Derbyshire makes Elizabeth feel like a thief: "But surely. . . I may enter his county with impunity, and rob it of a few petrified spars without his perceiving me" (PP, 239). She seems to be afraid of encountering, if not the horrors of a Gothic castle, at least the resentment of a stern aristocrat.

When Elizabeth and the Gardiners reach his home, what they see is definitely picturesque, so that instead of stepping into a Gothic romance, they seem to be about to enter a sentimental idyll:

> They gradually ascended for half a mile, and then found themselves at the top of a considerable eminence, where the wood ceased, and the eye was instantly caught by Pemberley House, situated on the opposite side of a valley, into which a road with some abruptness wound. It was a large, handsome, stone building, standing well on rising ground, and backed by a ridge of high woody hills;--and in front, a stream of some natural importance was swelled into greater, but without any artificial appearance. Its banks were neither formal, nor falsely adorned. Elizabeth was delighted. She had never seen a place for which nature had done more, or where natural beauty had been so little counteracted by an awkward taste. They were all of them warm in their admiration; and at that moment she felt, that to be mistress of Pemberley might be something! (PP, 245)

This place is unparalleled by any other, at least of those Elizabeth has seen. It is reached "with some abruptness"; time, therefore, seems about to be stopped by one of those "sudden" moments of romance "where the normal, pragmatic and premeditated course of events is interrupted" (FTCN, 92). When they reach the house they find themselves in an indoor setting as full of the refined mingling of "art and nature" as the outside; as Katrin Burlin remarks, as the visitors move from window to window the scenery seems to be animated, composing itself into "tableau after tableau."[62] There is only one problem with this near-magic "picture of perfection": as the home of a man who spoke to Elizabeth of "the inferiority of your connections," Pemberley could not have admitted people "in trade" such as the Gardiners in any other capacity than as passing, anonymous travelers. It is this recollection that saves Elizabeth from "something like regret."[63] As mistress of all this romantic grandeur, "my uncle and aunt would have been lost to me: I should not have been allowed to invite them" (PP, 246). These are not just any uncle and aunt to Elizabeth; Mrs Gardiner, especially, has occasionally played the role Elizabeth's mother was so unfit to perform. A place that cannot receive them cannot have any real value for her. Thus, the romantic image of the opulent home the sentimental heroine acquires when she marries loses almost all its charm.

The meaning of Pemberley and of what it "might be" to be its mistress is about to undergo a significant transformation, however. For Mrs Reynolds, the housekeeper, more humble and polite than Elizabeth would have fancied for the job at such a house, speaks of Darcy in glowing terms. He is not just a liberal, kind master and landlord, "affable to the poor"; as a child, he was never cross, but rather "the sweetest-tempered, most generous-hearted boy in the world" (PP, 249). This view may not be completely coherent with Darcy's own self-appraisal, for he will later recognize his debt to Elizabeth for his transformation and confess, "I have been a selfish being all my life, in practice, though not in principle. As a child I was taught what was *right*, but I was not taught to correct my temper" (PP, 369). But Mrs Reynolds' praise is not aimed at providing *the* correct, incontrovertible judgment on Darcy. Rather, it fulfills two functions: First, it shows that Darcy can establish relationships of esteem and affection with those under his power. Second, it turns this power upside down by showing Pemberley from the viewpoint of a servant, provoking Elizabeth's thought, in free indirect style, that servants' opinions (though presumably no more prone to be absolutely certain than anybody else's) can be both important and intelligent: "What praise is more valuable than the praise of an intelligent servant?" (PP, 250). Darcy's power, then, is regarded from the vantage point of the common people, of those who will benefit or suffer from his doing "good or evil" (PP, 251), and who reserve the right to judge him for it, to "give him a good name"-- or a bad one if he earns it, it is implied (PP, 249).

This perspective on Pemberley is totally new in the novel. When we first hear of Darcy's home it appears as the "noble place" coveted by Miss Bingley. (Bingley, to his sister's horror, seems to degrade Pemberley by suggesting he would buy it if Darcy would sell it, when the sycohphantic Miss Bingley suggests Bingley should use it as a model for his own home. Such a sale is not a possibility, says she, implying that tradition and high birth cannot be bought--and unwittingly casting aspersions on herself, whose family was once in trade.) It is simultaneously shown as a source of vanity for Darcy, for it is "the work of many generations" (PP, 38). As such it will continue to be seen by Lady Catherine, who considers it so superior an emblem of high birth as to be "polluted" if Elizabeth marries Darcy (cf. PP, 357). However, if Pemberley's lineage is impeccable, from the viewpoint of what sort of "community," of relationships among people, Pemberley has promoted, we cannot consider its past in a favorable light. There it was that little Darcy was taught "to think meanly" of everyone outside his family circle, while hypocritical little Wickham won the love of his father's master (a kind but unwise old man, it would seem) through fraudulent means (PP, 200). At Pemberley Georgiana, Darcy's sister, seems to have been the victim of her family's conceptions of accomplished women, perhaps "the product of too much formal training on her stately brother's part."[64] Indeed, she is awkwardly, painfully shy before strangers (PP, 261), and in awe of her brother (PP, 388). Finally, at Pemberley even Bingley has felt Darcy to be a little too imposing, since he jokingly calls Darcy "an aweful object . . . , at his own house especially, and of a Sunday evening when he has nothing to do" (PP, 50-51).

Nevertheless, as Darcy changes, so does the meaning and significance of his home in the novel. This change, as we have seen, is evident to Elizabeth at Pemberley for the first time. And almost its first manifestation is his attitude to the Gardiners, whom he initially takes "for people of fashion." When he finds they are precisely those people whose relation to Elizabeth had once made him regret admiring her he is surprised, but he is now capable of judging Mr Gardiner for "his intelligence, his taste. . ., his good manners," rather than his blood line or his involvement in commerce (PP, 255). After Darcy and Elizabeth get married, the Gardiners continue to be their frequent visitors, and the four remain "on the most intimate terms. Darcy, as well as Elizabeth, really loved them" (PP, 388). In showing love and "warmest gratitude" toward the Gardiners, in becoming their intimate friends, Darcy is adopting Elizabeth's standards and placing personal merits before social class. The old Pemberley, then, is not imposing its own traditional structure on the lives of the Darcys before accepting Elizabeth as its mistress. On the contrary, the "purely human relations" typical of festive utopia win over rank and hierarchy as the basis for interpersonal relationships, and a new Pemberley is born. The death and rebirth of Permberley do not produce, it is true, a grotesque collective feast, but a sort of Platonic aristocracy, a redefinition of superiority and elegance, no longer based on social class or origin, but on personal merit. And yet the greatest joy this world has to offer is precisely heightened fellowship among those capable of communing with others.

In accordance with the birth of a new order, Elizabeth's visit to Pemberley becomes associated to abundant food (PP, 268), a triumphal banquet representing the victory of life over death (cf. RHW, 283). Nina Auerbach has pointed out the profusion of food at Pemberley, and the fact that this abundance carries over to Longbourn later on, when Bingley and Darcy come to dinner (cf. PP, 342). Indeed, the unprecedentedly "fat haunch" of venison, "roasted to a turn," the soup, the partridges, everything Mrs Bennet serves on that occasion, appears much more luxuriant, more detailed than any previous Longbourn or Netherfield dinner. But this change need not be due, as Auerbach holds, merely to the presence of the two suitors, signifying that "men can bring what seems a cornucopian abundance to the scanty Bennet dinner table."[65] Rather, the "beautiful pyramids of grapes, nectarines, and peaches" that make guests gather around the table at Pemberley, like the success of Mrs Bennet's dinner party, can be seen within the context of the festive atmosphere of the last volume, which is fast turning into a carnivalesque banquet.

As we have seen, after Elizabeth returns from Pemberley she faces many discomforts and "mortifications"; many of these contribute to take "from the season of courtship much of its pleasure," but they add "to the hope of the future" (PP, 384). The "family party" that will assemble at Pemberley in the narrator's words in the final chapter becomes a metaphor for the resolution of relationships, which paints a picture of utopian happiness. It is, however, a mode of happiness that contains no romanticization, no "alien miraculous world" capable of supplying what was wanting in unworthy characters, nor even capable of hardening those too soft at heart. In spite of the hero's and the heroine's improvement, many deficiencies remain. Thus, for instance, in a direct address to the reader the narrator informs us that Mrs Bennet will continue to be as vapid and ridiculous as ever:

> I wish I could say, for the sake of [Mrs Bennet's] family, that the accomplishment of her earnest desire in the establishment of so many of her children, produced so happy an effect as to make her a sensible, amiable, well-informed woman for the rest of her life; though perhaps it was lucky for her husband, who might not have relished domestic felicity in so unusual a form, that she was still occasionally nervous and invariably silly. (PP, 385)

Nor will the Wickhams be reformed; rather, they will continue to be impudent and selfish. Lydia's letter to Elizabeth on her marriage, purportedly aimed at wishing the latter joy, shows the former's attempts to cash in on her new relationship to Darcy in order to obtain "a place at court" for Wickham. That Lydia fully realizes the shamelessness of such a request after Wickham's treatment of Darcy is clear from her closing line, "however, do not speak to Mr Darcy about it, if you had rather not" (PP, 386). Of course, Elizabeth "had much rather not," but on occasion she will send some money to these impecunious, improvident relatives. The Wickhams' real penance, so notoriously absent after their wrongdoings, will lie simply in their fault itself: their being unable to experience any real love ("His affection for her soon sunk into indifference; hers lasted a little longer" (PP, 387)). Nevertheless, Lydia does not fulfill stern moralists' expectations, for she does not become adulterous.

Other characters similarly retain their failings. If marriage does not reform the Wickhams, it cannot harden the Bingleys, who will be still too mild, too kindhearted, and therefore easy game for the freeloading Wickhams. Miss Bingley will still be mercenary and hypocritical, while the rift with supercilious Lady Catherine will be patched up, but only so that she may ascertain "that pollution which [Pemberley's] woods had received from the presence of such a mistress" and from the Gardiners' frequent visits (PP, 388).

By contrast to the world of hollow social conventions symbolized by the Miss Bingleys and Lady Catherines of the world, however, at Pemberley a new community has arisen, a novel world of love and equality. This universe provides a good environment for women, for we find fretful Kitty mended, Georgiana Darcy become a new younger sister and profitting from Elizabeth's instructions, and Elizabeth freely laughing, while Darcy, who during courtship "had yet to learn to be laught at" (PP, 371), can now become "the object of open pleasantry" without losing his dignity (PP, 388). At Pemberley, with the Gardiners warmly loved and the Bingleys and the Darcys intimate and close neighbors, all the worthy characters enjoy their ability to commune with each other. Even Mr Bennet becomes a bit more sociable, since he "delighted in going to Pemberley, especially when he was least expected" (PP, 385). If happy endings are wish-fulfillment, then the wishes of the author of *Pride and Prejudice* may have included a good, nurturing environment for women, greater equality between males and females, the power of material abundance, and the joys of fellowship and love among people who choose community over the divisions created by traditional hierarchies of rank and status.

There are two worlds depicted in the novel's resolution: the official one of conventions and hierarchies, where human relationships are governed by a crass commercialism, and the extraofficial one of "new and purely human relations," the joyful world of the new Pemberley's carnivalesque utopia. The two are deeply opposed, and yet they are forced to coexist, even to mesh. In a sense, the generalized war with which the novel began has now sharpened as two well-defined camps have arisen. But the gay relativity that the whole process suffered by Elizabeth has so skillfully argued cannot be overruled. After all, Elizabeth has been the clown who had to be taught the same lessons her bantering meant for others. When she resumes her clowning, she remains a woman temperamentally suited for joyful self-assurance, but she is wiser now. And her wisdom has taken the form of a new readiness to remember how self shapes perception, how knowledge that appears objective is actually relative to personal circumstances.

Therefore, people in utopia must still not only be in conflict with the inimical world outside, but also with themselves, and with each other. Paraphrasing Elizabeth's reflections about Darcy's inevitable "triumph" had he known that she now loved him (PP, 311-2), we may say that while these characters are mortal, there must be war. Utopia, by definition a place which is not, seems to create a closing, but the merry war of ludicrous pride and prejudice, and thus the festive, ambivalent laughter at the inevitable partial blindness of mortals, must go on.

Just as the novel never allows one to escape into some realm protected from conflict and war, its scepticism also may extend to its own dialogic tendencies. For in spite of her mask of equalizing, self-deprecating clowning, Elizabeth will tend to adopt the same monologism she detests in Darcy. The arrogance typical of some males in patriarchy may infect the women who refuse to bow down, the novel seems to say. Both men and women may at some point need to learn to laugh (Darcy) or to recover laughter (Elizabeth). But even when these processes have already occurred, *Pride and Prejudice* does not allow its readers to rest assured in the security that they can be permanent. Rather, parallel to the utopian ebullience that promises that everything will be righted in this fictional world, in the conclusion we find the early premise of imperfection and impermanence still intact. From the beginning Elizabeth was aware of how much "people themselves alter" (PP, 43), and nothing in the resolution really undermines this early premise. By its very nature, utopia simply overleaps flaws and deficiencies without cancelling the problematic nature of the novel's fictional reality. In the end, in spite of the whole joyous turn of the conclusion, the initial ironies directed against those searching after universal truths are allowed to stand; but now one knows enough about the narrator's tendency to generalized suspicion to wonder whether she may not also suspect herself of a nostalgia for such truths.

NOTES

1. Brown, *Jane Austen's Novels,* p. 67.

2. F. Anne Payne, *Chaucer and Menippean Satire* (Madison, Wisconsin: The University of Wisconsin Press, 1981), p. 208.

3. It is ironic that Collins, who professes to despise novels, behaves like the caricature of a romantic hero when he proposes to Elizabeth, spouting conventions regarding courtship, proposals and "elegant females" one may find in sentimental novels.

4. Cf. Mary Russo, "Female Grotesques," in *Feminist Studies/Critical Studies.*

5. Nina Auerbach sees "Mrs Bennet's reign" as testimony to the idea that in Austen's novels "female power is effectively synonymous with power abused" ("Austen and Alcott on Matriarchy," in *Towards a Poetics of Fiction,* p. 274). Actually, Mrs Bennet's position as homemaker can hardly be seen as a position of power, for she is completely dependent on her husband's whims. Also, the novel provides a strong maternal figure in Mrs Gardiner, who, after all, is remarkable enough to warn Elizabeth against falling in love without causing offence, in "a wonderful instance of advice being given on such a point, without being resented" (pp. 144-5).

6. Compare Mrs Bennet, for instance, to the wife in Goldsmith's *The Vicar of Wakefield,* where the protagonist is forced to correct his wife and daughters when they dress in absurd finery to attend the village church; the females are fully submissive to the superior wisdom of their father and husband.

7. For an excellent historical survey of such concepts of women in English literature, see Sandra Gilbert and Susan Gubar, *The Madwoman in the Attic,* Chapter I.

8. Susan Gubar, "The Female Monster in Augustan Satire," *Signs,* 3 (Winter 1977), p. 393.

9. B. C. Southam, "Introduction," *Jane Austen: The Critical Heritage,* ed. B. C. Southam (London: Routledge and Kegan Paul, 1968), pp. 9-10.

10. The episode in which Elizabeth Bennet first appears (a Meryton assembly at which Darcy tells Bingley Elizabeth is "not handsome enough to tempt" him to dance), for instance, bears a dialogic contrast to a scene in *Evelina* in which the title character also overhears two men making comments about her at a ball (*Evelina*, p. 89). For a perceptive, yet rather traditionalistic discussion of Elizabeth Bennet as an "anti-Evelina," see Kenneth Moler, *Jane Austen's Art of Allusion*, pp. 97-101.

11. Marian E. Fowler, "The Feminist Bias of *Pride and Prejudice*," *Dalhousie Review*, 57 (1977), p. 56.

12. For a cogent view of the similarities between views held by contemporary feminists such as Mary Wollstonecraft, Priscilla Wakefield, and Catherine Graham, and many of the positions and attitudes of Elizabeth Bennet, see Marian E. Fowler, "The Feminist Bias of *Pride and Prejudice*."

13. Cf. Bakhtin's discussion of Goethe's description of Roman carnival (RHW, 248).

14. For a discussion of *Pride and Prejudice* as the story of the humbling of a "patrician hero" in the Richardson-Burney tradition, with a concomittant "partial reformation" of the heroine as an "anti-Evelina," see Kenneth Moler, *Jane Austen's Art of Allusion*, pp. 75-108.

15. Actually, it is not Darcy's intention to show contempt for her, but Elizabeth is too prejudiced against him to admit that he admires her.

16. Bakhtin's phrase to describe the speech of clowns (DN, 405).

17. It is such a type of communication that Roman Jakobson calls "phatic," recognizing its important social function in keeping the channels among interlocutors open. (Cf. "Linguistics and Poetics," in *Language and Literature*, ed. Krystina Pomorska and Stephen Rudi (Cambridge, Mass.: Belknap Press, 1987), pp. 62-94; first published in *Style in Language*, ed. T. A. Sebeok (Cambridge, Mass.: MIT Press, 1961), pp. 350-77).

18. The importance of this question for the interpretation of the novel has long been recognized, though different critics have used different names for what I am referring to as "person" and "community." Samuel Kliger (see "Jane Austen's *Pride and Prejudice* in the Eighteenth Century Mode," in *Pride and Prejudice*, Norton Critical Edition, ed. Donald Gray (New York: W. W. Norton & Co., 1966), pp. 352-61) refers to the "art-nature" dichotomy, a terminology partially adopted by Kenneth Moler (cf. *Jane*

Austen's Art of Allusion, p. 104). Dorothy Van Ghent places the question in the context of the reconciliation of sensitive individuals with the terms of social existence (Cf. "On *Pride and Prejudice*," in *Pride and Prejudice*, Norton Critical Edition, p. 362.) Marvin Mudrick refers to the social pressures that tend to limit the individual's freedom of choice ("Irony as Discrimination," p. 95). Alistair Duckworth concludes that the novel balances the claims of self and society (*The Improvement of the Estate*, p. 142). Julia Prewitt Brown asserts that Jane Austen was concerned in *Pride and Prejudice* with the need for social rituals and moral edicts, though she recognizes that the elevation of the moral intelligence of the society largely depends on the malleability of individual beings (*Jane Austen's Novels*, p. 78). Finally, Mary Poovey states that in *Pride and Prejudice* "marriage remains for Austen the ideal paradigm of the most perfect fusion between the individual and society" (*The Proper Lady and the Woman Writer* (Chicago: Univerity of Chicago Press, 1984), p. 203).

19. Marvin Mudrick, "Irony as Discrimination," p. 96.

20. See Alistair Duckworth, *Improvement of the Estate*, p. 142.

21. See Kenneth Moler, *Jane Austen's Art of Allusion*, p. 104.

22. See Julia Prewitt Brown, *Jane Austen's Novels*, pp. 75-78.

23. Claudia Johnson, *Jane Austen: Women, Politics and the Novel*, p. 77.

24. Mikhail Bakhtin, "Epic and the Novel," *Dialogic Imagination*, p. 39.

25. Bakhtin, "From the Prehistory of Novelistic Discourse," *Dialogic Imagination*, p. 47.

26. Mary Poovey, *The Proper Lady and the Woman Writer*, p. 194.

27. I am using this term in the Bakhtinian sense of "an utterance that belongs, by its grammatical (syntactic) and compositional markers, to a single speaker, but that actually contains mixed within it two utterances, two speech manners, two styles, two 'languages,' two semantic and axiological belief systems" (DN, 304).

28. This presence of a collective voice is, according to Bakhtin, "especially characteristic of comic style in which someone else's speech is dominant." Bakhtin extensively uses Dickens' *Little Dorrit* to provide examples of this hybrid construction in which "current opinion" mingles with

"authorial speech." It is interesting to note in these examples the incidence of the words "everybody" and "nobody," which appear in Austen as markers of the collective voice (see Bakhtin, DN, 302-8).

29. It is this aspect of Darcy's character that is stressed by some critics; for instance, Alistair Duckworth presents him as a defender of "the norms by which men have lived for generations" and which "are in danger of neglect and destruction" (see *The Improvement of the Estate*, pp. 127-131.)

30. As it has been repeatedly said, Mr Bennet's retreat from parental responsability into cynical solipsism is one of the ways in which the novel makes a statement regarding everyone's social duties and accountability. See Julia Prewitt Brown on Mr Bennet's "spiritual lassitude" (*Jane Austen's Novels*, p. 75); also Alistair Duckworth on Mr. Bennet's "chosen freedom from social commitment" (*The Improvement of the Estate*, p. 128)). Even Marvin Mudrick, though blaming Mr Bennet's cynicism partly on the tyranny of social that make divorce impossible, refers to this character's self-enclosure in "his own irrevocable folly" ("Irony as Discrimination," p. 88).

31. This typical Austenian emphasis on the importance of strong allegiance to a community should not be misunderstood as identical to the idealization of country life that was a commonplace in eighteenth-century literature. As Frank Bradbrook observes, Austen shows a more balanced view of the relative merits of London and country life than Goldsmith or Cowper. Thus, while a snob like Miss Bingley, scorns the country, talking of Elizabeth's "country town indifference to decorum," an ignoramus like Mrs Bennet believes London has no other advantage over the country than the shops and public places. A more sensible position is that shown by Bingley who sees that country and capital each have their advantages (although he ends, like most of Austen's sensible characters, "by marrying and settling in the country"- Cf. Frank Bradbrook, *Jane Austen and Her Predecessors* (Cambridge: Cambridge University Press, 1966), pp. 39-41).

32. These two passages have been interpreted as individualistic acts of *linguistic* boldness and unconventionality on the part of Elizabeth, for she uses word that can elsewhere carry the stigma of ignorance or vulgarity (Norman Page, *The Language of Jane Austen* (Oxford: Basil Blackwell, 1972), p. 29). I think she is undeniably bold in braving such a stigma, but it must not be forgotten that she is doing so by employing, precisely, unpretentious, *conventional* languaje, and on occasions when she is in the presence of dignified impertinence and pride that would scorn such language as common.

33. See V.N. Volosinov, *Marxism and the Philosophy of Language* (Cambridge, Mass: Harvard University Press, 1986), p. 34.

34. I am using the term in the sense of a speech act as defined py John Searle: an illocution by which we commit ourselves to doing things (cf. "A Taxonomy of Speech Acts." in *Expression and Meaning* (Cambridge: Cambridge University Press, 1976), p. 29).

35. V.S. Pritchett sees a resemblance between that visit and a naval battle: notice there how the positions of the people in the drawing room are made certain, where Elizabeth like a frigate has to run between the lines. Pritchett, furthermore, thinks of Austen as a war-novelist, formed by the Napoleonic wars, knowing directly of prize money, the shortage of men, the economic crisis and changes in the value of capital (*George Meredith and English Comedy* (New York: Random House, 1969), p. 28.

36. Critics have found in this passage echoes of the confrontation between Burney's Cecilia and Mrs Delvile (cf. Q.D. Leavis, p. 71) while others have recognized Austen's debts to Burney and the differences between the two (cf. for instance, Frank Bradbrook, *Jane Austen and her Predecessors*, p. 98). Other critics have pointed out similarities between this episode and the clash between Richardson's Pamela and Lady Davers (cf. Jocelyn Harris, *Jane Austen's Art of Memory* (Cambridge: Cambridge University Press, 1989), p. 41). One may also trace in the dialogue between Lady Catherine and Elizabeth strong influences of the interview between Charlotte Smith's Emmeline and Lady Montreville. The latter's description as accustomed to undisputed power in her own family and as expecting from everybody an acquiescence as blind as she got from her tradesmen and servants could be applied to Lady Catherine, who, following Austen's customary style, is shown acting in this manner rather than described as such. The lady's insults, threats and boasts and her insistence ("I will hear no objection") are very similar to Lady Catherine's; Emmeline's reply, when Lady Montreville accuses her of lying to conceal her knowledge of Delamere's whereabouts ("If, however, I did know, it is not such treatment, Madam, that should compel me to give any information") could be a predecessor of Elizabeth's response to Lady Catherine's impertinent questions: "But you are not entitled to know [my concerns]; nor will such behavior as this ever induce me to be explicit." Finally, in both meetings it is the young lady who cuts the dialogue when she feels insulted (cf. PP, 352-8, and *Emmeline*, Vol. II Ch. ii, pp. 132-5). Elizabeth, however, never trembles or feels hardly able to stand, as Emmeline does at the beginning.

37. As Claudia Johnson observes, in keeping with the liberal tradition of moral philosophy to which *Pride and Prejudice* is affiliated, happiness is something many of the characters feel they have a basic right to. Indeed, in all of Austen's novels, but especially in *Pride and Prejudice*, pursuing happiness is the business of life (Claudia Johnson, *Jane Austen*, pp. 81, 80).

38. Claudia Johnson, *Jane Austen*, p. 73.

39. It is significant that, when Mr Bennet is criticized for his neglect of parental duties, it is not done as censure of his abdication of authority, but in terms of his breach of conjugal obligation in continually ridiculing his wife in front of his daughters (PP. 236).

40. Susan Morgan, *In the Meantime: Character and Perception in Jane Austen's Fiction* (Chicago: University of Chicago Press, 1980, p. 78).

41. Andrew H. Wright, "Heroines, Heroes and Villains in *Pride and Prejudice*," in *Twentieth-Century Interpretations of Pride and Prejudice*, ed. E. Rubinstein (Englewood Cliffs, N.J.: Prentice-Hall, 1969), pp. 97-8.

42. M.M. Bakhtin, "From Notes Made in 1970-1," in *Speech Genres*, pp. 132-5.

43. Lloyd W. Brown, *Bits of Ivory*, p. 121-3.

44. In spite of its seeming ahistoricity, the first person plural in generalizatios, with its presumption of universal equality, may be justified when the topic is the relativity of perceptions and judgments. Our perceptions are all influenced by our personal situations; one's gender, class, generation, nationality, political allegiances, etc., color one's lenses and are refracted through one's speech, but no one can escape the influence of these multiple determinations, in one form or another. On the other hand, no one can escape the force of "centripetal," homogenizing forces either.

45. Ivor Morris, *Mr Collins Considered* (London: Routledge and Kegan Paul, 1987, p. 5)

46. The implication, of course, is that Jane **had** been assailed by attentions from Miss Bingley. Again, we see that even the friendly attentions a person may receive from new acquaintances can be described in military terms as an" assailing." This realization leads us to even greater awareness of the pervading presence of war in the novel's universe.

47. Julia Prewitt Brown, *Jane Austen's Novels*, pp. 65-7.

48. It is significant that the narrator is proposing that Elizabeth's clarity of perception may be compromised by her esteem for Wickham, and thus *apparently* recommending the strict application of a moral position, which should be used to judge both Charlotte and Wickham with the same severity; and yet she recognizes her own fallibility by the use of a probabilistic word such as "perhaps."

49. It seems important to point out that this ironic surmise on the part of the narrator comes after Darcy has changed, showing himself in the best possible light as polite host to Elizabeth and the Gardiners. Darcy is being regarded favorably at this point in the action. The fact that his plans have influenced his perceptions and beliefs is not presented as an aspersion on his character, but as further proof of a generalized condition of humanity.

50. Trying to arrive at a definitive, impartial conclusion about Darcy's merit on the basis of the text's constant relativization has led some critics astray. Nina Auerbach, for instance, concludes that "Darcy's [childhood] is a muddled contradiction." Auerbach contrasts Mrs Reynold's portrait of Darcy as a sweet-tempered child (pp. 248-9) and Darcy's own representation of himself as "selfish and overbearing," "caring for none one outside my family circle" (PP, 369), and finds them irreconcilable (cf. "Austen and Alcott on Matriarchy," in *Towards a Poetic or Fiction*, p. 276). What Auerbach fails to take into consideration is the fact that Mrs Reynolds was part of the circle of intimates to whom Darcy showed deference, and that she was undoubtedly also partly influenced by the fact that heavis a liberal master; as Mrs Gardiner hints, such a virtue has great weight in the feelings of a servant (p. 258). In the end, no appraisal of Darcy, or of anyone else in the novel, is absolutely trustworthy.

51. Bakhtin has given the name of "character zone" to this coloring of narratorial pronouncements by the style of a character appearing in a passage (cf. DN. 316).

52. M.M. Bakhtin, "From Notes Made in 1970-1," in *Speech Genres*, p. 135.

53. Samuel Kliger has pointed out that Darcy's refusal to clear himself publicly of Wickham's charges shows Darcy's adherence to the fundamental principle of *noblesse oblige* which is never to complain, never to explain. ("Jane Austen's *Pride and Prejudice*, in the Eighteenth Century Mode," in *Pride and Prejudice*, Norton Critical Edition, p. 360). What

this critic does not remark is that, by the same principle, Darcy's long letter explaining his actions shows a turn away from such a lofty sense of pride.

54. Death from laughter is one of the forms of gay death, one of the typical images of carnival, according to Bakhtin (RHW, 408).

55. This passage exhibits a marvelous irony, for it shows how human beings will seek certainty even from such an unlikely source as frustration. Elizabeth has just learned her own fallibility, but she would belie her human condition if she did not strive for some assurance of the happy completion of her plans in the future, interpreting vexation as an offering to the gods, thus reassuring herself thatevery thing else will march smoothly.

56. Among notable exceptions to this view we find Walter Scott's. This novelist, in an unsigned review of *Emma* published in *Quarterly Review* provides the following famous comment: "[Elizabeth] does not perceive that she has done a foolish thing [in refusing Darcys hand] until she accidentally visits a very handsome seat and grounds belonging to her admirer." (Jane Austen: *The Critical Heritage*, p. 65). From this perspective (if it is serious), Pemberley appears as a symbol of merely monetary and social advancement, and Elizabeth, more than prudent, seems mercenary.

57. Frank Braddbrook, *Jane Austen and her Predecessors*, p. 59.

58. Cf. Alistair Duckvorth, *The Improvement of Estate*, p. 129.

59. Tony Tanner, p. 128.

60. Nina Auerbach, p. 275.

61. Katrin R. Burlin, "Pictures of Perfection at Pemberley," in *Jane Austen: New Perspectives*, p. 155.

62. Katrin Burlin, p. 156.

63. It is characteristic of this novel that the "lucky recollection" does not act itself magically, as if a spell were broken. Rather, the phrase "This was a lucky recollection- it saved her from something like regret" has a certain ironic flavor: the regret is not completely dispelled. This irony works as a foreshadowing hint, looking forward to Elizabeth's falling in love, and it also gives testimony of the heady power of romantic notions, never totally dissipated even when prosaic reality asserts itself.

64. Katrin R. Burlin, p. 164.

65. Nina Auerbach, p. 271.

Chapter 5
"Emma": Gender, Class and Carnivalesque Discourse

Of the three novels included in the present study, *Emma* is the one begun when Austen was older;[1] it was finished only two years before her death.[2] The presence of carnivalesque elements in it would therefore indicate that carnival was not merely a youthful tendency in Austen, or one which she gradually abandoned as she matured. Indeed, carnival is a powerful ingredient in this novel, and it appears bound up with a profound dialogism. In *Emma* we find a kaleidoscopic array of voices; even more than in other works by Austen, analysis of the narratorial discourse reveals how the narrator's voice combines with the protagonist's and that of other characters in an intricate overlaying of styles and ideologies.

The situation in *Emma*, moreover, is more complex than in any other of Austen's novels, and the heroine is more frequently mistaken and more responsible for the problems she encounters than Elizabeth Bennet or Catherine Morland is for the ones each has to face. Emma Woodhouse's faults and errors cannot be attributed solely to the clowning role she plays in the novel. But if Emma is more personally reprehensible than the hero, Mr Knightley, his shortcomings are more significant, for they show the prejudice, blindness and inflexibility that affect even the most benevolent of patriarchs. The complexity of the moral universe in *Emma* involves the novel in a succession of qualifications and counter-qualifications of ideological positions;

the result is a many-layered irony and a greater ambivalence than can be found in Austen's preceding works.

Part of this complexity is based on the contrast between the heroine's subordinate social position by reason of gender and her prominence as one of Highbury's highest-ranking citizens in terms of social class. While Elizabeth Bennet must hold her own against social forces at play in country villages, forces inimical to single young women in possession of very little fortune, and Catherine Morland must contend, in addition, with the generalized contempt directed against very young and inexperienced females, Emma Woodhouse is placed in a position of privilege at the center of her social world. From the viewpoint of Bakhtinian carnival, Emma's presiding at her home, Hartfield, is one of the conditions making it a world-upside-down with strong matriarchal tendencies. If in *Northanger Abbey* the ending is the most utopian of all of Austen's novels, and in *Pride and Prejudice* utopia begins with Elizabeth's visit to Pemberley, in *Emma* the story begins with the protagonist's partial loss of the nearly utopian situation she has enjoyed for years. Emma, let us remember, "seemed to unite some of the best blessings of existence"; as the novel opens we are told "she had lived nearly twenty-one years in the world with very little to distress or vex her." Although Austen mentions "the evils of Emma's situation," these are the disadvantages of a highly privileged person: "the power of having rather too much her own way, and a disposition to think a little too well of herself" (E, 5). The novel ends ambivalently, in what may be seen as either a further loss or a recovery of her former ideal situation.

In other Austen's novels, carnival is found mainly in the functions played by the characters as clowns or fools, in certain twists of their interactions and their development, in parody, in the gay ambivalence between laughter at the absurdities of social intercourse, on the one hand, and a sense of agape and community, on the other. Although these ingredients are indeed present in *Emma*, its deepest carnivalesque ironies are found in the speech and thought of the characters and in the narratorial discourse itself. The novel excels its predecessors in the originality of its narrator's voice, a voice at once sophisticated and eccentric, sharply astute in its mockery underneath its apparent restraint. Even more unique, indeed extraordinary, is the way in which this voice mingles and alternates with the protagonist's style and perspective, engaging in carnivalesque dialogue with her (and more briefly with a few major characters). In addition, the narrative discourse leads the reader in a process of deep identification with a character whose attitudes and actions are simultaneously, although indirectly, being disparaged. This extended and often paradoxical interaction among narrator, characters and reader may lead us on a path of amused discovery of the complexities of the speaking subject, of how often there are several different and even opposed perspectives at work in an utterance, of the wisdom of skepticism regarding many moral and intellectual certainties.

By means of the peculiarities of this dialogue, the novel's narrative style, even more than that of any other of Austen's works, often resonates with some of the most basic characteristics of carnival laughter (cf. RHW, 10-12). Indeed, the novel's ideological stance is "popular" in the sense that it sides with a dominated group, women, for *Emma,* unlike the vast majority of novels from the same period, allows itself to be interpreted in many respects as feminist. Its laughter is universal in the sense that every one is included, since all characters, from the naive Harriet Smith to the strong and sensible Mr Knightley, are laughed at by turns. It is self-directed, for the narrator fuses her voice with Emma's and then laughs at her. It is charged with philosophic tensions, calling for the reader's reflections about human consciousness and dialogue itself.

It must be admitted that, mixed with these elements, there are some ingredients of the novel's style that seem very far from carnival. One of these is the tendency to litotes, to the subtle, light touch of understatement. This tendency, stronger perhaps than in the other two works, is evident in such delicate (yet ultimately demolishing) appraisals of the characters as the narrator's stating about the simpleminded Mr Woodhouse that "his talents could not have recommended him" (E, 7), or the observation that "though [the first Mrs Weston] had one sort of spirit, she had not the best," said of Mr Weston's ill-natured, demanding first wife. Or the remark, when Miss Bates attributes her own keen interest in Mr Elton's affairs to Jane, that "Jane's curiosity did not appear of that absorbing nature as wholly to occupy her" (E, 174).

Furthermore, there are aspects of Emma's initial and final situations that Bakhtinian categories do not seem to fit. From the perspective of both class and gender, the ideological world in *Emma* exhibits a tendency to inertia that Bakhtin recognizes as part of social language, but which he does not discuss in any detail.[3] Foucauldian categories are needed in order to analyze the discourse of Emma's conservative social and political role in managing Hartfield, her clash with the *petite bourgeoise* housewives who labor "toward the acquisition of social and political status,"[4] and her interacting with servants and the indigent. And yet, in a certain sense, the social power invested in her, which she upholds even while resisting some of its implications, is inimical to her independence and self-determination. Indeed, her position in the world defines her as one who can possess power only in a domestic context. In the end, Emma will willingly enter into a marital relationship more egalitarian than most, but framed by a social context severely limiting for women. The special circumstances surrounding her marriage, however, will once again be related to carnivalesque elements that allow the conclusion to be interpreted as a cunning utopian move against male dominance. In general, *Emma*'s laughing spirit contains elements that can only be explained by recurring to carnivalesque categories.

As the novel opens, Emma Woodhouse, twenty years old, is undergoing a crisis typical of middle-age: she has been busy managing her household for years, but now her last dependent, Miss Taylor (actually her governess), is married and gone. Emma is left with only the male head of the household for company, but he composes himself "to sleep after dinner," and Emma has then "only to sit and think of what she had lost" (E, 6). Our heroine suffers from what today's women's magazines call "empty-nest syndrome" before she even contemplates marriage.

This situation is one of the ways in which Emma's home, Hartfield, constitutes a "world-upside-down" similar to that found in carnivalesque broadsheets. In Hartfield, Emma is responsible for the welfare of the household; she has been "mistress of the house and of you all" since she was twelve (E, 37). As Emma herself observes, "few married women are half as much mistress of their husband's house as I am of Hartfield" (E, 84). Her father, "a valetudinarian all his life" (E, 7), acts rather like the stereotype of a phobic old woman. Instead of commanding and protecting his home and his children, as one would expect of a patriarch, he constantly needs to be humored, handled, comforted. At Hartfield, then, conventional images are reversed: male becomes female, a child rules for years over adults, the father obeys the daughter. Furthermore, Mr Woodhouse, rather than seek to "establish" his daughters, as other parents do, was sadly grieved when his eldest daughter, Isabella, married; even now, nine years later, he has not become reconciled to her marriage (E, 8). He hates marriage in general and becomes depressed "by the idea of his daughter's attachment to her husband" (E, 80). Emma, for her part, is the opposite of most young ladies in her determination of never marrying; initially she is as certain that marriage is not for her as her father could wish (cf. E, 84).

But Emma is destined to find love and marry. The reader's attitude to Emma's marriage may be related to how one reacts to inversion, incongruity and laughter in this work. If we agree with Wayne C. Booth that the "rightness of [Emma's] marriage" represents "a conclusion to all the comic wrongness that had gone before,"[5] we may then conveniently overlook, as Booth does, Knightley's decision to leave Donwell Abbey, his home and the largest estate in the vicinity of Highbury, in order to move into Hartfield after his marriage. This decision does not only appear unwise in the managerial eyes of William Larkins, Knightley's steward, and it not only exposes him to the scorn of the Eltons of this world (cf. E, 469); indeed, in most circumstances, impartial observers would find little "rightness" in the need for a 38-year-old bachelor of independent means to leave his well-established home to reside with his father-in-law, a hypochondriac and almost pathological worrywart. If, considering the consequences of this marriage for Emma's life and dwelling on the affirmation of Mr Woodhouse's rights to be coddled contained in the conclusion, we interpret the novel from a straightforward psychological perspective, we may have to agree with Bernard Paris that "the high spirits of the last several chapters are considerably dampened by the prospect of the newly-weds having to humor Mr Woodhouse for as long as he lives."[6] If, on the other hand, we consider Emma's marriage a sad surrender to Mr Knightley, "one of the abettors of Emma's unhappiness," with Allison Sulloway we may see Austen's "overt desire to amuse her readers" as a cover for the "secretly subversive, secretly Romantic" intentions of the work.[7]

And yet a reading may be possible that will respond positively both to the text's explicit claims regarding characters' worth and to its humor. It may be possible to consider the marriage, if certainly not an answer to all of Emma's needs, at least personally salutary, and at the same time share the novel's simultaneous sympathy for Emma ("an excellent creature"—E, 39), Mr Knightley ("sensible," "cheerful"—E, 9, "always so kind..., so truly considerate to every body,"—E, 450), and Mr Woodhouse ("everywhere beloved for the friendliness of his heart and his amiable temper" —E, 7). To accept all this, we need to pay attention, *pace* Paris, to the novel's laughter, and to see it not, as Booth holds, as a reaction to wrongness,[8] or, with Sulloway, as a cover for serious intent. We need to find in the fabric of the novel one strand of that "peculiar logic of the inside out (*a l'envers*)" that Bakhtin described as characteristic of carnival (RHW, 11). We need to see the novel's inversions, the humiliations of the major characters, the rather generalized susceptibility to folly, as calling for our laughter, for an attitude of ambivalent and yet contestatory hilarity.

Carnival laughter, the great leveler, shows us the world "in its droll aspect, in its gay relativity" (RHW, 11). And indeed, Highbury is full of incongruity, of masks and fools and mésalliances. Furthermore, some aspects of Emma's character may be best understood in relation to her unwitting role in a carnival pageantry, a comic procession in which the townspeople unknowingly participate. In addition to the collective show of ludicrous disharmony, the narrator's mimicry of characters' speech brings carnivalesque disturbance into the apparent correction of the narrative discourse. Carnival is also present in the comic effect achieved by the dialogic interrelation of languages and voices of different characters.

The characters, however, take themselves quite seriously. With the possible exception of the novel's clowns (Frank Churchill, aware of his roles and playing them with gusto, and Emma, aware of *some* of her own roles, but more often of those *others* unconsciously play), each character thinks he/she is acting in the most serious manner possible, doing his/her best to uphold a static official ideology. Whenever Mr Elton is gallant to women or "good to the poor," when Mrs Elton self-importantly presides at social functions (as Miss Bates would say, she is the queen, and "we all follow in her train"—E, 329), when she patronizes Jane Fairfax or parades her devotion to her "caro sposo," whenever Emma resents Mrs Elton's pre-eminence as bride, when she is crowned by Frank at Box Hill as the real sovereign who "wherever she is, presides" (E, 369), when she is later uncrowned by Mr Knightley, when she patronizes and instructs Harriet, when she plots to make a match between Harriet and Mr Elton, when Mr Knightley lectures Emma although he knows from long experience how often it has only made her more stubborn, they could all be seen as engaged in a collective pageant in which participants see themselves in serious clothes. As they interact, the reader may discover that actually everyone, public included, is, if not stark naked, unwittingly wearing motley dress.

In fact, the novel's characters can be regarded as a comic entourage for Emma, defining and being defined by her. The Highbury parading in *Emma* is not the village striving to become a town; of the mundane concerns of its streets we have only a single vivid portrait, as Emma looks out at "the busiest part of Highbury" (E, 233) from the door at Ford's while Harriet makes some purchases.[9] Although the characters' lives show many symptoms of the social and economic changes of the times, what the novel seems primarily concerned with is the semiotics of interactions and social relations among the village's leading citizens as they revolve around Emma. Within this semiotic system, an outstounding role is played by several clowns and fools.

Highbury's fools, highly enjoyable in themselves, demand of the reader an ambivalent attitude of that "true open seriousness" tending to liberate from intolerance and dogmatism in ways similar to the effects of the popular laughter of Renaissance literature and culture (cf. RHW, 120-3). In *Emma* we are taught not only to tolerate, but to discover truth in the mouths of, characters whose intelligence seems negligible, who would be despised from a worldly viewpoint. Miss Bates, for example, a poor, plain, unintelligent old maid, whose speech appears to be a steady stream of nonsense, is actually an important source of insights into characters' relations. As Mary Lascelles has said, her chatter can be characterized as "limpid confusion" helping us to understand, in its modeling of "very low relief," the "finest incricacies of the plot."[10]

One of the ways in which such characters make significant contributions to the novel's semantic universe is by unwittingly pointing to the protagonist's mistakes. From the beginning Emma is enthroned at the center of the narrative as the most astute character in the novel; and yet the least gifted, most ingenuous ones could often teach her a thing or two, if she cared to listen. Harriet Smith, for instance, is not only a comic example of what dullness Mrs Goddard's school could produce; she also reveals important aspects of the action. For example, her naive reactions to Emma's manipulations often unconsciously suggest the improbability of the match Emma proposes for her and consequently the illogic of Emma's positions. Harriet lacks the discursive self-assurance of the educated bourgeoisie; her modesty alone would make her ineligible to the role of wife of a man as vain as Mr Elton. Ironically, Emma, though in many ways Mr Elton's superior, is as sure of her own opinions as such a role could demand. Thus, Harriet damns Emma with lively praise when she naively says, "How nicely you talk; I love to hear you. You understand every thing. You and Mr Elton are one as clever as the other" (E, 76). Again, when Emma explains to Harriet the solution to Mr Elton's charade as *courtship*, and insists that it was "written for you and to you," Harriet's reply becomes, on second reading, a pointed reproach to Emma for putting such things into Harriet's head: "Whatever you say is always right, . . . but otherwise I could not have imagined it. . . It is a sort of thing which nobody could have expected. I am sure a month ago, I had no more idea myself!" (E, 74)

Another of the novel's fools, Mr Woodhouse, is comic himself in his fears, which move him to seek neurotic refuge in inactivity and in routine contacts with old friends. He needs so much time to adapt to the smallest change that he proposes, instead of Emma's attending the Coles' dinner party, their coming to Hartfield "one afternoon next summer. . . to take their tea with us" (E, 209). His peculiar ways represent a carnivalesque inversion of common stereotypes about typical male and female conduct. Like a delicate lady, he cannot bear to watch the rough play Mr Knightley takes part in with his brother's children (E, 81); he shuns male rituals, joining the ladies instead of remaining with the gentlemen after dinner (cf. E, 122). His failure as a traditional father and his transgression of gender roles would make him contemptible from what Bakhtin calls "the point of view of 'classic' aesthetics, the aesthetics of the ready-made and the completed" (RHW, 25), which demands a unitary response from readers, and also tends to uphold patriarchal ideals. But this novel asks us to laugh at him and simultaneously to regard him with tenderness, as Mr Knightley and Emma do, to react ambivalently to his fragile androgynous stance and to "his habits of gentle selfishness" (E, 8). In *Emma*'s anti-patriarchal world a vulnerable, tender being, who hurts no one and wishes everybody's good, deserves to be protected, no matter how ridiculous or how boring.

Mr Woodhouse also plays important semiotic functions in the novel. One of his roles in the Highbury pageantry leads to the disclosure of the comic aspect of social intercourse. Playing host to the newlywed Eltons and other friends, he feels obliged, as usual, to make "the circle of his guests, . . . paying his particular compliment to the ladies" (E, 294). Once he has repeated his polite formulas ("You do us a great deal of honor to-day, I am sure"), "The kind-hearted, polite old man might then sit down and feel he had done his duty, and made every fair lady welcome and easy" (E, 295). He is motivated by his belief that "Young ladies are delicate plants" (E, 294); his simplemindedness mimics and thus unveils the silliness of such gallantry.

At times, however, Mr Woodhouse's ludicrousness is capable of unwittingly producing what Bakhtin would call "prosaic 'estrangement' of the discourse of conventional pathos" (DN, 402), and of doing so at Emma's expense. Such is the case when Emma proposes to "do [Mr Elton] a service" and "look about for a wife for him." Her speech ironically mixes conventional pathos ("when he joined [the Westons'] hands today, he looked so very much as if he would like to have the same kind office done for him!") with some prosaic details about Mr Elton's "having fitted up his house so comfortably that it would be a shame to have him single any longer." Mr Woodhouse replies by equating the service of finding him a wife with that of feeding him once as a guest: "if you want to shew him any attention, my dear, ask him to come and dine with us some day. That will be a much better thing" (E, 14).

In the preceding passage, Emma's clowning, her devaluing marriage in her allusion to mundane reasons for marrying, is only half-hearted, for Emma's romantic notions will lead her to take seriously the task of making a match for Mr Elton. And yet Emma is quite capable of mimicking the verbal foibles of the man she intends to see married to her friend Harriet Smith, laughing at his excessive gallantry (cf. E, 49). In these, as in many instances, even while she uses her wit, her partial knowledge of the situation (her blindness to Mr Elton's intentions of marrying *her*, rather than Harriet) directs some of the irony against her. One central point, then, in a careful reading of the text is the interaction of her laughter and ours with her and at her, and ultimately (not least when irony is directed against the super-excellent Mr Knightley) at ourselves.

As J.J. Burrows has said, Emma's laughter could only be obscured "in the gloomy climate of much modern criticism." Burrows' catalogue of some salient uses of Emma's wit can be read bears some consideration:

> Even when she is laughing at others, one can make no worse objection than Mrs Weston: "For shame, Emma! Do not mimic her. You divert me against my conscience" (225). . . And when she turns her wit against herself she is more irresistible than ever. Thus, when Mrs Weston suddenly discovers "that Mrs Elton must be asked to begin the ball," Emma hears "the sad truth with fortitude" and wryly decides it is "almost enough to make her think of marrying" (325). To Mr Knightley's remark that, instead of scolding her, he will leave her to her own reflections, she replies, "Can you trust me with such flatterers?" (330). And again, when Mr Knightley asks in mock indignation, "What do you deserve?", she replies, "Oh! I always deserve the best treatment because I never put up with any other" (474).[11]

Interesting though this portrait of Emma's characteristic mixture of vanity and ironic self-disparagement is, her ability to laugh at herself as much as at others is not simply entertaining, as Burrows' commentary would seem to indicate, not merely what Bakhtin would term "gay, fanciful, recreational drollery deprived of philosophic content" (RHW, 12). In her case, the philosophic content is indeed present in Emma's awareness of the contingency and seemingly invincible heterogeneity of this world, an awareness that can move her both to laughter and to tears. Witness Emma's reflections on the subject of Mr Knightley and Harriet Smith, to her

> an union to distance every wonder of the kind . . . Could it be?—No, it was impossible. And yet it was far, very far, from impossible . . . Was it new for any thing in this world to be unequal, inconsistent, incongruous—or for chance and circumstance (as second causes) to direct human fate? (E, 413)

Here Emma has been misled by Harriet's hopes, in turn fed by Mr Knightley's ill-judged, though well-intentioned attention to Harriet in behalf of Robert Martin. Mr Knightley, it should be remembered, at Donwell talked to Harriet "in a very particular way indeed," by her own account (E, 410). He himself acknowledges having "taken some pains for [Emma's] sake, and for Robert Martin's sake . . . to get acquainted with her" (E, 474). He could not have chosen a worst moment to try his hand at matchmaking, for his "pains" are interpreted by Harriet as a sign of his love for her. The chain of mistakes, whose conclusion gives rise to Emma's reflections on the tendency to incongruity and disorder "in this world," confirms the justice of her conception of human fate.

   This conception stands in clear contrast to Knightley's idea of the orderliness of the universe, an idea he exhibits on many occasions, though never as decidedly as when he surmises that Mrs Elton must treat Jane Fairfax, her superior both in "mind and manner," with deference: "no degree of vanity can prevent her acknowledging her own comparative littleness" (E, 287). Another important speech showing Mr Knightley's simplistic confidence that virtue will assert itself and inevitably triumph comes when he criticizes Frank Churchill for not coming to visit his stepmother, as is his duty: "a man," says Mr Knightley, "can always do . . . his duty . . . not by manoeuvering and finessing, but by vigour and resolution" (E, 146). It never dawns on Mr Knightley that a clear-cut chance to do his duty is not a God-given possibility for every male, that a man can be as dependent and tied to others' wills and whims as a woman. From what we know of Mr and Mrs Churchill we may surmise they are no more likely to bow down before reason and nature than Mrs Elton.[12] In summary, in Mr Knightley's opinion, first, superior and inferior beings are readily classifiable, and second, moral inferiority will naturally yield to superiority and to a gentlemanly sense of duty.

   With the firsts point, Emma not only agrees; she also adds to Mr Knightley's sense of a moral hierarchy a much more marked discrimination among social classes than he would ever accept, showing a snobbish attitude the novel seems designed to undercut. But she is too much aware of the world's incongruity to share Mr Knightley's opinion about the second point.

She cannot believe in the natural and inevitable triumph of Jane Fairfax's moral and intellectual superiority over Mrs Elton, for she has "no faith in Mrs Elton's acknowledging herself the inferior in thought, word or deed; or in her being under any restraint beyond her own scanty rule of good-breeding" (E, 288). In this case, Mr Knightley could not be more mistaken, as several exchanges between Mrs Elton and Miss Fairfax in subsequent chapters will show. Mrs Elton is not only not awed by Miss Fairfax, but considers herself "Lady Patroness," calls Jane familiarly by her first name, and generally meddles in her affairs so shamelessly that on two occasions, at least, it seems "more than [Jane] could bear" (E, 359—cf. E, 296). Nevertheless, Mr Knightley has an ingenuous confidence not only in the natural influence of superiority over inferiority, but also in the power of good to triumph over evil, and in the inevitably favorable outcome of every dutiful deed. In his view, "Respect for right conduct is felt by every body" (E, 147). Mr Knightley could make his the words of another famous Knight, proclaiming that "the Firste Moevere of the cause above" created order, by which "men wel discerne" that He "stable is and eterne."[13] Emma might agree regarding the attributes of the "First Moevere,"[14] but not that order is readily discernible in our earthly realm of "second causes" (cf. E, 413).

The many contrasts found in the novel, between characters and their circumstances, among characters, in the contradictory qualities of individual characters, confirm the suspicion that the narrator shares Emma's views. Such contrasts, moreover, are more festive than serious, as is characteristic of "carnivalistic mésalliances." In this category of "the carnivalization of literature," according to Bakhtin, things which were in an official, hierarchical worldview ordered, "self-enclosed," and distant are jumbled and drawn into unseemly contact: "Carnival brings together, unifies, weds, and combines the sacred with the profane, the lofty with the low, the great with the insignificant, and the wise with the stupid" (PDP, 122-3).

As an example of carnivalesque mésalliances in *Emma* we may cite Emma's relationship with her father, in which sacred filial devotion is "wedded" to the laughable inferiority of the father's abilities. Mr Woodhouse is "no companion for her," cannot "meet her in conversation, rational or playful" (E, 7), and he demonstrates his obtuseness in a thousand amusing exchanges. Other carnivalesque contrasts include the one between Mr Woodhouse's "apologies and civil hesitations" and Mr Knightley's plainness and straightforwardness (cf. E, 57-58), the opposition of Mr John Knightley's surly view of Christmas dinners and Mr Elton's delight in dining out (E, 113-6), or the contrast between Mr Elton's saccharine charade and Mr Martin's sensible, sensitive letter proposing to Harriet (cf. E, 76). (The latter contrast is joined to elements of inversion, for Mr Elton, the educated man, produces the less tasteful piece of writing, while Mr Martin, a yeoman farmer, is a much better writer.)

Of course, the many mésalliances in the novel cannot be seen as equivalent or even analogous, for there are also various degrees of inequalities. One of the most striking disparities is the almost brutal contrast between Mrs Elton's vulgarity and Jane Fairfax's patient "sense" and elegance. This contrast, in turn, serves as foil to that between Emma herself and Mrs Elton; the former contrast is much more substantial than the latter, however, for, as has been often pointed out,[15] superior though Emma is, there are more similarities between Emma and Mrs Elton (both snobbish and patronizing) than the protagonist herself would admit or even imagine.

The difference between Mrs Elton and Emma is shown by such details as the latter's "good grace" in refusing to counter the former's popularity with any indication of her real impression of Mr Elton's new bride. This attitude stands in contrast to Mrs Elton's "ill-will" towards Emma and her "sneering and negligent" manners towards Harriet (cf. E, 281). And yet Mrs Elton does some good where Emma is negligent, for, in spite of the evils of Mrs Elton's patronizing Jane Fairfax, the latter finds some relief from the narrowness of her home and companions in accepting Mrs Elton's attentions. Emma, unable or unwilling to recognize Jane's needs, is astonished that the latter should "chuse the mortification of Mrs Elton's notice," but both Mrs Weston and Mr Knightley remind her that Jane must harbor a "very natural wish of a little change" (E, 285-6). Mrs Elton, furthermore, plays an important disruptive function by unsettling the social hierarchy Emma would like to believe immutable. In this sense she is another unruly woman, less sympathetically seen perhaps than others created by Austen, but indeed necessary to the author's purpose.

Other notable mésalliances are related to incompatible qualities joined in a single character, such as "the seeming incongruity of gentle manners and a conceited head" in Mr Elton (E, 136). The most evident mésalliances, however, are not merely comic, but occasionally also irritating. Such is the case of Emma's application of her superior intelligence to matchmaking, and her reiterated misuse of her talents to find arguments to justify unjustifiable behavior (although it is hard to agree with Mr Knightley's concluding remark when he rebukes her for "abusing the reason you have": "Better be without sense than misapply it as you do"—E, 64).

In one case, a profound difference between a character's merits and her circumstances seems so unfair that there is no comic effect whatsoever. Such is the case of the contrast between Jane Fairfax's elegance and her miserable surroundings and between her superior abilities and the fate she narrowly escapes, disparity which, coupled with Jane's constant endurance of Miss Bates' maddeningly dull chatter, moves Emma to make another contrast "between Mrs Churchill's importance in the world and Jane Fairfax's. . .: one was every thing, the other nothing—and she sat musing on the difference of woman's destiny" (E, 384).

There is also "difference" in the fabric of Highbury's social relations. Although the text seems to endorse Mr Knightley's tendency to stress the bonds of community against the class distinctions Emma likes to make, it also suggests that many of the social situations depicted are inherently unjust. The education many women receive, for example, is sadly inadequate; thus, Mrs Goddard's school, where Harriet Smith studied, is a place "where girls might be sent to be out of the way and scramble themselves into a little education, without any danger of coming back prodigies" (E, 220). A good education, though rare, cannot save such women as Jane Fairfax from the "misery of victims" who must "sell their intellect" in the "governess-trade" (E, 300-1). Some critics seem to feel a need to apologize for Jane's "exaggeration" as "a measure of the bitterness of her enforced gratitude, not an indication of insensibility."[16] And yet the situation of a governess was peculiarly dire. If we compare it to the economic and social privations of a male tutor, we may see little difference. But a female's immobility and dependence made the ambiguous situation of a private instructor, neither a member of the higher nor of the lower classes, desperately lonely in the case of a woman. Of course, governesses were not flogged, and though they might be seduced or raped and then despised, most of their material conditions were superior to slaves'. But in the very material sense of a lack of communication with peers, being a governess was indeed worse than being a slave.

Other negative predicaments in Highbury include the poverty of Miss Bates and the scorn heaped on old maids (E, 85), or the situation of "Poor old John" Adby, Miss Bates' father's clerk, now bed-ridden and destitute, and dependent on charity (E, 383). In spite of Mr Knightley's or Emma's good intentions, in Highbury those made weak through the action of time or social rules are not well provided for.

Even among those who enjoy economic and/or social prominence, social relations are not always based on shared interests. One of the central conflicts in Highbury is the struggle between the gentry, for which birth and tradition are basic, and new forces claiming status on the grounds of fortune and conspicuous consumption. This conflict is played out primarily in the war between Emma, representing the old order, and Mrs Elton, representing the new. Emma's role as Highbury's leading lady is acknowledged by Miss Bates, for instance; but younger citizens seem to be losing a sense of the social gulf between the old name of the Woodhouses and the "new money" (even though its amount is not enormous) of a Miss Hawkins. The Mrs Coles and Mrs Perrys of the town no longer find it impossible that Mr Elton should be Emma's consort, and even Miss Bates concedes, in her typical fragmentary style, that "nobody could wonder if Mr Elton should have aspired—" (E, 176). Emma's snobbish claim to the right to preside is increasingly being undermined by two facts: from the viewpoint of personal merit, Jane Fairfax seems superior, and from a social standpoint, the grounds on which the Woodhouses base their primacy are being superseded by new social realities.

The ultimate irony of her situation is that Emma, who feels so much above the competition between the Coles, the Perrys and the Eltons, is being unwittingly assimilated into it. Emma's blindness becomes evident in the episode of the Coles' dinner party. She initially assumes that the social-climbing Coles "could hardly presume to invite" the families she considers "regular and best." At first Emma regrets the Coles might not understand her "social cut",[17] for "her father's known habits would be giving her refusal less meaning than she could wish." Comically, this regret turns into anxiety when everyone is invited but the Woodhouses. The idea of her best friends gathering at the Coles changes her mind so much that "when the insult came at last, it found her very differently affected." Professing to be ready to decline the long-awaited invitation, Emma finally lets herself be talked into accepting (E, 207-8). In this case her love of company triumphs over her snobbery; this outcome cannot obscure the reader's impression that Emma, even while feeling so superior, is actually in danger of becoming socially irrelevant. The narrator's amusement over Emma's mistaken perceptions is finely restrained but evident in her report of Emma's retrospections about the party:

> Emma did not repent her condescension in going to the Coles'. The visit afforded her many pleasant recollections the next day; and all she might be supposed to have lost on the side of *dignified seclusion*, must be amply repaid in the *splendour of popularity*. *She must have delighted the Coles—worthy people, who deserved to be made happy! And left a name behind her that would not soon die away.* (E, 231—emphasis added)

In this passage, the "double-voiced discourse" in the portions I have underlined, combining as they do Emma's own self-satisfied thoughts and the narrator's laughter, is further proof of the constant relation between irony and poliphony in *Emma*. If the delusion of grandeur is a requisite part of the proper attitude of the powerful, Emma is well-equipped to lead. However, she will need to hold her own against Mrs Elton, whose condescension is quite as active.

Even the friendliest forms of social interactions, furthermore, rarely evince the order of right reason. Few neighbors are aware of the great distance between Emma, who rarely practices her music, and Jane Fairfax, a talented musician (cf. E, 232). Highbury neighbors are so little discriminating that they take it for granted that Mrs Elton "must be as clever and as agreeable as she professed herself." Her husband may be excused for thinking he had "brought such a woman to Highbury as not even Miss Woodhouse would equal," but Mrs Elton's "little judgment" and condescension towards her new "country neighbourhood" make her popularity among those she patronizes one more proof of the invincible folly of humankind (cf. E, 281). Moreover, many of the Highbury neighbors are incurably meddlesome, much given to gossip and to "forc[ing] themselves anywhere" (E, 390-1). In sum, one aspect of the movements of Emma's "sets" of friends and acquaintances is the active display of carnivalesque contrasts under an appearance of tranquil homogeneity and decorum,[18] a collective exhibition orchestrated around the protagonist by people indispensable to her, even loved by her, but ludicrous and blind as Emma herself will prove to be.

In spite of her many mistakes, Emma, unlike Mr Knightley,[19] will not refuse to dwell on all the "difference" she sees around her. With regard to this attitude, Emma's voice is closer than any other character's to the narrating voice, which is so adept at depicting the characters' incongruities in prose that combines their speech with exposition or narration. Emma, for her part, is the only character capable of duplicating Miss Bates' style, or of mimicking Mr Elton's characteristic phrase.[20] Ironically, the character most often laughed at by the narrator is Emma herself, although the lens through which we see most of the action is Emma's consciousness. As we see her mistakes we come to realize that she is, as David Lodge puts it, "an unreliable focalizing character. The effect is not only a multiplication of ironies and reversals but also an intensification of what Henry James called the sense of felt life."[21] Indeed, to see the action unfold through Emma's eyes and yet to realize how deeply mistaken she is creates a most interesting tension in the reader between identification with Emma and censure of her erring ways. Through this means the narrator's laughter acquires the taste of carnivalesque self-mockery; inasmuch as we identify with the protagonist, our laughter as readers becomes self-mocking as well. Indeed, it is not possible to characterize the unique flavor of the narrating voice, to capture fully the quality of relations among narrator, Emma and the reader without recurring to the concept of carnival.

In the very complexity and ambivalence of the narrator's own discourse, in the "clowning" through which the narrator's irony mingles with the character's own self-consciousness, we find what Volosinov calls the "simultaneous participation of two speech acts" in the narrative utterance. This merging of two acts, two speakers, two attitudes, can lead to "identification" between narrator and hero, or to "interference" or distance between the two, as each of the two acts merging in a single utterance appears to be "differently oriented in its expressivity." These phenomena are related to a form of reported speech Volosinov calls "quasi-direct discourse"[22] ("free indirect speech" and "free indirect style" in other authors) and of other forms of reported speech.[23] This type of discourse allows the narrator to report Emma's thoughts in such a way that the supposed original statement, as it might have crossed the character's mind, is still discernible through the sentence as it stands, in a kind of discursive pentimento.

Free indirect speech can be regarded as the result of a linguistic mixture of direct and indirect styles of reporting (*oration recta* and *oratio obliqua* respectively). For example, in such a passage as "She watched [Frank] well. It was a clear thing he was less in love [with her] than he had been" (E, 316), we can discern the joining of elements from what a direct report of Emma's thoughts would be ("She watched him well. 'It is a clear thing he is less in love with me than he has been,' she thought") and from an indirect one ("She watched him well, and concluded that he was clearly less in love with her than he had been"). The actual passage, in free indirect speech, shares with the hypothetical version in direct speech the syntax of the quoted conclusion, although of course the reporting phrase "she thought" has been eliminated. It also shares with the version in indirect speech the verb tenses and the pronouns. This stylistic mixture creates in the reader a sense of both sharing the character's thoughts from within and being guided by the narrator's impressions. In Emma's case, at least, the effect is usually of both identification and ironic "interference." On a second reading of the novel the irony of the report of Emma's thoughts quoted above becomes more evident, for we know Frank cannot be "less in love" with Emma, since he has never loved her.

Nevertheless, the formal linguistic aspects of this rhetorical phenomenon cannot explain many other instances of similar phenomena. Most of the narration is focalized through Emma's consciousness, even when the linguistic evidence is not as clear. Very often, if the reader realizes (perhaps in a second reading) that long stretches of the text are written from Emma's viewpoint and do not present the narrator's own opinions of each situation, it is not due to any linguistic marks, but because what is said can only be believed by the protagonist. Such is the case, for instance, when we are told that "it was particularly necessary to brace [Harriet] up with a few decisive expressions" in order to convince her she must reject Mr Martin's proposal (E, 55). Actually, Emma's "assistance" in making up Harriet's mind for her is not only not necessary, but will prove damaging to her young friend's happiness. On such occasions, the narrator's refraining from providing any signal about the inappropriateness of Emma's point of view and choice of words is what makes the text so finely ironic, so gayly ambivalent, so sly in its mockery.

Sometimes a phrase will be ambiguous, so that on a first reading one might believe the narrator shares Emma's views on what is taking place. Thus, when we find out that Emma's "plans and proceedings" regarding Mr Elton and Harriet "were more and more justified and endeared to her by the general appearances of the next few days" (E, 69), the phrasing and the very absence of narratorial comment allow the reader at first to assume that Emma *is* justified. Only later will the reader be certain that Emma is wrong about this whole matter of a match between Harriet and Mr Elton. (To some readers, the fact that Mr Knightley has disagreed with Emma on this matter is positive proof from the beginning that she must be wrong. But if one does not start from the premise that a young woman's opinion must invariably be less reliable than that of a man seventeen years her senior, one may need additional evidence to decide.) When Emma is fully convinced of what she *wants* to believe, the report of a situation will often be couched in the words Emma would use. This is what happens when, at one point, Emma comes out of a room to meet Mr Elton and Harriet and we read that "The lovers were standing together at one of the windows" (E, 90), even though they are "lovers" only in Emma's estimation. On more than one occasion, the narrating voice appears to follow Emma's understanding of a situation. Thus, for instance, the episode in which Emma sketches Harriet's portrait and Mr Elton sighs out his admiration contains many expressions that adopt Emma's apraisal of Mr Elton's "love and complaisance" or "very promising attachment" (E, 47). The narrator appears to be taken in as much as Emma; such an attitude is typical of the clown, who acts the fool in order to laugh at sentimentality and false pathos. Of course, once Mr Elton's real intentions come out, the ambiguity of such expressions becomes evident: Mr Elton's attitude pointed to his love and admiration for the artist, not for the model.

However, it would be totally wrong to decide that the novel's narrator is unreliable, or wishes to trick readers in order to surprise or shock them later. What the narrating voice is doing is mimicking Emma's accents and opinions, teaching us to love her and simultaneously to laugh at her, showing us her strengths as well as her weaknesses. As we follow the action through Emma's eyes and mind, we discover her elegant wit, her intelligence, her benevolent (if not always beneficent) interest in the well-being of others. We acquire, moreover, what Claudia Johnson has called the same "confidence in [the] basic soundness [of Emma's authority]" that moves Mrs Weston to say of Emma, "She has qualities which may be trusted; she will never lead anyone really wrong; she will make no lasting blunder" (E, 40).[24]

And yet there is no denying Emma's snobbery, her horror of what she calls "confusion of rank," her abhorrence of mixing with families that are not "proper" (E, 198). Among her less attractive qualities is her envy of Jane Fairfax, who excells as a musical performer, whereas Emma's lack of discipline only allows her to play "the little things which are generally acceptable" (E, 227). This envy animates her suspicion of Jane's love for Mr Dixon, which in turn moves her to question Miss Bates with "the insidious design of further discovery" (E, 160).

In spite of Emma's serious faults, we are taught to love her because there is love of her in the voice that narrates. Such an attitude can only stem from a philosophical, carnivalesque awareness of the occasional pettiness and jealousy of even the best of mortals. The narrator can be seen to be constantly laughing at Emma's false certainties. This laughter is never more pointed than when Emma amuses "herself in the consideration of the blunders which often arise from a partial knowledge of circumstances, of the mistakes which people of high aspirations to judgment are for ever falling into" (E, 112). In this passage, she is laughing at Mr John Knightley for warning her, at the moment she is most persuaded that Mr Elton loves Harriet, that the young man seems to be courting Emma herself. She does not at the moment believe Mr John Knightley, but the blunder, of course, is hers. Once we know all this, the narrator's report of Emma's amused "consideration of the blunders. . . ," acquires some of the indirect, cryptic but biting, mocking flavor of some of the speeches by Lear's Fool. That Emma can be at the same time so cherished and so ludicrously mistaken is only possible through the gay ambivalence of a carnivalesque narrative attitude.

One result of this subtle but demolishing mimicry of the protagonist with whom readers are made to identify is to allow readers to feel all the more strongly how vain and fallible human beings can be, just as the reports of her envious neglect of Jane Fairfax, at a time when readers have already been taught to see the whole narrative world through her eyes, point to the pettiness and jealousy of humanity. Such ambivalent feelings are perfectly in keeping with the iconoclastic, anti-establishment bent of carnival rites and art. This irreverent, anti-official attitude, Bakhtin has told us, is never gratuitous, but is always imbued with both gaiety and philosophic content. Emma's own tendency to laugh at herself, for example, may lead readers to see her laughter as a wise response to the realization of how difficult it is to reach any level of certainty or to avoid mistakes.

The sense of the unavoidability of human error is reinforced by several factors. For one thing, most of the characters in the novel are wrong, at one point or another, about what others feel. To name but a few of the mistakes they make in this comedy of errors: Emma thinks Mr Elton is courting Harriet, while Mr Elton thinks Emma is encouraging him as Emma's suitor; Mr Knightley thinks Emma loves Frank, Mr and Mrs Weston think Emma and Frank are falling in love with each other, and even Jane Fairfax thinks Emma is attracted to Frank, while all the time Emma is hoping Frank will fall in love with Harriet; during a leavetaking visit he pays her, Emma thinks Frank is hinting at his love for Emma, while Frank thinks Emma has discovered he is in love with Jane Fairfax; Emma later thinks Harriet loves Frank, while Harriet thinks Emma knows that Harriet is in love with Mr Knightley. But the errors do not simply stem from what Graham Hough has called "conjectural analyses of other people's dispositions."[25] The most prominent mistakes are made by the two major characters about their own feelings: for a long time, both Emma and Mr Knightley remain blind to their own feelings of love for each other. As these errors accumulate, we sense not only the characters' difficulties as they attempt to interpret the feelings of others and even their own, but also the relativity of each character's appraisal of any situation.

The novel's carnivalesque sense of gay relativity is reinforced by the narrator's comments, on those few occasions when she speaks for herself. Taking the perspective of an interested bystander, or perhaps an unobtrusive, occasional participant in a general conversation, the narrator sometimes provides brief appraisals of small incidents or situations, or ironic surmises about the characters' thoughts; these occasional narratorial comments may serve to show how different perspectives will yield opposite views of the same situation. Thus, at one point, she comments,

> The ladies here probably exchanged looks which meant, 'Men never know when things are dirty or not,' and the gentlemen perhaps thought each to himself, 'Women will have their little nonsenses and needless cares.'" (E, 253)

The narrator also occasionally begins a chapter with an ironic phrase such as, "Human nature is so well-disposed towards those who are in interesting situations that a young person who either marries or dies is sure of being kindly spoken of" (E, 181). This jocose coupling of marriage and death throws a glance of gay relativity on the stereotypical tenderness with which newly-wed young people are generally regarded.

The narrator's voice can be heard not only in these few "solo" interventions, but also in the mixture of her own attitude and a character's. As an instance of "speech interference," this type of report often becomes a form of mimicry that points to the narrator's disapproval. For example, slight explicit criticism of a character's attitudes may be coupled with an ironic imitation of his/her style. Such is the case when expository prose slides into Emma's lame excuses to avoid visiting Mrs and Miss Bates:

> She had many a hint from Mr Knightley and some from her own heart, as to her deficiency—but none were equal to counteract the persuasion of its being very disagreeable,—a waste of time—tiresome women—and all the horror of being in danger of falling in with the second rate and third rate of Highbury"(E, 155).[26]

The sentence fragments indicate Emma's own lack of conviction; that incoherence dissolves into fluidity when Emma expresses her sense of social superiority.

As similar fragmented presentations of characters' utterances appear repeatedly in the text, their ironic effect can best be likened to the vocal modulation with which we mimic someone else's speech. Sometimes the mimicry is aimed at the collectivity, as happens when all of Highbury exacerbates Harriet's hopeless regard for Mr Elton by recurrently singing the praises of "Miss Hawkins' happiness," and by "continual repetition of how much [Mr Elton] seemed attached!—his air as he walked by the house—the very sitting of his hat, being all in proof of how much he was in love!" (E, 184). Sometimes a report reaches us filtered through a double layer of ironies. When Emma overhears Mrs Elton pressing Jane to accept a "situation" as governess, we sense not only the narrator's irony aimed at Mrs Elton's snobbish criteria but also at Emma's intense dislike of the speaker: the job "was not with Mrs Suckling, was not with Mrs Bragge, but in felicity and splendour fell short only of them: it was with a cousin of Mrs Bragge, an acquaintance of Mrs Suckling . . . *Delightful, charming, first circles, spheres, lines, ranks, every thing*—and Mrs Elton was wild to have the offer closed with immediately" (E, 359—emphasis added). The narrator is reporting Mrs Elton's meddling through the filter of Emma's attitude, employing Emma's sarcastic mental accents as she overhears Mrs Elton's effusions.

Throughout the novel, fragmented speech appears very often in dialogue, usually to comic effect. Indeed, I believe no other novel by Austen contains as many passages of fragmented speech. In addition to the examples already mentioned, Emma's speech is often mimicked by means of this device (cf. for instance, her dismissing Harriet's praise of Mr and Miss Martin's kindness—E, 179); Harriet herself speaks in fragments when agigated; Mrs Elton's self-important chatter is often rendered by means of this device. In addition to Miss Bates' characteristic use of fragments I will merely mention the long, contradictory, incoherent conversation, led by Mrs Elton, as Mr Knightley's guests gather strawberries in the Abbey's gardens (E, 358-9); Frank's ill-humored mutterings after his quarrel with Jane when she leaves Donwell Abbey as he arrives ("I met *one* as I came—Madness in this weather!—absolute madness!"—E, 363-4); Emma's sentimental self-reproach after Box Hill ("Miss Bates should never again—no, never!"—E, 377); Mr Knightley's melodramatic incoherence, stemming from heartfelt compassion for Emma and from anger towards Frank when he thinks she has been jilted ("The feelings of the warmest friendship—Indignation—Abominable scoundrel!"—E, 426). (Although Mr Knightley's effusions are moving, his incoherent use of clichés ("Time, my dearest Emma, time will heal the wound—Your own excellent sense—your exertions for your father's sake—I know you will not allow yourself—") is also, in typical carnivalesque fashion, slightly comic, for actually Emma does not love Frank.) In all these examples, fragmentation works to produce, even in silent reading, a strong accoustic image that increases the impression of narratorial verbal mimicry.

In addition to free indirect speech and fragmentation, Austen often uses other devices that produce a carnivalesque impression of narratorial clowning. As she "creates the image of a language" in *Emma* through what Bakhtin would call "dialogized interrelation of languages" (DN, 358), her narrator's voice seems bent on uncrowning the heroine and hero as much as on mocking lesser characters. One device by which she achieves this is hybridization; others include the juxtaposition of dialogic exchanges in contrast to each other.

The first of these two devices achieves its effects through "double-accented, double-styled hybrid constructions" similar to those Bakhtin describes in Dickens (DN, 304-5). In these cases, the combination of "two utterances, two speech manners, two styles, two 'languages'" seems to operate more through ideological difference than in the use of fragmentation. And yet the analogy to mimicry still seems valid. I have underlined the phrases quoted below (taken from a narratorial report of collective reactions to the prospective visit of Mrs Elton's brother and sister, the Sucklings) to represent the stress they seem to invite in oral reading: "After being fed with *hopes of a speedy visit* from Mr and Mrs Suckling, the Highbury world were *obliged to endure the mortification* of hearing that they could not possibly come till the autumn. No such *importation of novelties* could *enrich their intellectual stores* at present" (E, 352—emphasis added). Without even mentioning Mrs Elton until the following paragraph, the narrator seems to be simultaneously laughing at her patronizing airs and at Highbury gullibility, by embedding the language of Mrs Elton's self-importance in a framework of serious reporting. In the portions underlined, the snobbery and the irony seem to have merged into each word.

One of the mechanisms by which the text prepares readers to interpret the phrases underlined in the pasage just quoted as evidence of Mrs Elton's self-aggrandizing is the description of Mrs Elton's condescension towards Highbury on previous occasions (cf. E, 281). Thus, description predisposes the reader to a certain interpretation of subsequent situations. A similar device, by which a text effects a debasing, uncrowning mimicry is what Volosinov calls "preset direct discourse," in which the juxtaposition of different types of discourse, their flowing out of and into each other, produce "a sort of reciprocal infectiousness between the reporting context and the reported speech."[27] Thus, for instance, in the novel's first chapter the narrator comments that Mr Woodhouse has "habits of gentle selfishness," inspiring in him the idea that Miss Taylor, in marrying, "had done as bad a thing for herself as for them." When, a moment later, the old man's exclaims, "Poor Miss Taylor! . . . What a pity it is that Mr Weston ever thought of her!" (E, 8), the reader knows not to give credit to his appraisal of the situation. In fact, the reader's perceptions of all of Mr Woodhouse's speeches in that first chapter are colored by the previous descriptions of his habits, fears, kindness and limitations.

In a similar way, the preceding narration "presets the apperception" of the first conversation between Mr Knightley and Emma. When Mr Knightley challenges Emma, claiming the "merit" she is so proud of, having predicted that Mr Weston would marry Miss Taylor, was only "a lucky guess" (E, 13), one has a strong inclination to believe him, since the narrator has warned us about Emma's "disposition to think a little too well of herself" (E, 5). At the same time, a large portion of the chapter has described Emma's meditation on the loss of Miss Taylor's company, and yet her unselfish exertions to raise her father's spirits, so the reader tends to empathize with her. And then she counters Mr Knightley's challenge, "And have you never known the pleasure and triumph of a lucky guess? I pity you—I thought you cleverer—for depend upon it, a lucky guess is never merely luck. There is always some talent in it" (E, 13). This retort indeed seems cleverer than Mr Knightley's exercise of ordinary common sense. How we react to her impudence before an older male must depend on how we feel about women's independence, but her wit is clearly closer to the narrator's, who from the first page has regaled us with such fine ironies as the statement that "The danger [posed by Emma's "having rather too much her own way" and by her thinking "a little too well of herself"], however, was . . . so unperceived, that they did not by any means rank as misfortunes with her" (E, 5-6). Thus the narration preceding her conversation with Knightley subtly directs our sympathy. In Volosinov's terms, "The basic themes of the impending direct discourse are anticipated by the context and are colored by the author's intonations."[28]

The interesting thing here is that this sympathy is directed simultaneously toward both characters' direct discourse, although in this conversation they take opposite sides. Emma's style, her wit, matches the narrator's own, while Mr Knightley, "one of the few people who could see faults in Emma Woodhouse" (E. 11) resembles the narrator in this very fact. The narrator, in typical carnivalesque ambivalence, both laughs at Emma for her ability to deceive herself, and fondly admires her wit and the strength of her spirit.

Emma's self-deception is never more evident than when she makes a conscious effort to avoid falling into previous mistakes, thinking herself cured of her tendencies to manipulate Harriet Smith's affections. The passage in question not only highlights Emma's weakness, but also tends to "preset the reader's apperceptions" of a passage in the next chapter, where Mr Knightley's mental processes show some similarities to Emma's. In the first of these two passages, both in the form of free indirect report (or "quasi-direct speech"), Emma considers whether to react to Harriet's remarks under her breath about someone she secretly admires, someone "so superior to Mr Elton!" Emma sits in doubt: "Should . . . she let it pass?" Possible evils occur to her; for one thing, Emma fears falling into "frequent discussion of hopes and chances" of Harriet's love such as they had in the past about Mr Elton, discussions which have led Harriet into unrequited love for the Highbury vicar. On the other hand, Harriet "might think her cold or angry" if she remains silent. Emma decides "it would be wiser for her to say and know at once, all that she meant to say and know. Plain dealing was always best" (E, 341). Emma's applying "the judicious law of her own brain" about how much to say makes them speak at cross-purposes, Harriet thinking of Mr Knightley while Emma believes she is referring to Frank Churchill. Words like "wiser," "plain-dealing," and "judicious" sound ironic in the reader's ear. And yet there is no doubt that Emma sincerely believes she is taking the most prudent course of action. The passage may be read as an invitation to laugh at the jumbled situation of humanity, apt to fall most ludicrously while trying hardest to do the right thing.

But Emma is not the only character who does damage precisely when she attempts to do her best. Perhaps the deepest carnivalesque irony is found in the fact that the wisest, most prudent, most stable character, Mr Knightley, is led by his love for Emma and his blindness to his own feelings to create a further comedy of errors. Emma's interference and her mistaking Harriet's meaning in Vol. III, Ch. IV will cause the two women much pain later on; similarly, Mr Knightley's interference and his mistaking Emma's meaning in the following chapter will cause them both needless pain. Mr Knightley, wishing to give Emma a hint of the intimacy he has sensed between Frank and Jane, convinces himself he must break his own rule of non-interference. Much as Emma thought she was only moved by a desire to protect Harriet, blinding herself to the persistence of her urge to manipulate Harriet's life, Mr Knightley will not admit to himself that his own love of Emma partly motivates him. As we witness Mr Knightley's inner deliberations reported in free indirect speech, the narrating voice seems to subtly mimic his mental process. Unable to accept the humbling urgings of his jealousy of Frank Churchill, Mr Knightley will rationalize his own needs to observe her reaction to his suspicions:

> He sat a little while in doubt. A variety of evils crossed his mind. Interference— fruitless interference. Emma's confusion, and the acknowledged intimacy [with Frank], seemed to declare her affection engaged. Yet he would speak. He owed it to her to risk anything rather than her welfare. (E, 350)

He only hurts himself further by speaking, for he interprets her laughing assurance that Frank cannot be in love with Jane as evidence that there may be an understanding between Emma and Frank. Actually, Emma, though convinced Frank loves her, does not want this love; rather, she already wishes Harriet and Frank's eventual mariage.

Thus, while most of the novel's narration mimics Emma in reporting her thoughts, when the focus shifts to other characters' perspectives, those characters are mimicked (and uncrowned) as well. His/her thoughts become expressions, not of an author's "categorical word," but of the character's "adventitious, subjective state."[29] No character, then, escapes the narrator's irony, not even Mr Knightley, considered by some critics the author's surrogate.[30] As one critic points out, "Knightley represents an integrity of personality and honesty of action that are exemplary in the novel. But even these virtues are incomplete in a world in which complete truth is 'very seldom' found in human disclosure."[31] Laughter at Knightley, who would almost qualify as "the best of men," as the hero is usually called in sentimental fiction, contrasts with that aura of perfection created in many novels by the narrator's repetition of that superlative commendation and by the heroine's fawning devotion to the hero.

Both through the handling of discourse and the depiction of characters and their social milieu, *Emma* invites the reader to see this world and its inhabitants as comically blind, and yet to "doat" on some of them, "faults and all," as Mr Knightley would say (cf. E, 462). Both Emma and Mr Knightley are set up as admirable, and then mocked; their "crowning and uncrowning," as Bakhtin would call it, shows that an awareness of the "joyful relativity of all structure and order, of all authority and all hierarchical positions" (PDP, 124) is one of the ingredients in the text's composition.

Of course, we do not laugh as often at Knightley as we do at Mrs Elton, for instance, or in the same way. The narrator shows a marked fondness for the former and a distaste for the latter. Both, however, are indispensable to her purposes. Mrs Elton, self-important, vulgar, condescending, disrupts the quiet, rustic world of Highbury and unveils for us the bland and blind naivete of its inhabitants. Even those who, like Knightley, are not taken in by her, partially share in the villagers' lack of sophistication. Mr Knightley, for instance, can on occasion sound unimaginative and dull. Thus, if Mrs Elton's "idea of the simple and the natural" ("a table spread in the shade") is the result of romantic fashion, *his* ("the table spread in the dining-room [is more appropriate for] gentlemen and ladies, with their servants and furniture"— E, 357) smacks of stiff, uninteresting habit; the phrase makes the people sound as heavy as the furniture. Only Emma is at the same time original, skeptical and shrewd, and yet she also is blinded, not by naive faith, but by her own vanity. *Emma* asks us to laugh by turns at everyone; its laughter, capable of including now a character, now another, and even the narrating voice, is the opposite of the exclusion by reason of class Emma would constantly put into effect.

On the other hand, Mr Knightley also makes profound mistakes. Critics who see his perspective as uniformly normative must disregard his self-criticism at the end of the novel. The passage is reminiscent of Darcy's confession to Elizabeth in one of the final chapters in *Pride and Prejudice.* In a conversation introduced by Emma's reference to a French novel, Mme. de Genlis' *Adelaide and Theodore*, Emma and Mr Knightley discuss the value of sternness in correcting children, the explicit topic of much of the French work. In the passage in question, Emma is referring to Mrs Weston's newborn girl: Mrs Weston, Emma's former governess, "has had the advantage of practicing on me, like la Baronne d'Almane on la Comtesses d'Ostalis, [two characters in *Adelaide and Theodore*] and we shall now see her own little Adelaide educated on a more perfect plan" (E, 461). On this occasion, Mr Knightley takes the opposite view to the one he has held all along. He holds that Mrs Weston will spoil her daughter even more than she spoilt Emma, but he not only avers that "nothing very bad" will happen to a spoilt child, for she "will be disagreeable in infancy and correct herself as she grows older" (E, 461); he now even criticizes the way he used to lecture Emma as she was growing up, while Emma defends it. In Austen's characteristically subtle style, the mentor and his pupil reverse positions, and yet the change is natural, smooth, unstriking. Nevertheless, the reference to *Adelaide and Theodore* signals the significance of this reversal. A careful reading reveals the many contrasts and parallels between Emma and the French work, raising the question of parody.

In *Emma* parody of sentimental fiction seems evident in Emma's quixotic notions of Harriet Smith's unknown origin and Jane Fairfax's supposed adulterous interest in Mr Dixon. As Mary Lascelles remarks, "Such a young woman as Emma . . . could have become acquainted with illegitimacy as an interesting situation, infidelity as a comic incident, only in her reading." Although Lascelles surmised that in providing Emma with bookish follies, "Jane Austen had no particular novel . . . in mind,"[32] others have compared this novel to earlier ones. Kenneth Moler, for instance, has pointed out the similarities and differences between *Emma* and two contemporary parodies, Charlotte Lenox's *The Female Quixote* (1752) and Eaton Stannard Barrett's *The Heroine* (1813).[33] Margaret Kirkham has also shown several points of comparison between *Emma* and Kotzebue's *The Birthday* (translated by Thomas Didbin in 1799), most notably in the two heroines' belief "that they cannot marry because of their duty to their invalid fathers."[34] The contrast between the two works allows Kirkham to conclude that Emma, in her "role of devoted daughter, comes quite close to a sentimental stereotype." Austen's objective, concludes Kirkham, is "to criticise the romanticisation of devoted daughters."[35]

None of these critical works, however, do more than mention Emma's allusion to Mme. de Genlis' *Adelaide and Theodore*.[36] Although this is the only novel Emma refers to directly, I have been unable to find in the critical literature any exploration of the influences or refractions the French novel may have had on Austen's.[37] Nevertheless, Austen's work enters into dialogue with Mme. de Genlis' novel in many ways. For one thing, Emma and Adelaide share certain characteristics: they are both beautiful young women who seem unaware of their beauty (Emma, though "very handsome . . . appears to be little occupied with it" (E, 39); Adelaide is "very pretty . . . but never seems to think about it."[38] They are also similar in their character and intelligence; it is Adelaide's peculiar gift, like Emma's, that she can adroitly mimic others (cf. E, 49, 225; AT, I, 143 (I, 250-1)). And each carries her devotion to her progenitor to the point of refusing to marry until her fiancé promises to live at his father-in-law's home (E, 449; AT, III, 257-8 (IV, 331-45)). Furthermore, the pedagogic relationship between the Baroness and her daughter can be compared not only to that between Emma and Harriet, but also to the one Knightley had with Emma in her childhood. We may apply to the complex network of relationships between *Emma* and the French novel Bakhtin's description of the carnivalistic nature of parody in classical antiquity: "Parodying is the creation of a *decrowning double*: it is that 'same world turned inside out.' For this reason parody is ambivalent." In the Roman carnival, "various images (for examples, pairs of various sorts) parodied one another variously and from various points of view," creating "an entire system of crooked mirrors, elongating, diminishing, distorting in various directions and to various degrees" (PDP, 127). In *Emma* the relationships between Harriet and Emma, Emma and Mr Knightley, Emma and Mrs Weston, reproduce in diverse distortions the one between Mme d'Almane and the Comtesse, and between the Baroness and Adelaide. On the other hand, contrasts between circumstances in the two works are equally interesting: for instance, while the Baroness dedicates herself to Adelaide's education and rules her with an iron hand, affirming that a child governing a parent (or a wife ruling her husband) constitutes a form of "usurpation . . . naturally odious" (AT, I, 30 (I, 225)), Emma, as we have said, has presided at Hartfield since she was twelve, and is obliged by her father's simplemindedness to handle him as though he were the child (cf. E, 37).

The points of possible comparison and contrast are more than circumstancial, however. At the thematic level, both novels refer repeatedly to the influence the relationship between mentors and children or young people has on their education. In several episodes, we find this relationship exalted in *Adelaide and Theodore* and subjected to skeptical scrutiny in *Emma*. For example, certain situations in which Harriet finds herself bear comparison to similar ones lived by Adelaide, with Emma playing the role the Baroness d'Almane, Adelaide's mother, plays in the French novel. Probably the most striking similarity between Mme d'Almane and Emma is their penchant for matchmaking. Just as the Baroness d'Almane maneuvers in various ways in order to direct Adelaide's romantic feelings, Emma strives to govern Harriet's erotic interests. At a certain point, Harriet confesses to Emma that she has been keeping "most precious treasures" related to Mr Elton, and disposes of them in her presence (E, 337-40); on a similar occasion, Adelaide, following her mother's hint, decides to fight against "the slightest inclination" toward a young man, and thus relinquishes to her mother a "pretty box" containing "remembrances" of the young man (AT, III, 180 (IV, 181)). However, while in *Adelaide and Theodore* Mme. d'Almane rejoices in this new evidence of her success as educator, in *Emma* the heroine is shamed by this evidence of her misdirection of Harriet's affections, for Mr Elton has not only indignantly rejected Harriet, but also shown his shabby moral values. The results of the two incidents are also widely different. When she counsels her daughter not to give in to her feelings, the Baroness is merely testing Adelaide, whom she always unabashedly manipulates; the mother does mean to make a match between Adelaide and the young man she loves. Whereas in *Emma* all attempts at the manipulation of Harriet's affections end in fiascos, in the French novel the mother's actions are completely sucessful.

Emma's allusion to *Adelaide and Theodore* leads to Mr Knightley's meaningful reappraisal of his own role with regard to Emma's personal growth. While the Baroness continually advises her friend and her niece steadfastly to watch and punish their respective children (see, for instance, AT, I, 216 (I, 223)), warning now one, now the other of the two mothers against "spoiling a child, and indulging all its whims" (AT, II, 93 (II, 358)), Mr Knightley finally recognizes that his own stern attitude of the past, his interference in Emma's education, "was quite as likely to do harm as good." Emma's protest that she has benefitted from "the assistance of all your endeavors to counteract the indulgence of other people" moves Mr Knightley to reminisce, in that very conversation introduced by Emma's allusion to *Adelaide and Theodore*:

> "How often, when you were a girl, have you said to me, with one of your saucy looks—'Mr Knightley, I am going to do so and so, Papa says I may,' or 'I have Miss Taylor's leave'—something which, you knew, I did not approve. In such cases my interference was giving you two bad feelings instead of one." (E, 462)

In the last sentence a distorted echo may be heard of the Baroness' view that if a child compensates for submission to her mother by becoming even more intractable with others, then "instead of curing her of one vice you only make her guilty of more" (AT, I, 216 (I, 233)). The two passages, each showing a child relating alternately to a strict and to more lenient adults, are perfectly corresponding inversions of each other: while Adelaide submits to her mother and lords it over her governess, Emma is indulged by her father and her governess and then flaunts her liberties before Mr Knightley; while the Baroness recommends strongly subduing an "imperious mind," Mr Knightley is proposing non-intervention, admitting that his "disagreeable" lectures to Emma were self-defeating: "I do not believe I did you any good" (E, 462). Children, Mr Knightley has come to realize, ought to be given principles and then allowed to exercise their own good sense, even if the "self-correcting" process entails their making mistakes along the way. Because of its explicit ideologic content, this "echo" of the French novel in *Emma* would be more properly classified as what Bakhtin calls "hidden polemic" than as either simple allusion or parody. The episode does, as Bakhtin would say, strike "a polemical blow. . . at the other [work's] discourse on the same theme" (PDP, 195).

But, one might ask, has Emma not learned from Mr Knightley's lectures, even as an adult, most notably during the famous outing to Box Hill? The latter episode shows an interesting resemblance to one in which Adelaide joins in a joke against her governess, Miss Bridget. Let us briefly recount the two episodes, in order to compare attitudes toward the heroine's moral education in each novel. At Box Hill, her vanity flattered by Frank Churchill's attentions, Emma has misapplied her wit, cruelly making fun of that incurable bore, Miss Bates, who is nevertheless a kindly, loving person. Drawing her aside, Mr Knightley once more reproves her, "I cannot see you acting wrong without a remonstrance. How could you be so unfeeling to Miss Bates?" Emma first replies that Miss Bates probably "did not understand me," and then argues that she deserves to be laughed at, for "what is good and what is ridiculous are most unfortunately blended in her." Mr Knightley reveals that Miss Bates "has felt your full meaning," and after acknolwedging her weaknesses, observes that her poverty

> "should secure your compassion. It was badly done indeed!—*You*, whom she had known from an infant, whom she had seen grow up from a period when her notice was an honour, to have *you* now, in thoughtless spirits, and the pride of the moment, laugh at her, humble her . . . This is not pleasant to *you*, Emma, and it is very far from pleasant to me; but I must, I will —I will tell *you* truths while I can." (E, 374-5 (Stress added.))

Emma's reaction "of anger against herself, mortification, and deep concern" is immediate. As she rides home, Emma is grieved "for having taken no leave of" Mr Knightley; she is also fully contrite: "How could she have been so brutal, so cruel toward Miss Bates" (E, 376). Although it is implied she seldom cries, Emma feels "tears running down her face almost all the way home." That evening she resolves "to call upon [Miss Bates] the very next morning": "If attention, in future, could do away the past, she might hope to be forgiven" (E, 377).

In *Adelaide and Theodore*, the girl is gulty of putting a portrait of the Emperor Vespasian, whom Miss Bridget, the stern and very plain English governess, is said to resemble, in her own chamber, where the governess will see it and feel offended. When the Baroness reproaches Adelaide, suggesting that she "did it out of ill-nature," Adelaide replies that Miss Bridget is wrong "to mind what people say about [her] person." Mme d'Almane, however, retorts that Miss Bridget's weakness does not justify Adelaide's ridicule. The Baroness then affirms that Miss Bridget has felt wounded by Adelaide's offence:

> *You*, who owe friendship, respect, gratitude to Miss Bridget, *you* make her uneasy, *you* laugh at that which gives her pain, and *you* wish to make her appear ridiculous. If you were a few years older, this fault, which is a very serious one, would prove at the same time that you had a bad heart, and that you wanted

understanding. At these words Adelaide burst into tears.—Ah, mamma, how shall I repair my fault! . . . In showing Miss Bridget a sincere repentance. (AT, I, 182 (I, 321-2)— Stress in the original))

Finally, Adelaide resolves to exert herself from then on to obtain Miss Bridget's pardon.

At the level of discourse, the two passages quoted show a similar structure: the two mentors depict the action by which the heroine has laughed at the older woman, addressing the heroine directly and repeating the second person pronoun, in order to accuse her of insensitivity and to impress on her the circumstances that demand the older woman to be shown gratitude rather than ridicule. The two episodes, taken globally, also exhibit several parallels: both start with the heroine ridiculing an older, single woman of limited means; both end when the heroine resolves to gain the older woman's pardon by repeatedly showing her affectionate deference in the future. But before yielding, the heroine's defense refers to a weakness in the object of mockery. The mentor's rebuttal includes the following arguments: a) the victim's flaw does not justify the heroine's cruelty, b) the victim has been wounded in her feelings, c) the longstanding personal relationship between heroine and victim is a circumstance aggravating the fault committed. The last argument is dwelt on, playing upon the heroine's guilty feelings; the fear of appearing to disadvantage in the mentor's eyes increases her remorse, and she weeps.

In both novels, furthermore, the fault is stressed and even exaggerated by the mentor, who sees him/herself as totally unselfish, but appears unconsciously moved by more than concern for the heroine's moral welfare. The additional motivation, in the case of Mme d'Almane, is her reiterated tendency to prove her power over her daughter; in the case of Mr Knightley, it is his need to assert his intimate tie to Emma at a time when Frank seems to be gaining ground with her. As he will later come to realize, if his many interventions in the past did any good, it was not because they led to Emma's personal improvement; rather, "The good was all to myself, by making you an object of tenderest affection to me" (E, 462). There are significant differences, however, between the two episodes, for Mme d'Almane, unlike Mr Knightley, never gains any such insight into herself, nor does Mme de Genlis' narrator ever suggest that she should. And while Mme d'Almane rejoices in having rebuked Adelaide, Mr Knightley's immediate reaction is more mixed. Although he looks at Emma "with a glow of regard" when he learns she has visited Miss Bates in repentance (E, 385), his gratification is dampened by jealousy of Frank. Mr Knightley's having played the stern parent to Emma must pain him, for he has never acted as a man in love with her; Frank has apparently had no rival. Emma herself feels his sermon on Box Hill could not "issue from any feeling softer than upright justice and clear-sighted good will.—She had no hope" of his loving her (E, 416).

Mr Knightley's failure to "court" Emma is part of his inability to mold his discourse to fit fully a specific interactive purpose, an interlocutor's needs. As Emma says, his manner is "downright, decided, commanding" (E, 34); he is always "entirely convinced that [his] opinions [are] right and [his] adversary's wrong" (E, 67); he is, moreover, as Emma ironically tells him, "very fond of bending little minds" (E, 147). In spite of his plain, direct style of speaking, however, he has unconsciously used the regard she has for him to shame her into seeing things his way, and exaggerated her "offence" out of jealousy. His plain-dealing, in sum, has partly been unconscious manipulation. But he may now regret his sermonizing: if he had shown Emma how his affection had been changing into love, they (as well as Jane and Harriet) might have been spared much grief.

When Knightley learns of Frank's secret engagement to Jane and is assured by Emma she has never loved Frank, he proposes. As he speaks, he disparages *and* justifies his own "manner," the style of his discourse when addressing Emma:

> "I cannot make speeches, Emma . . . If I loved you less I might be able to talk about it more. But you know what I am.—You hear nothing but truth from me.—I have blamed you, and lectured you, and you have borne it as no other woman in England would have borne it.—Bear with the truths I would tell you now, dearest Emma, as well as you have borne with them. The manner, perhaps, may have as little to recommend them. God knows, I have been an indifferent lover.—But you understand me.—Yes, you see, you understand my feelings— and will return them if you can. At present, I ask only to hear, once to hear your voice." (E, 430)

The very fact that Mr Knightley derogates his present manner, supposing it to be the same as in the past, shows that his discourse *has* changed. The accusatory "you" of his Box Hill speech has been replaced by a "you" as recipient of an apology, as object of actions of which he now accuses himself. He used to be certain of expressing "upright justice" and universal precepts; he is now concerned with her understanding him. He has formerly expected her to answer his reproaches; now he forbears to frame her reply, asking her only to let him hear her voice. While Adelaide's mother reaffirms her parental attitude after the "Emperor Vespasian" episode, for Mr Knightley the Box Hill incident represents the last paternal lecture he will address to Emma. After he proposes and is accepted, he hopes their relationship will be based on equal "truth and sincerity with each other" (E, 446).

Emma, on the other hand, shares his aspiration but also realizes, with the narrator, that "Seldom, very seldom, does complete truth belong to any human disclosure; seldom can it happen that something is not a little disguised, or a little mistaken" (E, 431). With this reservation, she obviously agrees that their relationship in the future should be as open and as equal as possible. Although Emma finally accepts that Mr Knightley's appraisal of many situations (notably the desirability of Harriet's marrying Mr Martin) has been correct, she soon shows she will not rely on her future husband's infallibility. Thus, she laughingly doubts Mr Knightley's report that Harriet has accepted Mr Martin, supposing that Knightley has, "in the confusion of so many subjects," mistaken Mr Martin's words: "It was not Harriet's hand that he was certain of—it was the dimensions of some famous ox." When Mr Knightley protests against her supposing him "so great a blockhead," she insists, rather than retracting, "You must give me a plain, direct, answer." It is soon established both that Mr Knightley's report is correct, and that Emma will not trust his world implicitly, but will always reserve the right to judge for herself (E, 473-4). (Marilyn Butler interprets this incident as evidence that, even after Emma has improved through submission to Mr Knightley, she occasionally "slides back from [a] . . . clearer moral perception."[39] It is not clear why Emma's considering the possibility Mr Knightley might have mistaken Mr Martin's meaning can be seen as cloudy moral perception, unless Butler considers any challenge to Mr Knightley's infallibility as reprehensible.)

This is the end to Mr Knightley's sermonizing. *Emma*, it would seem, tends to regard the pedagogic role in general, and the figure of the romantic hero as the heroine's mentor in particular, in an ironic light. Emma learns from her own reflections on her experience, aided, but not determined, by the principles she has been taught; as he admits himself, Mr Knightley's penchant for lecturing her has been little more than meddling (cf. E, 462). By the end of the novel he seems to be closer than at the beginning to a view expressed by another of Austen's heroines, Elizabeth Bennet: "We all love to instruct, though we can teach only what is not worth knowing" (PP, 343). His changed views underscore the ways in which the novel's dialogue with *Adelaide and Theodore* pokes fun at the conventional morality of idealized filial devotion and feminine submission to both parents and husband. Indeed, the contrast between the two works provides further evidence of Mr Knightley's fallibility.

In addition to parodical dialogue with *Adelaide and Theodore*, Austen uses other forms of dialogue with literary languages in *Emma*, incorporating the characters' tendency to view their experience through the filter of fictionalizations. Emma, for example, sees herself both as Harriet's fairy godmother, deciding to "improve her" by keeping her away from her low former friends and introducing her "into good society" (E, 23). She also considers herself Harriet's knightly savior from the assault, not of giants or villains, but of the Martins, in the image Emma construes of them as matchmaking, social-climbing egoists: Emma "did suspect *danger to her poor little friend from all {the Martins'} hospitality and kindness*—and that, if she were not taken care of, she might be required to *sink herself forever*" (E, 28—stress added). The novel's ironic view of Emma's attitudes of this kind often constitutes a "double-voiced discourse of pathos" (cf. DN, 394), in which Emma's romanticizations appear colored by the narrator's tongue-in-cheek report, as is evident in the phrases underlined above.

Emma is not the only character who interprets her world through fictionalizations. Harriet, for instance, in addition to keeping a box of mementos associated with the man she loves, just as Adelaide did, constructs other situations she is living through as episodes of sentimental fiction. In one incident, she cannot bear to have anyone read the little charade Emma has convinced her is Mr Elton's covert declaration of love; Emma her-self must argue her out of such "consciousness" and "refinements" (E, 77). Emma's lecture in this episode shows her awareness of the ludicrousness of novel-induced aspirations to *bon ton*; as Bakhtin points out, romances tend to idealize relationships in order to distance themselves from everyday life, providing a dis-course opposed to "vulgar discourse and its coarse ways" (DN, 384). On another occasion, Harriet avers she "will never marry," since she is in love with a man so infinitely superior "to all the rest of the world" (E, 339). (At this point, Emma, thinking she is referring to Frank, counters Harriet's silent-lifelong-devotion motif with a restatement of the *Pamela* fiction, raising Harriet's hopes by saying, "there have been matches of greater disparity"— E, 342). Similarly, Frank Churchill's letter explaining himself to Mrs Weston is full of romanticizations; one example is his assertion that if Jane had refused to enter into a secret engagement with him, he would have gone mad (E, 437).

This use of the language and conceptions of sentimental fictions is not limited to young women and romantic young men, however. Mr Knightley himself makes up a fictionalization of his own when he attempts to console Emma for what he thinks is her broken heart over Frank's engagement. His language, in which Frank appears as the blackest villain ("Time, my dearest Emma, time will heal the wound . . . Abominable scoundrel!), while he regards Emma as "this sweetest and best of all creatures, faultless in spite of all her faults" (E, 433), bears the stamp of sentimental fiction. He even fictionalizes Jane Fairfax's future as Frank's wife, apostrophizing her and elegizing before Emma: "Jane, Jane, you will be a miserable creature" (E, 426). The narrator's ironic view of Mr Knightley's fictionalizations is evident in the mocking conclusion to the chapter, summarizing the action:

[Mr Knightley] had found [Emma] agitated and low—Frank Churchill was a villain.—He heard her declare that she had never loved him. Frank Churchill's character was not desperate.—She was his own Emma, by hand and word, when they returned into the house; and if he could have thought of Frank Churchill then, he might have deemed him a very good sort of fellow. (E, 433)

This entire chapter is full of similar ironies; the narrator's voice becomes more evidently parodical when she reveals that Emma had not "the heroism of sentiment" nor the "simple sublimity" of refusing Mr Knightley because her friend Harriet loved him (E, 431). A similar intention to mock the elegant coherence of novelistic episodes of proposal can be found in the famous narration of Emma's response to Mr Knightley's proposal, "What did she say? Just what she ought, of course. A lady always does" (E, 431). The merging of irony and emotional restraint in this passage may serve to illustrate Bakhtin's assertion that novelistic pathos, "if it is authentic, shies away from a discourse that is *openly* emotional, not yet separated from its subject" (DN, 395). Nevertheless, the generalized use of romanticizations by the major characters in *Emma* suggests that, in Austen's view, the effect of novels on our understanding of the world is wider and perhaps more inescapable than it would at first appear.

Austen's characters understand their world through conventions, not only those derived from fictional literature, but also those present in everyday discourse, those mental and linguistic constructions that have been called scripts and frames by cognitive psychologists.[40] The utterance by the novel's characters of such conventional, axiomatic-sounding labels and social norms, is usually countered ironically either by Emma or the narrator, or, in double irony, by both. In this sense, the text enters into dialogue with conventional languages, laughing at them as inescapable, commonplace conceptions of the world that tend to impoverish the mind, turning people into ludicrous automatons and self-important fools. Thus, in Austen's narrative, words are engaged in what Bakhtin would call "a dialogue as a living rejoinder" (DN, 279)) to the speaking subject's alienation, to his/her acceptance of conventional, dominant languages.

The character who most often and evidently uses conventional frames is Mrs Elton, who clings to clichés ("Surry is the garden of England"—E, 273) as to dogmas and holds ludicrously stereotyped views of the proper way of doing things (such as the need for donkeys, bonnets and baskets as the "apparatus of happiness" for strawberry-gathering—E, 355-8), views that are usually tied to peculiar labels. To her, a drive in the countryside constitutes "exploring"; married women are divided into those who have and do not have "resources" that may allow them the independence of not needing "*the world* . . . —parties, balls, plays" (E, 276-7). She is also much given to using what Robert P. Abelson calls "categorical scripts," or the understanding of situations as generic types determining a form of behavior.[41] Thus, she insists that married women "are too apt to give up music" (E, 277), despairing of her own musical future so resolutely that she converts the cliché into a self-fulfilling prophecy.

As critics have repeatedly pointed out, many of Mrs Elton's foibles appear in less evident or less vulgar form in Emma; the use of scripts is no exception. In her lectures to Harriet Emma often resorts to unexceptionable, though misapplied, statements in the form of both categorical scripts ("A woman is not to marry a man merely because she is asked"—E, 54) and hypothetical ones, in which two or more alternatives and their consequences are contemplated[42] ("I lay it down as a general rule, Harriet, that if a woman *doubts* as to whether she should accept a man or not, she certainly ought to refuse him"—E, 52). Sometimes Mrs Elton's use of a categorical script is itself a signal to the reader of Emma's impending application of a similar one, in a case of the reader's "preset apperception" like the ones discussed above.

Such is the case in the episode in which Mrs Elton visits Hartfield for the first time. Mrs Elton's effusions about Hartfield lead her to predict her sister and brother-in-law will be "enchanted with it," and then to utter a categorical script, "People who have extensive grounds themselves are always pleased with any thing in the same style." Emma, who realizes such people care "very little for the extensive grounds of any body else," decides this "doubled-dyed" error is meant to disclose the grandeur of Mrs Elton's relatives, the Sucklings. As soon as Mrs Elton leaves, Emma mentally explodes:

"Insufferable woman!. . . Absolutely insufferable! . . . Much beyond my hopes. Harriet is disgraced by any comparison. Oh! what would Frank Churchill say to her, if he were here? . . . Ah, there I am—thinking of him directly. Always the first person to be thought of! How I catch myself out! Frank Churchill comes so regularly into my mind!" (E, 279)

In addition to other ironies aimed at Emma (her unwittingly confessing she had "hopes" of Mrs Elton being insufferable, probably in order to confirm Mr Elton's bad judgment in his choice of a bride), Emma's "catching herself out" is nearly as double-dyed an error as Mrs Elton's. Emma is mentally playing the novelistic role of a woman secretly in love, and she plays it with the aid of a categorical script about people we love as "Always the first to be thought of."

Mr Knightley also often resorts to scripts, as when he surmises that Frank, as "a young man brought up by those who are proud, luxurious and selfish" must have all the same failings (E, 145). In the matter of Frank's pride, at least, Mr Knightley proves to be wrong. He is also partly wrong when he uses another categorical script, "a man can always do. . . his duty [if he chooses]; not by manoeuvering and finessing, but by vigour and resolution" (E, 146) to condemn Frank for not coming earlier to pay a courtesy visit on Mrs Weston. Although it is true that Frank delays his visit unnecessarily, he does need "manoeuvering and finessing" in order to do what his aunt does not like, whether it is his duty or his pleasure. Indeed, much as he would like, for Jane Fairfax's sake, to come to Highbury more often and to stay for longer periods, he must stay at home in accordance with his aunt's wishes.

There are collective as well as individual uses of frames and scripts. All of Highbury sings the praises of "the handsome letter" written by Frank to Mrs Weston on the occasion of her marriage (E, 18); Mr Woodhouse uses the clichéd frame when reporting Highbury news to his older daughter, Isabella (E, 96). Mr Woodhouse, furthermore, very often refers to categorical scripts, whether they refer to young ladies as "delicate plants" (E, 294) or the proper etiquette in the treatment of brides. He does not realize that the rituals he observes with the naiveté of a clockwork doll in a child's pantomime have any meaning, or serve any purpose beyond the satisfaction they give from the familiarity of old use. Therefore, he cannot understand Emma when she tells him that his observance of the categorical script that "A bride . . . is always the first in company, let the others be who they may" might lead to more marriages, since "It is encouraging people to marry if you make so much of them." For him, his deference to brides is "mere common politeness and good-breeding and has nothing to do with any encouragement . . . to marry." Emma's witticisms on such forms of courtesy as "vanity baits for poor young ladies" merely make her father nervous (E, 280). And so Emma once more defers to his comfort and drops the matter, leaving it to the reader to reflect on whether such social carrots might have some influence on *her* vanity as much as on any other young lady's and move her to matrimony.

The need for such "vanity-baits" in a society where marriage can be very onerous to "poor young ladies" is another reflection we may derive from this pasage. On this basis, we may wonder whether the narrator's continued dialogue with dominant languages is not sometimes overpowered by the force of this dominance. For the novel, after all, does end with Emma marrying. All her powers as an "imaginist," all her wit and discernment, her vigor of mind and character, will not secure her any social position, any use of her talents, other than marriage. With regard to women's social role, we may wonder whether the "dialogic nature of language," the "struggle among socio-linguistic points of view" to which Bakhtin refers (DN, 273) does not most often end in monologic victory for the dominant ideology. And yet it is possible that the public significance of women's domestic role at the end of the eighteenth and the beginning of the nineteenth centuries may have been greater than we now imagine.

Elizabeth Langland's investigation of the socio-political function of housewives as it appears in nineteenth-century literature can help us to inquire into the novel's attitude to what Wollstonecraft would call married woman's "fulfilling the duties of her station." Although Langland's corpus was made up of Victorian novels and documents, many of her observations are applicable to *Emma*. In Victorian society, in spite of prevailing ideology which "held the house as haven, a private sphere opposed to the public sphere of commerce . . ., the house and its mistress in fact served as a significant adjunct to a man's business endeavors."[43] Middle-class women controlled significant "discursive practices" which helped to ensure bourgeois hegemony in Victorian England by guaranteeing their husbands' place in society. Among these we find strategies to manage lower-class dissent and mastery of rituals for status display. Several of these strategies and rituals are important aspects of Emma's activities as mistress of Hartfield, by which she played the social and political function of a middle-class housewife. (For *Emma* is unique as a novel in showing a single young lady living the social role she will play after marriage.) Emma, it is true, believes the Woodhouses' singular position as the number one family in pre- or near-industrial Highbury to be unalterable. At most, she might have to put an upstart in his/her place; she need not strive to hold a relation of equality among other middle-class social lions or of acceptance by aristocrats, as the typical middle-class Victorian would do. And yet Emma's world is changing, and she is being drawn into a struggle she deems to be beneath her.

In spite of the protagonist's blindness to the significance of her own social roles, the novel does recognize housewives' socio-political function. Emma herself is shown carrying out activities tending to the same ends Langland discovers in the actions of housewives in Victorian novels. As strategies for regulating the behavior of the lower classes Emma uses both philanthropy (cf. Emma's visit to the sick cottager, E, 83-87) and the management of her servants in similar ways to those used by Dickens' Esther Summerson in *Bleak House* or by Gaskell's Mrs Gibson in *Wives and Daughters*. Emma is a most efficient mistress, keeping her control over her housekeeper "in so regular a train" that she can only feel contempt for Mrs Elton's using such duties as an excuse to neglect her music (E, 278). Emma's superiority over Mrs Elton is similarly evident in the contrast between the latter's vulgar overuse of finery in dress (cf. E, 484) and the former's restraint, in accordance with the "simplicity is elegance" discourse of the high middle-class.[44]

She also exhibits her mastery of rituals for status display in her smooth handling of every aspect of her household. Emma is highly proficient in her role as hostess, for example, presiding over dinners and other social functions for which she furnishes abundant delicacies. She sees the dinners she provides for her "second set" of friends, for instance, as almost feudal patronage, rewards to loyal vassals who pay homage to her father (cf. E, 20). Her interest in showing her family's social prominence extends to a most modern tendency to conspicuous consumption. Thus, for instance, Emma, who sentimentalizes her own devotion to her father to the point of weeping over the idea of quitting him to get married "as a sin of thought" (E, 435), does not hesitate to persuade him, who hates change, to use a more fashionable, "large, modern circular table" instead of the old Pembroke he has dined on for forty years (E, 347).

In spite of Emma's unawareness of her participation in the competition for social prominence, there is no doubt that she can and does participate in the struggle for status. Indeed, she manages her servants, household consumption and charities efficiently enough to bolster her family's prestige. That she does it in a seemingly effortless manner only underscores her proficiency; indeed her powers seem superior to her role, which leads to pose a new problem, that of Emma's surplus of ability.

Although Emma executes her tasks to perfection, the text does not seem to endorse her social objectives. The reader is invited to view ironically the public role provided for middle-class women. For one thing, Emma's stress on hierarchy is one of the recurring points of contention with Mr Knightley, who emphasizes the equalizing bonds of community rather than social differences. Thus, while balancing his activity as a capitalist "gentleman farmer" with his nearly feudal concern with protecting impoverished neighbors like Miss Bates, he tries to include as many of his friends as he can in his definition of "gentlemen and ladies"; for instance, he defines Mr Martin as a "gentleman-farmer" (E, 62), while Emma places him among "the yeomanry" (E, 29). Miss Bates herself represents communal ties; as Julia Prewitt Brown puts it, "all classes join and cooperate in her ... Her small apartment joins the older gentry (the Woodhouses and Knightleys), the new rich (the Coles), and the lower-middle to lower-class townspeople and clerks."[45] This relative blindness to class distinctions appears as a positive attitude that is at odds with a defense of status such as Emma continually undertakes. In the end, Emma will accept the wisdom of many of Mr Knightley's attitudes toward social relations; the novel, shrewd as it is in its analysis of the intricacies of power, advocates a utopian sense of community in which exclusionary, hegemonic power is defeated.

On the other hand, the novel is imbued with a positive attitude to power in the sense of energy, force, dynamism, the ability and capacity to act in a decisive manner. And yet no socio-political or professional role is proposed for women as an alternative to the defense of the family's status. Does the novel, then, advocate no exercise of power (in the positive sense) for women? Is the proper course for Emma to accept women's traditional position of subordination and submission to men?

The issue of power in relationships between men and women is posed early, in the argument between Emma and Mr Knightley about Harriet Smith's rejection of Mr Martin's proposal. Once the issue is noted, its relevance to other episodes becomes evident. According to Emma, Harriet is too good for Mr Martin; this position, which is both snobbish and based on a romanticization of Harriet's unknown origin, she will ultimately reverse. Initially, however, she also holds that her friend can aspire to a man in a higher social position, such as Mr Elton. Mr Knightley disagrees with Emma on both points.

Foucault's categories of power are useful to explicate their difference in views, and to see the relevance of these issues to other episodes in the novel. (The following analysis, it must be noted, does not yet enter into what

Foucault in the same work refers to as "objective capacities"[46] and I have called "positive power," which in *Emma*, as in much of Austen's work, takes a carnivalesque, utopian form.) Foucault defines three techniques or forms of social power, as "domination (ethnic, social and religious)," as "exploitation [separating] individuals from what they produce," and as "that which ties the individual to himself and submits him to others" by producing a subjectivity prone to submission.[47]

In discussing the possibilities of Harriet's marriage to Mr Elton, Emma and Mr Knightley show different conceptions of what motivates men in choosing a wife. Both seem aware of the role played by social power in this choice, but they differ in their assessment of the type of power sought by men. While Emma believes men seek primarily the sense of power provided by lording it over a meek wife, Mr Knightley holds that "men of sense . . . do not want silly wives," and that Mr Elton is mostly interested in the economic and social power provided by a young woman's good fortune and class position (E, 60-68). In these terms, Emma considers the subjective power of making a woman submit a sufficient condition in a man's choice of a wife. Mr Knightley, on the other hand, denies that submissiveness has any attraction for sensible men, and holds that the forms of social and economic power Foucault calls domination and exploitation are the only relevant inducements when men such as Mr Elton choose a wife.

As it turns out, both are partly right and partly wrong. Mr Elton will not be drawn to Harriet's dependent, submissive attitudes, but to Emma's fortune and social position. The second woman he will choose, however, for all her claims to liveliness and independent "resources," delights in publicly professing "true conjugal obedience" to her "lord and master" (E, 457). Other relationships in the novel similarly disprove Emma and Mr Knightley by turns. Frank Churchill, contrary to Emma's strictures on the delight men find in compliant wives, has been attracted to Jane Fairfax precisely for her moral superiority; although her love for him moves her to consent to a secret engagement against her own sense of its wrongness, she often does not yield to him when her judgment tells her he is wrong. This is evident not only in their quarrel as she leaves the strawberry-picking party at Donwell Abbey, but also in her reproach when he indulges in recollections of episodes she considers shameful and thus best forgotten (E, 480). Frank himself readily admits Jane is much his superior (E, 479). It is true, as Margaret Kirkham notes, that in calling her "an angel" he gives evidence of a gallantry that can be seen as an inverted, chivalric form of sexism,[48] but this form of sexist power is not the same as tyranny over a meek wife. However, in spite of Mr Knightley's insisting that sensible men do not want silly wives, both Mrs John Knightley and Harriet Smith (later Mrs Robert Martin) are slow-witted and totally compliant. The former has a standard answer for everything her husband says: "Very true, my love" (E, 113). She resembles Mr Woodhouse in her poor intelligence (E, 92); like him, she often understands "only in part" (E, 95). And Harriet is so spineless and so slow she cannot decide such a simple matter as whether to have a purchase sent to Hartfield or to Mrs Goddard's (E, 235). In her relief when Emma decides for her we may see the success of the education Harriet has received; she is, in Foucault's terminology, subjectively "tied to herself" so strongly that she cannot act and therefore gratefully submits to others. She will make a very good wife, if the criterion is taken from Mr Knightley's ironic praise to Mrs Weston for her having learned "the very matrimonial point of submitting your own will and doing as you were bid" (E, 38).

If Mr Knightley cannot grant the attraction a woman submissive to the point of paralysis has for some men, it is both because he is less sexist himself and because his own sexist prejudice, such as it is, blinds him to the oppression of women around him. In spite of his enlightened aspirations to social equality and his endorsement of a rational attitude in women, Mr Knightley shows this prejudice in his surprising lack of liberality when appraising young ladies. Thus, he gives evidence of his prejudice against Harriet Smith when he avers that, in choosing her, "as a rational companion or useful helpmate [Mr Martin] could not do worse" (E, 61). This negative judgment is unfair, for Mr Martin could do much worse than choose Harriet, who is kind, principled and willing to learn, in spite of her shortcomings. Again, when Emma accuses Mr Knightley of believing that in any disagreement between them she must invariably be in the wrong, he counters, "I have still the advantage of you by sixteen years' experience, and by not being a pretty young woman and a spoiled child" (E, 99). Obviously, age, gender and beauty are hardly arguments; their invocation shows Mr Knightley's various prejudices.

In the end, Emma and Mr Knightley both will yield to each other, toning down their prejudices. Emma, who had earlier held it to be impossible for her to visit Mrs Robert Martin, of Abbey Mill Farm (E, 53), ends by looking forward, not just to Harriet's return from London to marry Robert Martin, but to getting to know Mr Martin himself (E, 475). And Mr Knightley finally admits he is "now very willing to grant you all Harriet's good qualities," among which he lists amiability, "very good notions [and] very seriously good principles" (E, 474). The text thus uses the longstanding argument between Mr Knightley and Emma over Harriet Smith to endorse the need for both greater openness to social mobility and a more enlightened attitude toward women's abilities.

One of Harriet's "good principles," praised by Mr Knightley, is her "placing her happiness in the affections and utility of domestic life," an attitude Emma has always explicitly upheld. Is this to be interpreted as endorsement of domestic life as the only right source of happiness for women? Indeed, no other social role for women is ever even considered in the novel. On the other hand, this position provides no solution for Emma's dissatisfaction with her domestic role. For Emma has needed more; from adolescence onwards, she has had the power of a socially respected middle-class housewife, and it has not been enough for her. She is lonely and unfulfilled after losing Miss Taylor's company, which provided the double pleasures of domestic intimacy and mild submission to Emma's personal power (cf. E, 5-6, 38).

Furthermore, much as Emma changes, she does not appear to have reached "the very material matrimonial point," described by Mr Knightley to Mrs Weston, "of submitting [her] own will and doing as [she] is bid" (E, 38). As Mr Knightley early recognizes, Harriet's charm for Emma is the power Emma can exercise over her. This inclination to control others is due to Emma's failing, which she must correct as the novel progresses, her "disposition to think a little too well of herself," fed by "the power of having rather too much her own way" (E, 5). Nevertheless, I believe we must distinguish between a love of power as moral defect in Emma and her need for a sphere of action demanding enough of her powers and personal abilities.

In spite of the views of critics who see morality in feminine submission, Emma's flaws, arrogance and willfullness, are not presented as more damnable in women than in men. Mr John Knightley, Knightley's younger brother, shares some of Emma's flaws; in his home his word is law, and he can little bear any doubts about the wisdom of his decisions (cf. E, 106). He is so self-centered he enjoys talking to few people outside his family. His wife, Isabella, "worships" him; her attitude, however, is presented as bad for her husband, for "His temper was not his great perfection," and "The extreme sweetness of her temper must hurt his." Both Emma and Mr Knightley are forced to step in to cover up for his "want of respectful forbearance toward" his father-in-law (E, 92-107). If the habit of controling others is bad for Emma, it is even less salutary for Mr John Knightley.

At the opposite extreme to Emma's vanity and love of power, we find the attitude that could make her resigned to the roles society offers to women. The best exponent of this attitude is Isabella, who, "passing her life with those she doated on, full of their merits, blind to their faults, and always innocently busy, might have been a model of right feminine happiness" (E, 140). However, as we have seen, this model of loving blindness only becomes possible because of Isabella's weakness of understanding (cf. E, 92). Although Emma, fully contrite after having led Harriet to fall in love with Mr Elton, and forced to tell her the news of his proposal to herself, feels temporarily attracted to the model of sweetness and tenderness represented by Harriet (as much as by Isabella and Mr Woodhouse himself (E, 269)), she quickly realizes, "It was rather late in the day to set about being simple-minded and ignorant" (E, 142).

Although Emma does aspire to become more "humble and discreet," her personal moral development will not supply greater attraction to the only form of work that is open to her. It is not that she does not enjoy looking after "the little affairs, arrangements, perplexities and pleasures of her father and herself," for she recognizes that on "all these little matters . . . the daily happiness of private life depends" (E, 117). But these "little matters," however enjoyable, are not enough to fill her life. A comparison between the degree to which work and public role make demands on objective and subjective relationships in her life and Mr Knightley's reveals great differences.

A useful tool for the comparison is Foucault's definition of "Power relations, relationships of communication, and objective capacities" as "three types of relationships which in fact always overlap one another, support one another reciprocally, and use each other mutually as means to an end."[49] Foucault defines capacity as a power "which is exerted over things and gives the ability to modify, use, consume, or destroy them"; relations of communication as those "which transmit information by means of a language, a system of signs, or any other symbolic medium"; and power relations as "relationships between partners," "an ensemble of actions which induce others and follow from one another"; indeed, the "exercise of power consists in guiding the possibility of conduct and putting in order the possible outcome."[50]

While Mr Knightley's work as a gentleman farmer and his role as a magistrate require his ingenuity (his "objective capacity") in solving either "some point of law" or "the plan of a drain, the change of a fence, the felling of a tree, and the destination of every acre for wheat, turnips, or spring corn" (E, 100) for economically productive purposes, Emma's decisions need not consult market prices or technological advances. At most she will exercise her ability to choose between sending the Bates family a leg or a whole hind quarter of a porker just killed at Hartfield (E, 172). While Mr Knightley will need to engage in frequent communications with both William Larkins, his steward, and his tenants (Robert Martin, for instance), Emma's conferences with her housekeeper are not mentioned except in the oblique allusion to such matters being "in so regular a train" that they required very little attention. While Mr Knightley needs to meet at the Crown with Mr Elton and other prominent citizens in order to exert a proper influence on the public affairs of Highbury (E, 456), and while the exercise of his power relations extends to preserving public order when threatened by such events as harassment of ladies by the gypsies (E, 334), Emma's power typically encompasses such issues as the possibility of reviving the old balls at the Crown (E, 198). The social importance of such issues has been pointed out above; however, in such a community as Highbury the politics of entertainment can hardly tax Emma's wits.

Prominent women in Highbury have power over servants as their "ideological Other,"[51] but are severely restricted both in choice (in contrast to men, who may choose between professions, women have a single role to play) and in the extent to which their abilities are exercised in discharge of their duties. Their work has a political significance, but the types of conduct they direct and the relations of communication they engage in are circumscribed to repetitive and often mechanical or trivial pursuits. Moreover, the novel recognizes the wife's generic role of submission to the husband's will as a social imperative (cf. Mr Knightley's allusion to "the very matrimonial point" of a wife "submitting [her] own will, and doing" as she is bid (E, 38)). Thus *Emma* paints a portrait of the middle-class housewife as a political player who works to preserve the hegemony of her class, but who is herself, by reason of gender, the male's "other" as "the one over whom power is exercised."[52]

Emma started, at twenty, suffering a mid-life crisis, feeling the typical emptiness of a housewife whose dependents have left and whose "spouse" (in Emma's peculiar case, her father plays the domestic role of master of the home of which she is mistress) can provide no real companionship. Although, at the end of the novel, her marriage to Knightley represents progress in her emotional and sexual life, as she gives up her illusion of being self-sufficient, of being able to satisfy her need for "objects" of her affection with occasional visits of her sister's family (cf. E, 85), her need for an outlet for her capacities ends only in frustration. By marrying an older man and presumably starting a family, Emma must be moving eventually toward a repetition of her sad situation at the beginning of the novel. Furthermore, by Mr Knightley's own standards, Emma is the loser in the practical aspect of her change in situation; while Miss Taylor, who "has been used to have two persons to please" in marrying Mr Weston must gain by having "but one" (E, 11), Emma's marriage represents an alteration in the opposite direction, from having one person to please to having two: her father and her husband.

And yet the text asks us to rejoice at her change, at "the perfect happiness of the union" (E, 484). The only positive answer to the dilemma might be found in viewing the resolution, Mr Knightley's decision to move into Hartfield, Emma's home, rather than ask the phobic Mr Woodhouse to move into Mr Knightley's home, Donwell Abbey, as a partial abolition of patriarchy, as a flight into matrilocal utopia. The novelist's decision to produce this move constitutes, as Julia Prewitt Brown observes, "a subtly feminist praise of Mr Knightley, whose practical sensibility does not include the traditional masculine insistence that his future wife leave her family to become Mrs Knightley, the mistress of Donwell."[53] But the move is even more significant if viewed as utopian, as marking a separation between the ordinary world, represented by Highbury, located in Surrey, England, and Hartfield as a non-place, an ideal society capable of producing "perfect happiness" (E, 484). In the world outside Hartfield, after all, other marriages are either unequal in virtue, like that of Frank and Jane, equal in folly, like the Eltons', or unequal in love, like the Westons'. Only in the union between Emma and Mr Knightley do we find "equal worth" (E, 465), equal respect, and equal love.

Mr Knightley's move to Hartfield reinforces the world-upside-down framework of the novel, set up by the domestic structure of Hartfield. Thus we find utopia and inversion shaping the festive laughter with which the novel ends; an analysis of the question of power has led us back to carnivalesque categories. The concept of carnival, then, is also relevant to the problem of women's subordination and women's relations to power as they are posed in *Emma*.

It is now time to go back to the question that led us to the discussion of power: is the hegemony of dominant languages in the end inescapable? The question may now be worded more precisely: is Emma's marriage a sign of the novelist's surrender to the ideology of male domination? Is the laughter of carnival merely a form of anaesthesia, an alienating illusion?

On the contrary, it is possible to see in *Emma* strategies of resistance to patriarchy that appear to unite astute reflections on women and power and the laughter of carnival. Patriarchal ideology appears in the end locked in a contradiction between the claims of father and future husband, for Mr Woodhouse cannot reconcile himself to Emma's marriage, even if she is to continue living at Hartfield. The solution, the wedge that breaks the insoluble dilemma, appears in a pedestrian *deus ex machina* in the form of a poultry pilferer in the neighborhood. Mr Woodhouse's fears make him eager to accept "his son-in-law's protection" to save him from "wretched alarm every night of his life" (E, 484). The ludicrous danger and the happy solution are marks of the narrator's levity, her irreverent, ironic bow before that apparent monolith, masculine strength.

The novel's last brush strokes unite in one paragraph Mrs Elton's triumph upon hearing of the shabbiness of the marriage ceremony ("Very little white satin, very few lace veils; a most pitiful business!"), the "band of true friends" and "the perfect happiness of the union" (E, 484). Thus we witness the last dance, the last group of figures in the pageant, incongruously mixing the motley forces of class conflict, loving community and the marriage union as utopian perfection.

NOTES

1. According to Cassandra Austen, *Emma* was composed between January 1814 and March 1815, when Jane Austen was 38-39. Even if we accept Q. D. Leavis' challenge to the received chronology, and her argument that *Emma* includes material that had earlier gone into *The Watsons*, the unfinished novel Austen worked on from 1803-4, when she was 28-29 (cf. "A Critical Theory of Jane Austen's Writings," *Scrutiny*, X (1941), we would still have to hold that *Emma* was begun later than either *Pride and Prejudice* or *Northanger Abbey*. *Pride and Prejudice* was begun in its original form as *First Impressions* when the author was 21, *Northanger Abbey* (first called *Susan*, later *Catherine*) was first drafted when she was 23. For a recent account of the traditional chronology, see A. Walton Litz, "A Chronology of Composition," *The Jane Austen Companion*, pp. 47-59.

2. "*Emma* was perhaps the *most* gradual performance of all Jane Austen's novels" (Margaret Kirkham, *Jane Austen: Feminism and Fiction*. p. 121).

3. Cf. Bakhtin's discussion of centripetal forces in language ("Discourse in the novel," DI, 27).

4. Elizabeth Langland, "Nobody's Angels: Domestic Ideology and Middle-Class Women in the Victorian Novel" (PMLA, Vol. 107, No. 2 (March, 1992)). I believe Langland's analysis can be successfully applied to the discursive situation of women in fictional works written some decades before the Victorian era.

5. Wayne C. Booth, *The Rhetoric of Fiction* (Chicago: The University of Chicago Press, 1961), p. 260

6. Bernard J. Paris, *Character and Conflict in Jane Austen's Novels*, (Detroit, Mich.: Wayne State University Press, 1978), p. 68.

7. Allison G. Sulloway, "Emma Woodhouse and *A Vindication of the Rights of Woman*,"*Wordsworth Circle* 7 (Autumn 1976), pp. 323, 325, 332.

8. Booth's assertion that the comic aspect of the novel is based on wrongness that is resolved in the conclusion seems to be based on an optimism both regarding certainty of right and wrong and the perfectibility of human beings that seems hard to square with the complexity and scepticism of Austen's text.

9. Emma sees an apothecary, a lawyer, a merchant's horses, "a butcher with his tray, a tidy old woman travelling homewards from shop with her full basket, two curs quarrelling over a dirty bone, and a string of dawdling children round the baker's little bow-window eyeing the gingerbread, and was amused enough" (E, 233). The concerns of these people, most of whom cannot make a social call on Emma, will not enter the novel directly; Emma dismisses the sisters of the "pert young lawyer" (E, 137) as "without exception the most vulgar girls in Highbury" (E, 233). But when our heroine, having learned her lesson, finally looks forward to getting to know Mr Robert Martin, a yeoman farmer (E, 475), we realize that *Emma* is partly about the rise of the yeomanry and tradesmen to a prominent place in Highbury. For an interesting though perhaps too traditional comparison between Austen and George Eliot on this point of including ordinary people below the middle class in fiction, see Frank W. Bradbrook, *Jane Austen: Emma* (London: Edward Arnold, 1961, pp. 43-4).

10. *Jane Austen and Her Art*, pp. 94-5.

11. J.J. Burrows, *Jane Austen's Emma* (Sydney: Sydney University Press, 1968, pp. 99-100).

12. For an interpretation of this passage opposite to my own, see Alistair Duckworth, *"Emma* and the Dangers of Individualism," *The Improvement of the Estate*, p. 167.

13. Geoffrey Chaucer, "The Knight's Tale,"*The Canterbury Tales*, eds. A. Kent Hieatt and Constance Hieatt (London: Bantam Books, 1984, pp.138-40). For a commentary on Chaucerian influences on another novel, *Persuasion*, see Jocelyn Harris' "Anne Elliot, the Wife of Bath and Other Friends," in *Jane Austen: New Perspectives*, pp. 273-93.

14. Although traditionally Theseus' First Mover speech has been interpreted as reflecting Chaucer's severely ordered cosmological view, recently many critics have argued for an ironic reading, a depiction of the universe as chaotic and Theseus speech as either a laudable attempt to create the illusion of symmetry or a tyrannical imposition of an ideology serving the interests of the aristocracy. For a discussion of the controversy and an interesting compromise, see Judith Ferster, *Chaucer on Interpretation*, (Cambridge: Cambridge University Press,1985) pp. 23-45.

15. See, for example, Alistair Duckworth's *"Emma* and the Dangers of Individualism," in *The Improvement of the Estate*, especially pp. 154-178.

16. Harry Knowles Girling, "Review" (of Gene Koppel's "The Religious
    Dimension of Jane Austen's Novels," *Eighteenth-Century Fiction*, Vol. I.
    No. 4 (July 1989), p. 351).

17. Cf. Elizabeth Langland's article "Nobody's Angels: Domestic Ideology
    and Middle-Class Women in the Victorian Novel," PMLA, Vol. 107,
    No. 2 (March 1992), pp. 290-304.

18. For a view for Highbury totally opposite to mine as the world of the
    pastoral idyll, see Lionel Trilling, "Emma and the Legend of Jane
    Austen," *Beyond Culture* (New York: Viking Press, 1965), especially pp.
    48-85.

19. One of the reasons why Mr Knightley is able to preserve his view of the
    world as well-ordered in the midst of so much evidence to the contrary
    is his determination, his concentration on is own purposes, his sturdy
    (and very attractive) imperviousness to little things . No two characters
    are more different than he and Miss Bates, but she does not irritate him.
    As Mrs Weston very aptly says, "She might talk on; and if he wanted to
    say any thing himself, he would only talk louder, and drown her voice"
    (E, 226). Such singlemindedness, however, will need some correction,
    and his views some expansion, as we shall see.

20. Graham Hough asserts that Mr Knightley establishes the stylistic
    pattern of the novel; his speech is identical to the objective narration
    with which the novel began. Although Mr Hough recognizes that "all
    characters we are to approve assimilate their speech to the objective," he
    considers the language of generalization and the narrator as somehow
    male-dominated, although he does not explain why generalizations are
    masculine ("Narrative and Dialogue in Jane Austen," *Critical Quarterly*,
    12, 1970, pp. 218-20).

21. David Lodge, "Jane Austen's Novels: Form and Structure," *The Jane
    Austen Companion*, ed. J. David Grey (New York: MacMillan, 1986), p.
    177.

22. See V. N. Volosinov, *Marxism and the Philosophy of Language*, tr. Ladislaw
    Mateika and I. R. Titunik (Cambridge, Mass: Harvard University Press,
    1986), pp. 109-159, especially pp. 136-7.

23. There is already a voluminous literature on this subject. Among the
    works I have found most helpful are, in addition to Volosinov's book, Roy
    Pascal's *The Dual Voice* (Manchester: Manchester University Press,
    1977), Dorrit Cohn's psychologically oriented study *Transparent Minds:*

Narrative Modes for Presenting Consciousness in Fiction (Princeton University Press, 1978), and the more formalistic work by Geoffrey Leech and Michael Short *Style in Fiction: A Linguistic Introduction to English Fictional Prose* (London: Longman, 1981). An excellent study on textual polyphony applying Bakhtin's and Volosinov's concepts to the investigation of reported speech in literary narrative is Graciela Reyes' *Polifonía Textual: La Citación en el relato literario* (Madrid: Editorial Gredos, 1984).

24. Claudia Johnson, *Jane Austen: Women, Politics and the Novel*, p. 128.

25. Graham Hough, "Narrative and Dialogue in Jane Austen," *Critical Quarterly* 12 (1970), 212.

26. This passage is a good example of what Volosinov calls the impressionistic modification of indirect discourse, in which thought or speech are "reported very freely, abbreviated, often only highlighting its themes and dominants... What comes through is the author's irony, his accentuation, his hand in ordering and abbreviating the material" (p. 133).

27. Volosinov, *Marxism and the Philosophy of Language*, p. 133.

28. Volosinov, p. 134.

29. Volosinov, pp. 158-9.

30. Thus, Maria Vaiana Taylor declares, Mr Knightley's "linguistic similarity to the narrator makes his the normative persuasive on the action. Indeed, in all matters moral, social or linguistic in *Emma*, Mr Knightley is a model" ("The Grammar of Conduct: Speech Act Theory and the Education of Emma Woodhouse," *Style*, Vol. XII, No. 4. (Fall 1978), p. 358). See also, for instance, Mark Schorer, "The Humiliation of Emma Woodhouse," in *Jane Austen: A Collection of Critical Essays*, ed. Ian Watt.

31. Charles A. Knight, "Irony and Mr. Knightley," *Studies in the Novel* 2 No. 1 (Spring 1970), pp. 191-2. For further discussion of some irrational elements in Mr Knightley see James R. Bennet, "Doating on You, Faults and All: Mr George Knightley," *Studies in the Novel* 5 (1973).

32. Lascelles, pp. 68-9.

33. Cf. *Jane Austen's Art of Allusion*, pp. 155-85.

34. Kirkham, p. 122.

35. Kirkham, p. 122.

36. In addition to the allusion to *Adelaide and Theodore* in *Emma*, Austen mentioned Mme de Genlis' *Les Veillées du Chateau* in a letter to her sister, Cassandra Austen, in 1800, briefly referring to "ideas worth transmitting." In another letter to Cassandra in 1807 she condemns Mme de Genlis' *Alphonsine* for its "indelicacies which disgrace a pen hitherto so pure." Finally, in 1816, in a letter to her niece, Caroline Austen, Jane Austen agrees that the way in which Mme de Genlis concludes "Olympe et Theophile," one of the tales in *Les Veillées du Chateau*, is "maddening. It really is too bad!— Not allowing them to be happy together when they *are* married." She continues to think of the rest of the work favorably enough to "lend your Aunt Frank the 1st vol. of *Les Veillées du Chateau* for Mary Jane to read. It will be some time before she comes to the horror of Olimpe" (See *Jane Austen's Letters*, ed. R.W. Chapman, (London: Oxford University Press, 1952), pp. 82, 173 and 450). I have found no allusions to *Adelaide and Theodore* in the letters.

37. Other critics who investigate Austen's sources also tend to either ignore Mme de Genlis' work or to merely mention Austen's allusions to it in her letters and in *Emma*. For example, R.W. Chapman notes references to *Alphosine* and *Les Veillées du Chateau* in addition to *Adelaide et Theodore* (*Jane Austen: Facts and Problems* (Oxford: Oxford University Press. 1948), p. 42). Frank Bradbrook's *Jane Austen and her Predecessors* (Cambridge: Cambridge University Press, 1966) merely mentions Chapman's mention, although he suggests, "The influence of French literature is difficult to estimate, but it is probably greater than has usuallly been assumed" (pp. 120-1). Bradbrook also includes, in Appendix I, Books for Young Ladies (pp. 141-2), a list of twenty-odd recommended readings taken from Clara Reeve's *The Progress of Romance* (1785), which includes *Adelaide and Theodore*. Neither Marilyn Butler's *Jane Austen and the War of Ideas* nor Claudia Johnson's *Jane Austen: Women, Politics and the Novel* mention any of Mme de Genlis' works.

38. Stephanie-Felicité du Crest de Saint-Aubin, Comtesse de Genlis, *Adelaide and Theodore or Letters on Education* (London: T. Cadell, 1788) Vol. I, p. 270. I have been able to find only one copy of the original novel in French, *Adele et Théodore, ou lettres sur l'education* (Quatrieme edition, revue, corrigé et augmenté. Paris: Imprimerie de Crapelet, 1801). In this edition, the passage in question can be found in Vol. II, lettre XXII, p. 95. Further references to this work will be included in the text, giving page numbers for both the English and the French editions.

39. *Jane Austen and the War of Ideas*, p. 259.

40. For a definition and broader discusion of frames, see M.A. Minsky, "A Framework for Representing Knowledge," in *The Psychology of Computer Vision,* ed. P. Winston (New York: McGraw-Hill, 1975). A useful discussion of scripts can ber found in Robert P. Abelson's "Script Processing in Attitude Formation and Decision Making," in *Basic Processes in Reading,* eds. David Laberge and S.J. Samuels (Hillsdale, N.J.: Lawrence Erlbaum Associates, 1977).

41. Cf. Abelson, pp. 35, 37.

42. Cf. Abelson, p. 37.

43. Langland, "Nobody's Angels: Domestic Ideology and Middle-Class Women in the Victorian Novel," p. 291.

44. As Langland observes, for Dorothea and Celia in *Middlemarch*, frippery was the ambition of a huckster's daughter ("Nobody's Angels," pp. 293-4).

45. *Jane Austen's Novels,* p. 112.

46. Michel Foucault, "The Subject and Power," in *Michel Foucault: Beyond Structuralism and Hermeneutics,* eds. Hubert L. Dreyfus and Paul Rabinow (Chicago: University of Chiago Press , 1983), p. 217-8.

47. Foucault, "Subject and Power," pp. 212.

48. *Jane Austen: Feminism and Fiction,* p. 113.

49. "Subject and Power," p. 217.

50. "Subject and Power," p. 221.

51. Langland, "Nobody's Angels," p. 296.

52. Foucault, "Subject and Power," p. 220.

53. *Jane Austen's Novels,* p. 124.

Chapter 6
Conclusion

The three novels that have been the object of this study all include important carnivalesque ingredients in their peculiar use of parody, their skepticism and gay relativity, their carnivalesque discourse. Parody is more prominent in *Northanger Abbey*, just as a skeptical approach to commonly held truths and individual perceptions is a central theme in *Pride and Prejudice*, and the handling of narratorial mimicry and carnivalesque, ironical discourse is more complex in *Emma* than in the other two works. All three novels, however, are similar in that they may be seen as explorations of roads to a carnivalesque utopia of feminine happiness, each following the course of a different woman. As literary creations, they exhibit Austen's cunning use of the available narrative and esthetic material to tell the stories of women without falling into traditional misogynist attitudes.

In *Northanger Abbey* Catherine Morland overcomes the silliness and ignorance her culture promotes in young women, innocently ignoring those conventions that could seriously thwart her while she sturdily and actively pursues her ends. Before Catherine and Henry grow morally and intellectually and marry, the two must encounter his father's crass patriarchal egotism and mercernary attitudes in a world where love is often a pretense masking greed. The novel takes them finally to "begin perfect happiness" (NA, 252) in a relationship which promises to allow the young woman to become morally independent, while the young man shows signs of losing the arrogance he had preserved in spite of relatively enlightened views regarding women.

In *Pride and Prejudice* the reader begins by laughing at universally acknowledged truths; then, through the process of growth of the intelligent, merry, yet often belligerent heroine, readers are led to explore the sway of monologic tendencies and the lure of illusive certainties as she clashes with an excessively proud man. The two, dealing with ideologies that regulate relations between classes and between genders, learn from each other, find love and finally marry. In the end they inhabit a world in which husband and wife relate as equals, and where worthy beings enjoy the possibility of happiness in loving relationships.

In *Emma* we discover the limitations encountered by a woman of superior wit and cleverness, kind but vain and wilfull, and given to mischievous laughter. In a society where there is no avenue open for the exercise of her powers, she clings to her snobbish assurance in the prominence of her class and family; she also amuses herself by trying to manipulate others, for she thinks herself capable of extraordinary perception. She will learn to distrust certainties, while the man who has been trying to instruct and guide her since her childhood will discover the folly of believing anyone can correct but her or his own self. In the end they will enter a *sui generis* married life, under special conditions that favor a relationship of equality in spite of his greater age and experience.

In the three novels hero and heroine must grow in some sense before they come together, but the world each couple enters in the end represents a unique form of flight from conditions adverse to women. I have described these fictional worlds of the novels' conclusions as carnivalesque utopias, as joyful, regenerative constructs, the result of inverting the anti-feminist rigors of official ideologies of Austen's times, while preserving many outer conditions of patriarchal society. Thus, after submitting her characters to uncrownings that turn upside down many of the conventions of sentimental novels (the victimized heroine, the perfect hero, sacred love), Austen adapts the device of the happy ending to her carnivalesque comedies. In them, the "perfect happiness" granted to the protagonists becomes a stylized rendering of happy endings, using meta-narrative devices calling attention to themselves and therefore drawing the reader, as a witness/participant, into the act of narrating.

This open avowal of the happy ending as a fiction does not in any sense diminish the novels' joyful, celebratory quality. Austen appears to have been fully aware of the escapist nature of the typical sentimental fiction; however, rather than decry its anti-rationalistic evasion, she, in typical carnivalesque fashion, prized its possibilities for feminist utopia. For example, she disliked one of the stories in Mme de Genlis' *Les Veillées du Chateau* because it ended unhappily; after many vicissitudes, the lovers marry but do not find happiness. (See Austen's *Letters*, p. 450). It seems likely that Austen's distaste for "the horror" of such an ending reflects her awareness that a tragic end defeats the purpose of such fiction.

Her own flights from reality, however, were much more complex than those of most sentimental novels. In her fiction she constructs a world in which the socio-economic and political events of her historical times take place only in the periphery, in a world from which women are excluded. But this historical reality is an invisible frame, or perhaps a lens through which everything is seen. Furthermore, in the fictional reality of the villages and towns she creates, the personal conflicts in the lives of the major characters are as crucial and as deeply penetrated by war and politics as "real, solemn" war and politics. And it is a fictional reality resting on an essential premise: feminine independence and equality, at least as utopian promise, are not to be barred from it. Thus, the many social constraints and obstacles to feminine happiness are not ignored as irrelevant to the fate of an idealized heroine, as it happens in typical sentimental fiction. Rather, they are recognized, examined, and then leapt over, as characters enter a non-world that is, for the very gaiety of its promises of "perfect happiness," a denunciation of the brutal restrictions placed on women in Austen's contemporary society.

Similarly, language in these novels shows a multiplicity of layers of meaning. The speech irregularities exhibited by the characters (fragmentation, ungrammaticality, paratactic, illogical effusions) are contained within hyper-correct, carefully structured sentences. But there is carnivalesque joy in the reiteration of these disruptive speeches, while the certainty that the narratorial correctness suggests is consistently undermined by irony as the narration superimposes different voices in a single word or statement. The characters' voices, with all their often erroneuous attitudes, appear mixed with, or overlayed on, the narrator's own, in a form of ironic, "double-voiced" discourse.

And so new layers of meaning are constantly generated; laughter renews itself, in a seemingly endless cycle between mocking the narrowness of official ideologies and possibly seeking some perfect certitude that is simultaneously suspected of being impossible. At the same time, Austen's fictions repeatedly record the ludicrous smallness of those who hold on to the illusion of a completed truth, a truth owned as basis for their individualistic, isolated private lives. To Austen we can apply, therefore, Bakhtin's description of typical Renaissance realism: "The ever-growing, inexhaustible, ever-laughing principle which uncrowns and renews is combined with its opposite: the petty, inert, 'material principle'" (RHW, 24) — only that the "material principle" Austen deals with is that which is typical, not of elitist class society, but of misogynous patriarchy. Indeed, in Austen the inexhaustibility is based precisely on the clash between and combination of these opposites, dogmatic, petty egotism and contestatory laughter, two ideological forces that coexist and endlessly battle each other.

BIBLIOGRAPHY

ABEL, Elizabeth, Hirsch, Marianne, and Langland, Elizabeth, "Introduction." In *The Voyage in: Fictions of Female Development*. Eds., Abel, Hirsch and Langland. Hanover: University Press of New England, 1983. 3-19.

ABELSON, Robert P., "Script Processing in Attitude Formation and Decision Making." In *Cognition and Social Behavior*. Eds. John S. Carroll and John W. Payne. Hillsdale, N.J.: Lawrence Erlbaum, 1977. 33-45.

ALLEN, B. Sprague, *Tides in English Taste*. Cambridge, Mass.: Harvard University Press, 1973.

ARMSTRONG, Nancy, *Desire and Domestic Fiction: A Political History of the Novel*. Oxford: Oxford University Press, 1987.

AUERBACH, Nina, "Austen and Alcott on Matriarchy." In *Towards a Poetics of Fiction*, Ed. Mark Spilka. Bloomington: Indiana University Press, 1977. 266-86.

AUSTEN, Henry, "Biographical Notice of the Author." In *The Novels of Jane Austen*. Ed. R.W. Chapman. Oxford: Oxford University Press, 1988. Vol. V. 3-9.

AUSTEN, Jane, *Jane Austen's Letters to Her Sister Cassandra and Others* . Ed. R.W. Chapman. Oxford: Oxford University Press, 1952.

_____ , *The Novels of Jane Austen*. Ed. R.W. Chapman. Oxford: Oxford University Press, 1988. Vols. I-VI.

_____ , *Pride and Prejudice*. Ed. David Grey, Norton Critical Edition. New York: Norton, 1966.

BABB, Howard S., *Jane Austen's Novels: the Fabric of Dialogue*. Columbus: Ohio State University Press, 1962.

BABCOCK, Barbara, Ed., *The Reversible World: Symbolic Inversion in Art and Society*. Ithaca and London: Cornell University Press, 1978.

BAKHTIN, Mikhail, "Discourse in the Novel." In *The Dialogic Imagination: Four Essays by M.M. Bakhtin*. Ed. Michael Holquist, tr. Caryl Emerson and Michael Holquist. Austin: Texas University Press, 1981. 259-422.

_____ , "Epic and the Novel." In *The Dialogic Imagination*. 3-40.

_____ , "Forms of Time and of the Chronotope in the Novel." In *The Dialogic Imagination*. 84-258.

_____ , "From the Prehistory of Novelistic Discourse." In *The Dialogic Imagination*. 41-83.

_____ , *Problems of Dostoevski's Poetics*. Ed. and tr. Caryl Emerson. Minneapolis: University of Minnesota Press, 1984.

_____ , *Rebelais and His World*. Tr. Helene Iswolsky. Bloomington: Indiana University Press, 1984. 248-50.

_____ , *Speech Genres and Other Late Essays*, Tr. Vern McGee, eds. Caryl Emerson and Michael Holquist. Austin: Texas University Press, 1986.

_____ , P.N. Medvedev, *The Formal Method in Literary Scholarship: A Critical Introduction to Sociological Poetics*. Tr. Albert J. Wehrle, Baltimore and London: The Johns Hopkins University Press, 1978.

BARTHES, Roland, "The Death of the Author." In *Image-Music-Text*. Tr. Stephen Heath. New York: Hill and Wang, 1977.

BENNET, James R,. "Doating on You, Faults and All: Mr George Knightley." *Studies in the Novel* 5 (Summer 1973): 248-50.

BERKELEY, George, "A Treatise Concerning the Principles of Human Knowledge," and "Three Dialogues between Phylas and Philonus, in Opposition to Sceptics and Atheists." In *The Empiricists.* New York: Anchor Books, 1974. 135-305.

BOOTH, Wayne C., "Freedom of Interpretation: Bakhtin and the Challenge of Feminist Criticism." *Critical Inquiry* 9 (September 1982): 45-76.

_____ , *A Rhetoric of Irony*. Chicago and London: The University of Chicago Press, 1974.

BRADBROOK, Frank W., *Jane Austen and her Predecessors*. Cambridge: Cambridge University Press, 1966.

_____ , *Jane Austen: Emma.* London: Edward Arnold, 1961.

BRONTE, Charlotte, *Jane Eyre.* London: Clarendon Press, 1969.

BROPHY, Bridget, "Jane Austen and the Stuarts." In *Critical Essays on Jane Austen.* Ed. B.C. Southan. 21-38.

BROWN, Julia Prewitt, *Jane Austen's Novels: Social Change and Literary Form.* Cambridge, Mass.: Harvard University Press, 1979.

BROWN, Lloyd W., "Jane Austen and the Feminist Tradition." *Nineteenth-Century Fiction* 28 (December, 1973): 321-38.

_____ , *Bits of Ivory.* Baton Rouge, Louisiana: Lousiana State University Press, 1963.

BURKE, Edmund, *Reflections on the Revolution in Frence.* Ed. G.A. Pecock. Indianapolis: Hacket, 1987.

BERLIN, Katrin R., "Pictures of Perfection at Pemberley." In *Jane Austen: New Perspectives.* Ed. Janet Todd. 155-70.

BURNEY, Fanny, *Camilla, or a Picture of Youth.* London: Oxford University Press, 1972.

_____ , *Cecilia.* London: George Bell & Sons, 1906.

_____ , *Evelina or the History of a Young Lady's Entrance into the World.* London: Oxford University Press, 1968.

BURROWS, J. J., *Jane Austen's Emma.* Sydney: Sydney University Press, 1968.

BUTLER, Marilyn, *Jane Austen and the War of Ideas.* Oxford: Clarendon Press, 1975.

BUTLER, Samuel, *Prose Observations.* ed. Hugh de Quehen. Oxford: Clarendon Press, 1979.

_____ , *Hudibras.* Ed. John Wilders. Oxford: Clarendon Press, 1967.

CHAPMAN, R. W., *Jane Austen: Facts and Problems.* Oxford: Oxford University Press, 1949.

CLARK, Alice, *Working Life of Women in the Seventeenth Century*. Reprints of
Economics Classics. New York: Frank Cass, 1968.

CONGREVE, William, *The Double-Dealer,* A Solar Press Facsimile. London:
Scholar Press, 1973.

COTTON, Daniel. *The Civilized Imagination: A Study of Anne Radcliffe, Jane
Austen and Sir Walter Scott.* Cambridge: Cambridge University Press,
1985.

DAVIS, Natalie Zemon, "Women on Top: Symbolic Sexual Inversion and
Political Disorder in Early Modern Europe." In *The Reversible World:
Symbolic Inversion in Art and Society*. Ithaca and London: Cornell
University Press, 1978. 147-90.

DE BEAUVOIR, Simone, *The Second Sex*. Tr. H.M. Parshley. Middlesex:
Penguin Books. 1977.

DE FOREST, Mary, "Review," *Eighteenth-Century Fiction*, Vol. I. (July 1989):
345-7.

DE GENLIS, Stephanie-Felicité, *Adelaide and Theodore or Letters on Education*.
London: T. Cadell, 1788.

DE LAURETIS, Teresa,. Ed. *Feminist Studies/Critical Studies*. Bloomington:
Indiana University Press, 1986.

DOODY, Margaret. "Jane Austen's Reading." *In The Jane Austen Companion*.
Ed. David Grey.

DRYDEN, John. "A Discourse Concerning the Original and Progress of
Satire." *Essays of John Dryden*. ed. W.P. Kerr. New York: Russell and
Russell, 1961. Vol. 1. 15-114.

_____ , "Mac Flecknoe." In *Dryden: Poems and Prose*. Middlesex, England:
Penguin Books. 1985.

DUCHWORTH, Alistair, *The Improvement of Estate*. Baltimore: The Johns
Hopkins University Press, 1971.

_____ , "Jane Austen and the Conflict of Interpretations." In *Jane Austen:
New Perspectives*. ed. Janet Todd. 39-48.

EDGEWORTH, Maria, *Belinda.* London: J.Johnson, 1801.

EHRENPREIS, Anne Henry, "Introduction." In Charlotte Smith's *Emmeline: The Orphan of the Castle.* London: Oxford University Press, 1971.

EMERSON, Carly, "Problems with Bakhtins Poetics." *Slavic and East European Journal.* 32 (Winter 1988): 503-25.

FERGUS, Jan, *Jane Austen and the Didactic Novel.* London: The Macmillan Press, 1983.

FERSTER, Judith, *Chaucer on Interpretation.* Cambridge: Cambridge University Press, 1985.

FIELDING, Henry, *The History of Tom Jones, a Foundling.* New York: Random House, 1948.

FOGEL, Aaron, "Coerced Speech and the Oedipus Dialogue Complex." In *Rethinking Bakhtin: Extensions and Challenges*, eds. Gary Saul Morson and Caryl Emerson. Evanston, Illinois: Northwestern University Press, 1989. 173-96.

FOUCAULT, Michel, *The Archaelogy of Knowledge.* Tr. A. M. Sheridan Smith. New York: Pantheon Books, 1972.

_____ , *Discipline and Punish.* Tr. Alan Sheridan. New York: Random House, 1979.

_____ , *The History of Sexuality.* Tr. Robert Hurley. New York: Vintage Books, 1980.

_____ , "The Subject and Power." In *Michel Foucault: Beyond Structuralism and Hermeneutics.* Eds. Hubert L. Dreyfus and Paul Rabinow. Chicago: University of Chicago Press , 1983. 208-26.

FOWLER, Marian E., "The Feminist Bias of *Pride and Prejudice*," *Dalhousie Review* 57 (1977): 47-64.

FULLBROOK, Kate, "Jane Austen and the Comic Negative." In *Women Reading Women's Writing.* Ed. Sue Roe. New York: St. Martin's Press, 1987.

GILBERT, Sandra and Gubar, Susan, *The Madwoman in the Attic.* New Haven: Yale University Press, 1979.

GOLDSMITH, Oliver, *The Vicar of Wakefield*. New York. J.H. Sears. 1939.

GREY, David, Ed. *The Jane Austen Companion*, New York: MacMillan, 1986.

_____ , Ed. Jane Austen's *Pride and Prejudice*. Norton Critical Edition. New York: Norton, 1966.

GROSSE, Marquis of, *Horrid Mysteries*. Tr. Peter Will London: Folio Press, 1968.

GUBAR, Susan, "The Female Monster in Augustan Satire." *Signs* 3. (Winter 1977): 380-94.

HARDING, D.W., "Regulated Hatred: An Aspect of the Work of Jane Austen." *Scrutiny* 8 (March, 1940): 346-62.

HARRIS, Jocelyn, "Anne Elliot, the Wife of Bath, and Other Friends." In *Jane Austen: New Perspectives*. Ed. Janet Todd. 273-93.

_____ , *Jane Austen's Art of Memory*. Cambridge: Cambridge University Press. 1989.

HAYS, Mary, *Memoirs of Emma Courtney*. New York: Garland Publischers, 1974.

HIRSCHKOP, Ken. "A Response to the Forum on Mikhail Bakhtin." In *Bakhtin: Essays and Dialogues on His Work*. Ed. Gary Saul Morson. Chicago and London: The University of Chicago Press, 1986. 73-80.

HONAN, Park, *Jane Austen: Her Life*. New York: St. Martin's Press, 1987.

HOUGH, Graham, "Narrative and Dialogue in Jane Austen." *Critical Quarterly* 12. (1970): 201-29.

JACK, Ian, *Augustan Satire: Intention and Idiom in English Poetry 1660-1750*. Oxford: Clarendon Press. 1952.

JAKOBSON, Roman, "Linguistics and Poetics." In *Language and Literature*. Eds. Krystina Pomorska and Stephen Rudit. Cambridge, Mass.: Belknap Press, 1987. 62-94.

JOHNSON, Claudia, *Jane Austen: Women, Politics and the Novel*. Chicago: University of Chicago Press, 1988.

KETTLE, Arnold, *An Introduction to the English Novel*. New York: Harper and Row, 1951.

KIRK, Eugene P., *Menippean Satire: An Annotated Catalogue of Texts and Criticism*. New York: Garland Publishers. 1980.

KIRKHAM, Margaret, *Jane Austen: Feminism and Fiction*. Sussex: The Harvester Press, 1983.

_____ , "The Austen Portraits and the Received Biography." In *Jane Austen: New Perspectives*. Ed. Jannet Todd. 29-38.

KLIGER, Samuel, "Jane Austen's *Pride and Prejudice*, in the Eighteenth Century Mode." In *Pride and Prejudice*. Norton Critical Edition, ed. Donald Grey. 352-62.

KNIGHT, Charles A., "Irony and Mr Knightley." *Studies in the Novel 2*, (Spring 1970): 185-93.

KUNZLE, David, "World Upside Down: The Iconography of a Eurepean Broadsheet Type." In *The Reversible World*. Ed. Barbara Babcock. 39-94.

LaCAPRA, Dominick, *Rethinking Intellectual History: Texts, Context, Language*. Ithaca: Cornell University Press. 1983.

LANGLAND, Elizabeth, *Society in the Novel*. Chapel Hill: North Carolina University Press, 1939.

_____ , "Nobody's Angels: Domestic Ideology and Middle-Class Women in the Victorian Novel." PMLA 107, No. 2 (March 1992): 290-304.

LASCELLES, Mary, *Jane Austen and Her Art*. London: Oxford University Press, 1939.

LEAVIS, Q.D., "A Critical Theory of Jane Austen's Writings." *Scrutiny* 10 (1942): 61-87.

LEWES, Henry. "The Novels of Jane Austen." Reprinted from *Blackwood Magazine* 86 (1859). In *Pride and Prejudice*. Ed. Donald J. Gray. Norton Critical Edition, New York: W.W. Norton. 1966. 323-31.

LITZ A., Walton, *Jane Austen: A Study of Her Artistic Development*. New York:

Oxford University Press, 1965.

LODGE, David, "Jane Austen's Novels: Form and Structure." In *The Jane Austen Companion*. Ed. David Grey.

LUCIAN, *True History and Lucius or the Ass.* Tr. Paul Turner. Bloomington: Indiana University Press, 1958.

McKEON, Richard, *"Pride and Prejudice*: Thought, Character, Argument and Plot." *Critical Inquiry* 5 (1979) 511-27.

MILLER, Nancy K. Changing the Subject: Authorship, Writing and the Reader." In *Femenist Studies/Critical Studies*. Ed. Teresa de Lauretis Bloomington: Indiana University Press, 1986. 102-120.

MINSKY, M.A. "A Framework for Representing Knowledge." In *The Psychology of Computer Vision*. Ed. P. Wiston. New York: McGraw-Hill. 1975.

MOLER, Kenneth, *Jane Austen's Art of Allusion*. Lincoln, Nebraska: University of Nebraska Press, 1968.

_____ , *Pride and Prejudice*: *A Study in Artistic Economy*. Boston: Twayne Publishers. 1989.

MONAGHAN, David, "Introduction: Jane Austen as a Social Novelist." In *Jane Austen in a Social Context*. Ed. David Monaghan. Totowa, N.J. Barnes & Noble, 1981.

_____ , "Jane Austen and the Feminist Critics." *A Room of One's Own*. 4 (Spring 1979): 282-310.

_____ , "Jane Austen and the Position of Women." In *Jane Austen in a Social Context*. Ed. David Monaghan.

MORGAN, Susan,. In *the Meantime: Character and Preception in Jane Austens Fiction*. Chicago: University of Chicago Press, 1980.

MORRIS, Ivor, *Mr Collins Considered*. London: Routledge and Kegan Paul, 1987.

MARSON, Gary Saul, Ed. *Bakhtin: Essays and Dialogues on His Work*. Chicago: University of Chicago Press, 1986.

_____ , and Emerson, Caryl. Eds *Rethinking Bakhtin: Extensions and Challenges.* Evanston, Illinois: Northwestern University Press. 1989.

MUDRICK, Marvin, *Jane Austen: Irony as Defense and Discovery.* Berkeley: University of California Press, 1952.

MUECKE, D.C., *The Compass of Irony.* London: Methuen, 1969.

_____ , *Irony and the Ironic.* London: Methuen, 1982.

NOKES, David, *Raillery and Rage: A Study of Eighteenth-Century Satire.* New York: St. Martin's Press, 1979.

NORBECK, Eduard, Ed. *The Anthropological Study of Human Play*, Rice University Studies, Vol. 60. No 3. Houston: Rice University Press, 1974. 1-94.

O'FAOLAIN,J. and Martines, L. *Not in God's Image: Women in History from the Greeks to the Victorians.* New York: 1973.

PAGE, Norman, *The Language of Jane Austen.* Oxford: Basil Blackwell, 1972.

PARIS, Bernard J., *Character and Conflict in Jane Austen's Novels.* Detroit, Mich.: Wayne State University Press, 1978.

PARSONS, Eliza, *The Castle of Wolfenback.* Ed. D.P. Varma, The Northanger Abbey Set of Jane Austen Horrid Novels. London: The Folio Press, 1968.

PAULSON, Ronald, *Popular and Polite Art in the Culture of Hogarth and Fielding.* Notre Dame, Ind.: University of Notre Dame Press. 1979.

PAYNE, F. Anne, *Chaucer and Menippean Satire.* Madison, Wisconsin: The University of Wisconsin Press, 1981.

PECHEY, Graham, "On the Borders of Bakhtin." In *Bakhtin and Cultural Theory.* Eds. Ken Hirschkop and David Shepherd. Manchester and New York: Manchester University Press, 1989. 39-67.

PHILIPPS, K.C., *Jane Austen's English.* London: Andre Deutsch, 1970.

POLHEMUS, Robert M., "Jane Austen's Comedy." In *The Jane Austen Companion.* Ed. David Grey.

POOVEY, Mary., *The Proper Lady and the Woman Writer.* Chicago: University of Chicago Press, 1984.

_____ , *Uneven Developments: The Ideological Work of Gender in Mid-Victorian England.* Chicago: University of Chicago Press, 1988.

PRITCHETT, V.S., *George Meredith and English Comedy.* New York: Random House, 1969.

PROPP, Vladimir, *Morphology of the Folktale.* Tr. Laurence Scott. Austin: University o Texas Press, 1968.

RICHARDSON, Samuel, *Clarissa, or the History of a Young Lady.* London: Dent & Sons, 1962.

_____ , *Pamela.* Oxford: Oxford University Press, 1964.

_____ , *Sir Charles Grandison.* London: H. Sotheran, 1884.

ROGERS, Katherine M., *Feminism in Eighteenth-Century England.* Urbana: University of Illinois, 1982.

_____ , *The Troublesome Helpmate: A History of Misoginy in Literature.* Seattle: University of Washingon Press, 1966.

RUSSO, Mary, "Female Grotesques." In *Femenist Studies/Critical Studies.* ed. Teresa de Lauretis. 213-29.

SACKS, Sheldon, *Fiction and the Shape of Belief.* Berkeley: University of California Press, 1966.

SHEIFLER, Ronald. "Irony and the Literaty Past: On *The Concept of Irony* and *The Mill on the Floss* ." In *Kierkegaard and Literature: Irony, Repetition and Criticism.* Eds. Ronald Schleifer and Robert Markley. Norman, Oklahoma: University of Oklahoma Press, 1984. 183-216.

SHORER, Mark, "The Humiliation of Emma Woodhouse." In *Jane Austen: A Collection of Critical Essays.* Ed. Ian Watt.

SEARLE, John. A., "Taxonomy of Speech Acts." In *Expression and Meaning.* Cambrige: Cambrige University Press, 1976.

SHOWALTER, Elaine., "Feminist Criticism in the Wilderness." In *Writing and Sexual Difference,* ed. Elizabeth Abel. Chicago: The University of Chicago Press, 1982.

SIMONS, Judy, *Fanny Burney.* Totowa, N.J.: Barnes & Noble, 1987.

SMITH, Charlotte, *Desmond.* New York: Garland Publishing Co., 1974.

_____ , *Emmeline: The Orphan of the Castle.* London: Oxford University Press, 1971.

_____ , *The Old Manor House.* London: Oxford University Press, 1969.

SOUTHAM, B.C. Ed. *Critical Essays on Jane Austen.* New York: Barnes and Noble, 1968.

_____ , "Criticism, 1870-1940." In *The Jane Austen Companion.* Ed. David Grey.

_____ , "Introduction." *Jane Austen, Northanger Abbey and Persuasion: a Casebook.* London: Macmillan Press, 1976.

SPACKS, Patricia Meyer, "Muted Discord: Generational Conflict in Jane Austen." In *Jane Austen in a Social Context,* ed. David Monaghan.

STEWART, Susan, *Nonsense: Aspects of Intertextuality in Folklore and Literature.* Baltimore: Johns Hopkins University Press, 1979.

_____ , "Bakhtin's Anti-Linguistics." In *Bakhtin: Essays and Dialogues on His Work.* Eds. Gary Saul Morson and Caryl Emerson. 41-58.

STONE, Lawrence, *The Family, Sex and Marriage in England 1500-1800.* New York: Harper Colophon Books,1979.

SULLOWAY, Allison G., "Emma Woodhouse and *A Vindication of the Rights of Woman.*" *Wordsworth Circle* 7 (Autumn 1976): 320-32.

_____ , *Jane Austen and the Province of Womanhood.* Philadelphia: University of Pennsylvania Press, 1989.

TANNER, Tony, *Jane Austen.* Cambridge, Mass: Harvard University Press, 1986.

TAVE, Stuart M., *The Amiable Humorist: A Study in the Comic Theory and Criticism of the Eighteenth and Early Nineteenth Centuries.* Chicago: The University of Chicago Press, 1960.

TERDIMAN, Richard, *Discourse/Counter-Discourse*. Ithaca: Cornell University Press. 1985.

THOMAS, Keith, "The Place of Laughter in Tudor and Stuart England." *Times Literary Supplement* (Jan. 21. 1977): 77-81.

THOMPSON, James, *Between Self and World*. University Park, Pa.: Pennsylvania State University, 1988.

TODD, Janet, Ed. *Jane Austen: New Perspectives*. New York: Holmes & Meier. 1983.

TOMPKINS, J.M.S., *The Popular Novel in England: 1770-1800*. Lincoln, Nebraska: University of Nebraska Press, 1961.

TRILLING, Lionel, "Emma and the Legend of Jane Austen." In *Beyond Culture*. New York: Viking Press, 1965. 31-55.

TURNER, Victor, *The Ritual Process*. Chicago: Aldine, 1969.

_____ , "Liminal to Liminoid in Play, Flow and Ritual: An Essay in Comparative Symbology." In *The Anthropological Study of Human Play*, Rice University Studies,. Ed. Edwar Norbeck, Vol. 60, No. 3. Houston: Rice University Press, 1974. 53-92.

VAN DIJK, Teun, *Macrostructures*. Hillsdale, N.J.: Lawrence Erlbaum Associates, 1980.

VAN GHENT, Dorothy, "On *Pride and Prejudice*." In *Pride and Prejudice*. Ed. Donald Grey. 362-73.

VOLOSINOV, V. N., *Marxism and the Philosophy of Language*. Cambridge, Mass: Harvard University Press, 1986,

WATT, Ian, "The Ironic Tradition in Augustan Prose from Swift to Johnson." In *Restoration and Augustan Prose*, Papers Delivered at the Third Clark Library Seminar. Los Angeles: William Andrews Clark Memorial Library.

_____ , "Introduction." In *Jane Austen: A Collection of Critical Essays*. Ed. Ian Watt. Englewood Cliff, N.J.: Prentice-Hall, 1963.

WILDERS, John, "Introduction," *Hudibras*. Ed. John Wilders. Oxford: Clarendon Press, 1967.

WILLIAMS, Raymond, *Culture and Society: 1780-1950*. New York: Columbia University Press, 1958.

_____ ,*The English Novel: From Dickens to Lawrence*. London: Chatto & Windus, 1970.

WILSON, Angus, "The Neighbourhood of Tombuctoo: Conflicts in Jane Austen's Novels." In *Critical Essays on Jane Austen*. ed. B.C. Southam. 182-99.

WOOLF, Virginia, "Jane Austen." In *Jane Austen: A Collection of Critical Essays*, Ed. Ian Watt.

WOLLSTONECRAFT, Mary, "Lessons." In William Godwin. Ed. *Posthumous Works of the Author of a Vindication of the Rights of Woman*. Clifton, N.J. Augustus M. Kelley, 1972.

_____ , *Mary, a Fiction*. London: Oxford University Press, 1976.

_____ , *A Vindication of the Rights of Woman*. New York: Garland Publishing, 1974.

_____ , *The Wrongs of Woman, or Maria*. In William Godwin. Ed. *Posthumous Works of the Author of a Vindication of the Rights of Woman*.

WRIGHT, Andrew H., "Heroines, Heroes and Villains in *Pride and Prejudice*." In *Twentieth-Century Interpretations of Pride and Prejudice*. Ed. E. Rubinstein. Englewood Cliffs, N.J.: Prentice-Hall, 1969.

Writing About Women
Feminist Literary Studies

This is a literary series devoted to feminist studies on past and contemporary women authors, exploring social, psychological, political, economic, and historical insights directed toward an interdisciplinary approach.

The series is dedicated to the memory of Simone de Beauvoir, early pioneer in feminist literary theory.

Persons wishing to have a manuscript considered for inclusion in the series should submit a letter of inquiry, including the title and a one-page abstract of the manuscript to the general editor:

Professor Esther K. Labovitz
Department of English
Pace University
Pace Plaza
New York, NY 10038
(212) 488-1416